CANADA

t Ripley

St Paul

Fort Mackinac

rt Des Moines

Fort Dearborn

Detroit

Fort Wayne

Boston

New York

Philadelphia

worth

St Louis

Jefferson Barracks

Fort Washington

Ohio

Richmond

ith

Tennessee

Savannah

Mississippi

Alabama

Mobile

w Orleans

Savannah

Tampa

t or Camp

n Transcontinental Trails

ional Frontiers

CUBA

Santiago de Cuba

The United States Cavalry:

An Illustrated History

The United States Cavalry

An Illustrated History

GREGORY J. W. URWIN

Color Illustrations by Ernest Lisle Reedstrom

BLANDFORD PRESS

POOLE   DORSET

First published in the U.K. 1983 by Blandford Press,
Link House, West Street, Poole, Dorset, BH15 1LL.

Copyright © 1983 Blandford Books Ltd
Reprinted 1984

Distributed in the United States by
Sterling Publishing Co., Inc.,
2 Park Avenue, New York, N.Y. 10016.

British Library Cataloguing in Publication Data

Urwin, Gregory J. W.
  The United States cavalry.
  1. United States, *Army*—History
  2. Cavalry—History
  I. Title
  357'.1'0973   UA30

ISBN 0 7137 1219 8

Typeset by Asco Trade Typesetting Ltd., Hong Kong
Printed by Graficromo S.A., Spain

Contents

Dedicated to
Dr Lawrence A. Frost

Scholar, Author, Healer, Mentor and Friend

Preface

An illustrated book on the United States Cavalry should not be regarded simply as the story of some colorful but insignificant sideshow in the American experience. From 1833 until 1917, the 'pony soldiers' were a vital branch of the U.S. Army, and they made important contributions to its many successes.

Furthermore, the mounted service produced a large number of America's greatest commanders. The names of men like 'Light Horse Harry' Lee, Richard M. Johnson, Stephen Watts Kearny, Alexander W. Doniphan, Robert E. Lee, Philip Kearny, Jeb Stuart, Nathan B. Forrest, Philip Henry Sheridan, George A. Custer, John S. Mosby, John H. Morgan, Ranald S. Mackenzie, Wesley Merritt, John J. Pershing, Jonathan M. Wainwright and George S. Patton will always figure prominently in their country's legend and lore.

This book is a balanced effort to capture the look and spirit of the U.S. Cavalry from the Revolution to the early days of World War 2, when it exchanged its horses for armored vehicles. The text concerns itself largely with the organization, campaigns, battles, and the character of the officers and men of the Army's mounted units. The uniforms, weapons and equipment the cavalrymen were issued are briefly described in the captions accompanying the color plates and other illustrations.

Although some may decry the attention given herein to American diplomacy and politics, the United States is a democracy, and the positions adopted by those parties or persons who vied for the favor of the electorate had a deciding influence on the shape of the Army and the nation's military policy. Anyone who neglects this point cannot fully understand the history of America's wars or armed forces.

Pictures often tell us as much about the past as words, and no effort was spared to uncover and then publish some of the finest illustrations of American cavalrymen now in existence.

Librarians and archivists are generally kind and ac-commodating individuals. My task of tracking down 100 black and white illustrations for this volume was greatly simplified by the generous response of nearly every such professional I contacted. Quite often, I received assistance that exceeded even the most stringent standards of professional courtesy. Among those who were so gracious I would like to name: Michael J. McAfee, Curator of the West Point Museum at the United States Military Academy; Michael J. Winey, Curator, U.S. Army Military History Institute; Richard B. Harrington, Curator of the Anne S. K. Brown Military Collection, Brown University Library; Jo Ann Tuckwood of the State Historical Society of Missouri; Heath Pemberton, Chief, Branch of History, Division of Publications, National Park Service; Warren E. Bielenberg, Acting Superintendent, Fort McHenry National Monument and Historic Shrine; John C. Curry, Assistant Archivist, Michigan State Archives; Monroe H. Fabian, Associate Curator, the National Portrait Gallery; Louisa Cunningham of the Yale University Art Gallery; and Nancy C. Kraybill, Curator of Collections, Monmouth County Historical Association.

Other persons whose splendid service is worthy of mention are: Joan M. Metzger of the Arizona Historical Society; Judith Ciampoli, Missouri Historical Society; Mary L. Williams, Park Ranger, Fort Davis National Historic Site; Michael E. Moss, Curator of Art, West Point Museum; Landon Chas. Reisinger, the Historical Society of York County; James B. Casey, Head Reference Librarian, the Western Reserve Historical Association; Karol A. Schmiegel of the Winterthur Museum; James B. Snider, Museum Curator, the Rutherford B. Hayes Presidential Center; James E. Mooney, Director of the Historical Society of Pennsylvania; Sam Daniel, Reference Librarian at the Library of Congress; Margaret Kaufman of the Valentine Museum; Jane C. Dickens, Chief, Defense Audiovisual Agency, Department of Defense; Helen

Sanger of the Frick Art Reference Library; and the staff of the National Archives Audiovisual Archives Division.

Many of the most precious treasures of American militaria are in the hands of private collectors, and I wish to convey my sincere thanks to a trio of gracious gentlemen who allowed some of the incomparable items from their collections to appear in these pages: Herb Peck, Jr, of Nashville, Tennessee; Bruce Jackson of the same city; and William H. Guthman of Westport, Connecticut. A commendation is due to Pamela Guthman and Linda Payne of Payne-Guthman Studios, Boston, Massachusetts, for their excellent photographs of articles from the Guthman Collection, which were made especially for this book.

In preparing the color plates for this volume, great reliance was placed on *The Horse Soldier*, the classic four-volume study by the late Randy Steffen. A few minor errors were found and corrected, and it is hoped that this offering does not include any of its own. *The Horse Soldier* portrays the American cavalryman as the regulations said he should have looked, while *The United States Cavalry: An Illustrated History* strives to present him as he actually appeared on campaign or in garrison.

This book could not have been possible without the research of the Company of Military Historians. Since its founding in 1949, the Company has elevated the study of American military uniforms to a high art and exacting science. Every study published on the subject since then has leaned heavily on the skill and knowledge of Company members. Even so, they rarely receive the credit they deserve. It would require a separate volume to list the Company plates and articles from the *Military Collector & Historian* that were tapped for this project, but perhaps that debt can best be paid by naming those peerless scholars whose contributions were so essential to this book's completion. They include H. Charles McBarron, Jr, Marko Zlatich, George Woodbridge, Charles H. Cureton, Frederick P. Todd, John R. Elting, Detmar H. Finke, George S. Pappas, Fairfax Downey, Randy Steffen, Philip R. N. Katcher, Rebecca Katcher, Joseph Hefter, James Stamatelos, Anne S. K. Brown, Michael J. McAfee, Clyde A. Risley, Peter F. Copeland, Harold L. Peterson, Joseph M. Thatcher, Frederic E. Ray,

Frederick T. Chapman, James P. Simpson, William Imrie, Roger D. Sturcke, Gordon Chappell and Gary Zaboly.

Whenever the work hit a snag, there were some special friends ready to pitch in and pull it clear: Dr Lawrence A. Frost, noted Custer scholar and the man who introduced the author to illustrator Lisle Reedstrom; Donald Burgess, the Editor-in-Chief of *Campaigns*, who was always quick to offer his encouragement and assistance; Michael Miller, the adjutant of the Northwestern Department of the Brigade of the American Revolution; Thomas Yoseloff, the head of Associated University Presses, who permitted the author to accept this assignment; and Michael David O'Leary, whose recommendation made it all possible.

I would like to offer my deepest thanks to my wife, Cathy Kunzinger Urwin, an historian in her own right, who took time off from her research to help correct the proofs. I would also like to thank my colleague at Saint Mary of the Plains College, Dr David J. Kovarovic, for his assistance and encouragement.

The artist is indebted to the following persons and organizations who served as his models and consultants for the color plates: Gib Crontz of Cedar Lake, Indiana; Mel Wakefield of Crown Point, Indiana; Robert Craig of Richmond, Indiana; Colonel C. Cosby Kerney of Danville, Indiana, and members of his United States Cavalry Association Reactivated; Phil Rodeghiero of Dolton, Illinois; the 37th Illinois Volunteer Infantry, Thomas's Mudsills; and William Graf of Iowa City, Iowa.

Lisle and I would like to express our deep gratitude to Barry Gregory and his colleagues at Blandford Press for presenting our work in such an attractive manner.

In addition to delving through various manuscript collections at several archives, over 350 printed sources were consulted to produce this volume, including compiled correspondence, journals, diaries, period newspapers, memoirs, regimental histories and congressional papers, not to mention dozens of secondary books and articles. Due to the space restrictions dictated by this popular format, a very select bibliography is appended to the text for those who desire to do more reading on the fascinating career of the U.S. Cavalry.

Gregory J. W. Urwin

1 The Continental Light Dragoons

1776-83

On 14 June 1775, barely two months after George III's light infantry traded shots with Massachusetts farmers at Lexington and Concord, the Second Continental Congress, which had been originally convened merely to coordinate colonial opposition to Imperial tax policies, adopted the forty ragamuffin New England militia regiments that were then besieging the King's troops in Boston as its own regular military force. This original Continental Army consisted almost entirely of line infantry, although the worthy gentlemen who were directing its fortunes from Philadelphia soon after created a regiment of riflemen and later added an artillery battalion to its ranks. Curiously enough, the congressional delegates gave little thought to the need for mounted units to defend the rebellious Thirteen Colonies, and the one time they did consider the idea they dismissed it out of hand.

Sometime in July 1775 a German hussar, fully dressed, armed and accoutred, strode into the halls of Congress and announced to the admiring members that he and fifty other veterans of the Seven Years War were ready to ride to Boston and fight the British. Temporarily dazzled by this display of martial grandeur and bravado, the congressmen authorized the formation of a Pennsylvania Hussar Company. Three weeks later, however, when they began to receive the extravagant bills incurred by this new outfit, the shocked representatives came to their senses and chose to dismiss the hussars.

Surprisingly, this frugal decision roused no protests from the Continental Army's recently appointed commander-in-chief, General George Washington. As a wealthy Virginia planter, Washington had been practically raised in the saddle, and he came from a class that prided itself on its knowledge of good horseflesh. Horse breeding and racing constituted a positive mania among the Virginia gentry, and no plantation was deemed complete without a stable and a respectable line of thoroughbreds. Whatever his natural predilic-

tions, Washington was soldier enough to realize that cavalrymen could only be of minimal use at the deadlocked siege of Boston, and he wisely avoided the expense of raising them.

Then on 17 March 1776, the British drastically altered the nature of the American War of Independence by evacuating Boston. It was apparent to General Washington that when they returned it would be to New York, the most strategic Rebel port on the Atlantic seaboard, and he promptly moved the Continental Army there to meet them. Faced now with guarding a vast coastline against enemy landings, Washington was pleased when Captain John Leary offered his Light Horse Troop of New York City, an 'independent' militia company consisting of forty light dragoons, for duty with the Grand Army.

'In a march they may be of the utmost service, in reconnoitering the Enemy and gaining Intelligence, and have it in their power to render many other Important benefits,' the Commander-in-Chief reported to Congress, and on 21 June he recommended that Captain Leary's troop be taken onto the Continental Establishment. Meanwhile, his subordinates were employing the services of two troops of light horse from King's County to patrol the western end of Long Island, and a company of mounted militia from Queen's County was also called into the field.

The next formation of Rebel cavalry to join the Grand Army did not elicit as appreciative a response from its leader. Back in May, as the Connecticut Assembly reorganized its militia for service with Washington, it took the individual troops of light horse that were attached to each of its infantry battalions and formed them into regiments of their own. Early in July, when it became clear that the colony's foot soldiers would not be able to march to New York at the appointed time, Governor Jonathan Trumbull, a venerable patriot, ordered three regiments of militia light horse under Lieutenant Colonel Thomas

Seymour to place themselves at Washington's disposal until Connecticut's infantry levies could arrive.

Moving out so quickly that they forgot to pack proper camp equipment, the Connecticut Light Horse, 400 to 500 strong, reached the Grand Army on 11 July 1776. Washington viewed their coming with mixed feelings. While he welcomed any addition in manpower, a dry summer had left barely enough forage on Manhattan for the Grand Army's artillery and transport animals, and Washington feared the mounts of the Connecticut cavalry would place too heavy a strain on his scanty resources. When he asked the troopers to stay themselves and send their steeds home, they sharply declined, but he was mollified by their offer to pay for the upkeep of their horses out of their own pockets. What really riled the Commander-in-Chief was their refusal to perform any tasks that took them off the backs of their chargers, claiming special privileges as granted by an ancient Connecticut militia law. On the evening of 15 July, Washington summoned Seymour and his field officers to headquarters for a good bawling out, sending them a curt note the next day that read in part: 'If your Men think themselves exempt from the common Duties of a Soldier, will not mount Guard, do Garrison Duty, or the Service seperate from their Horse, they can be no longer of Use here, where Horse cannot be brought to Action, and I do not care how soon they are dismissed.'

Some subsequent historians have blamed Washington's peremptory expulsion of the Connecticut Light Horse for the disaster that overtook the Grand Army six weeks later at the Battle of Long Island, when General William Howe sent a large British column deftly around the Rebels' left flank, inflicting over 1000 casualties and throwing the survivors into a humiliating rout. However, it is extremely doubtful that Seymour's troopers could have been of any real help that terrible 27 August. Some of them had participated in the conquest of Louisburg way back in 1745, and in general they were miserably armed. Even if Washington had kept them, these overaged warriors could not have survived for long without such necessities as tents, blankets, camp kettles and adequate forage.

Nevertheless, their feeble presence was to be missed in the string of major and minor American defeats that followed Long Island. Of the 32,000 Redcoats and Hessians that General Howe brought to capture New York, none had a more intimidating effect on the

The 3rd Continental Light Dragoons charge the 2nd Battalion of Foot Guards at the Battle of Guilford Court House, 15 March 1781. Painting by Don Troiani.

green Rebel soldiers than the couple of hundred English horsemen in Lieutenant Colonel Samuel Birch's 17th Light Dragoons. Their apprehension grew so noticeable that Washington felt impelled to issue a reassuring general order on 27 October 1776, in which he declared that the countryside was too broken by woods and stone walls for the British cavalry to operate effectively, and 'there is no Enemy more to be despised.' Then to further bolster his men's courage, Washington offered 'any brave parties, who will endeavour to surprise some of them,' a prize of $100 'for every Trooper, with his Horse and Accoutrements, which shall be brought in.'

The next day, 28 October, Washington dug in to give battle at White Plains, and he learned that brave words and cash rewards were no substitutes for a strong mounted arm. As the fight developed, the key to the Rebel position became Chatterton's Hill on the far right flank, which was held by two militia regiments and 1250 Continentals from New York, Connecticut, Maryland and Delaware. They drove back two attacks by British and Hessian regulars, but as they nerved themselves to meet a third assault, the air was split by the blare of trumpets, a rumble of kettledrums and the

17th Light Dragoons charged into the fray. The sight of those oncoming red-coated centaurs with their waving, wicked sabers was too much for the militia, and they took to their heels. To any observer watching from a safe distance, Chatterton's Hill exploded into a frenzied anthill, with the British riders dashing up the steep southern slopes and hundreds of terrified men and boys in homespun fleeing down the northern side. The Continentals, covered by Haslet's Delaware Regiment, made good their withdrawal, but the militia was cut to pieces and Washington lost another battle and nearly 300 men.

Roughly two weeks later, Howe captured 2837 Rebels at Fort Washington, the last American toehold in New York, and General Washington commenced his demoralizing retreat through the Jerseys. If the disintegrating Grand Army ever had need of cavalry, it was then, as it moved through that flat, open country. Providentially, help had arrived just in a nick of time. On 21 October, 1776, as the crisis around New York was nearing its climax. Governor Trumbull sent thirty-six-year-old Major Elisha Sheldon and his 5th Regiment of Connecticut Light Horse Militia to do what they could, and they reached White Plains on 1 November. Sheldon commanded no more than 125 officers and men, divided into seven weak troops. An officer with a Pennsylvania infantry battalion described them as 'beyond the meridian of life, without uniformity of clothing and discipline, and armed mostly with fowling pieces.' Their enlistments were due to expire on 25 December, but they were better than nothing, and Washington was glad to have them.

At the same time, the harried American Commander-in-Chief was heartened by the arrival of mounted reinforcements from his own native state. At the outbreak of the Revolutionary War, various counties in Virginia had raised troops of light horse for the purpose of home defense. In the middle of June 1776, the Virginia Convention gathered six of these volunteer formations into a full battalion under Major Theodoric Bland, an affluent physician and prominent Whig. As the tide of the war turned against the infant United States, Washington appealed for their assistance. That urgent request set up quite a debate among the rank and file of the Virginia Light Horse, for they had originally signed up merely to protect the Old Dominion. Service out of the state seemed an extreme step, but three troops left almost immediately, reaching the Grand Army between the end of October and

An American dragoon helmet of the style worn between 1778 and 1790 by Continental and militia units. It is of the basic jockey cap design, with a brass comb, band and chinstrap, and a horsehair crest dyed green.

the beginning of November. One of them was commanded by a twenty-year-old, Captain Henry Lee, who was destined to become the most brilliant American leader of horse in the course of the war. Eventually Governor Patrick Henry, Major Bland and his other officers prevailed upon the remainder to follow, and they joined up with Washington three months later.

At the beginning of December, just as he was about to put an end to his grueling retreat by crossing to the south side of the Delaware River, General Washington was met by the Philadelphia City Troop of Light Horse, three officers, twenty-two other ranks and a trumpeter led by Captain Samuel 'Quaker Sam' Morris. This elite militia unit had been founded on 17 November 1774, by twenty-eight wealthy young bucks who resided in America's largest city and who rode together regularly in the Gloucester Hunting Club. Each man paid all his own expenses, outfitting himself with a handsome brown regimental coat faced white, a leather cap, a carbine, two pistols, a broad-

sword, a cartridge box, a spirited horse and all its equipment. These patriotic gentlemen had escorted Washington on part of his journey to Boston right after he had been appointed commander-in-chief in June of the previous year, and now, as dark clouds settled over the Rebel cause, they bravely stepped forward, spurning even so much as a penny's payment for their labors.

During Washington's ensuing winter offensive, which neatly saved the newborn nation from an untimely end, the Philadelphia City Troop of Light Horse played a conspicuous part. At the surprise attack on Trenton early on 26 December, it furnished the

One of the Brunswick broadswords taken from the Dragoon Regiment Prinz Ludwig at the Battle of Bennington in 1777. On 9 February 1778, 149 of these double-edged weapons were issued to the 2nd Continental Light Dragoons. The scabbard was made out of wood, covered with black leather and bound in brass.

Commander-in-Chief with a bodyguard and couriers. Four days later half the troop captured an enemy patrol of a dozen men from the 16th Light Dragoons. At the Battle of Princeton, 3 January 1777, 'Quaker Sam' and his bold lads covered a Rebel battery and prevented it from being overrun by British cavalry.

General Washington had been in sore need of their services, for when its term of duty had run out on Christmas Day, only twenty-four troopers of the 5th Regiment of Connecticut Light Horse Militia chose to remain with the Continental Army. As soon as the active campaigning ceased for the winter, the Philadelphia cavaliers were discharged, but the Commander-in-Chief had already taken firm steps to fill the gap they left.

'From the Experience I have had in this Campaign, of the Utility of Horse,' Washington wrote Congress on 11 December 1776, 'I am Convinced there is no carrying on the War without them, and I would therefore recommend the Establishment of one or more Corps ... in Addition to those already raised in Virginia.' He then advised that Major Sheldon be put in 'command of a Regiment of Horse on the Continental Establishment,' and the accommodating legislators acceded to his wishes by raising that officer to the rank of lieutenant colonel-commandant the very next day. On 16 December, the Commander-in-Chief sent him speeding back to Connecticut to form his regiment, authorizing him to recruit six troops, each to consist of a captain, a lieutenant, a cornet, a quartermaster, two sergeants, two corporals, a trumpeter, a farrier and thirty-four privates. Sheldon was also to have a major and a staff of an adjutant, a regimental surgeon and a surgeon's mate.

On 24 December, as a part of the near-dictatorial powers granted to Washington in the midst of the winter emergency, Congress empowered him to raise a total of 3000 light horse. In the course of the next month, he authorized the establishment of four cavalry regiments, and then he informed his political superiors that he would wait to see how difficult it would be to outfit them before he commissioned officers for any more. Bland's Virginia Light Horse became the 1st Regiment of Continental Light Dragoons, and Elisha Sheldon's command was designated as the 2nd. The two remaining regiments went to members of the Commander-in-Chief's official family. Colonel George Baylor, who was put in charge of the 3rd Regiment of Continental Light Dragoons, had served

Thomas Young Seymour was a lieutenant and a troop commander in the 2nd Continental Light Dragoons. This 1793 miniature painted by John Trumbull shows Seymour wearing a blue-faced-buff coat with the high collar that was introduced after the Revolution, but the brass French dragoon helmet with the light blue turban appears just as Seymour wore it in the 1770s.

Washington as an aide through the first two years of the war. Stephen Moylan, colonel of the 4th Continental Light Dragoons, was an Irish Roman Catholic whose sterling qualities had allowed him to overcome the prevalent religious prejudices of the day to land such trusted positions as Muster-Master General and Colonel-Quartermaster-General of the Grand Army.

On 14 March 1777, Congress approved a new table of organization for the four cavalry regiments that had been submitted earlier by General Washington. Each regiment was to be commanded by a colonel, a lieutenant colonel and a major, assisted by one adjutant, a quartermaster, a paymaster, a surgeon and his mate, a chaplain, a saddler, a riding master, a trumpet major

Colonel George Baylor, the first commander of the 3rd Continental Light Dragoons, in a miniature executed by Charles Willson Peale during the winter of 1777–8. Baylor's uniform includes a white regimental coat with blue facings. His epaulettes, buttons and the lace edging his collar and distinctive lapels are silver. Note the black swordbelt under his coat.

PLATE 1: WASHINGTON'S FIRST CAVALRY, 1776–7

1. Private, Light Horse Troop of Philadelphia, 1776–7: *From contemporary descriptions and paintings. Members of this exclusive gentlemen's club provided their own uniforms and equipment, including the finest British arms.* **2. Private, Captain Henry Lee's 5th Troop, 1st Continental Light Dragoons, 1776–7:** *The Virginia state public store issued brown coats to this regiment's 1st Troop; and blue coats with red collars and cuffs to the 2nd, 3rd and 4th. Although the record is mute on what uniform the 5th and 6th Troops had, it was probably the coat pictured here. A return of 10 May 1777 revealed that thirty-two spears were distributed to the 1st and 5th Troops.* **3. Private, 1st Continental Light Dragoons, 1777:** *Based on Colonel Theodoric Bland's 'Regimental Order' of 13 April 1777. Interrupted lapels and green hearts on the elbows gave this unit's regimentals a unique appearance. All ranks wore green waistcoats. Hardy leather breeches were favored by cavalrymen on both sides during the Revolution.*

was not above exerting his influence to secure commissions for relatives and friends.

Finding officers was never much of a problem, but filling the ranks was another matter entirely. Recruits were dear enough to every branch of the Continental Army, but the cavalry faced the double dilemma of acquiring and equipping both men and mounts. Horses were especially hard to procure, and the situation was exacerbated as the war went on and the value of Continental currency dwindled down to virtual nothingness.

By 16 June 1777, Colonel Sheldon had only been able to send sixteen complete dragoons to Washington's headquarters at Peekskill. Searching out volunteers in Virginia, Colonel Baylor got just a single troop of his regiment manned and mounted by that time, not counting the troop of Virginia light horsemen under Captain George Lewis, which had been a part of the Commander-in-Chief's bodyguard and was now annexed to the 3rd Continental Light Dragoons. Lewis's troop continued to protect Washington's person and headquarters well into September 1778, and as a tribute to their dedication to the great man, the whole of Baylor's Horse was known as 'Lady Washington's Own'. The 3rd Dragoons did not reach a respectable size until the middle of August 1777, when

and four unpaid 'supernumeraries'. Following the English practice, the regiments were divided into six troops that were supposed to contain one captain, one lieutenant, one cornet, one quartermaster sergeant, one drill or orderly sergeant, four corporals, one trumpeter, one farrier, one armorer and thirty-two privates. The Commander-in-Chief appointed all the field officers, but he permitted the four colonels to select their respective company officers – although he reserved the right to veto any choices he thought unsuitable, and he

1. Private, Light Horse Troop of
   Philadelphia, 1776-7

2. Private, Captain Henry Lee's 5th Troop,
   1st Continental Light Dragoons, 1776-7

3. Private, 1st Continental Light
   Dragoons, 1777

The regimental colors of Pulaski's Legion. Made from crimson silk by the Moravian Sisters of Bethlehem, Pennsylvania, this banner was embroidered in gold. One side bears an all-seeing eye framed by a triangle (representing the Christian Trinity), a circle of thirteen stars and the motto NON ALIUS REGIT (NO OTHER REIGNS). There are exploding grenades in each corner. On the other side are the initials US, surrounded by the motto UNITA VIRTUS FORCIOR (UNITY MAKES VALOR STRONGER). The flag is twenty inches square, with a silver fringe. It was originally carried on a lance by one of Pulaski's cavalrymen.

eighty mounted militia from North Carolina that had arrived at Philadelphia were incorporated into its ranks. Sending out his recruiters into both Pennsylvania and Maryland, and aided by enormous grants appropriated by Congress, Colonel Moylan had much better luck. He was able to get 180 of the officers and men of his 4th Regiment of Continental Light Dragoons into the field by the beginning of June.

As General Sir William Howe, lately knighted for his exploits of the previous year, gave signs of resuming operations, Washington, all too aware of his lack of cavalry, gave vent to his anxieties and unloosed his famous temper. On 17 June, he angrily ordered Sheldon to forward all his men to the Main Army at once, whether they were mounted or not. Four days later, four troops of the 2nd Dragoons, led by Benjamin Tallmadge, the senior captain, and his troop mounted entirely on 'dapple gray horses ... with black straps and black bear skin holster-covers', set out from Wethersfield, Connecticut. Despite the Commander-in-Chief's stern mandate, Colonel Sheldon was unable to reach him with the rest of the regiment until the end of July, although it should be pointed out that he sent Lieutenant Thomas Young Seymour's troop up to Albany to fight in the Saratoga Campaign and had to keep some troopers on the east side of the Hudson to guard against British incursions to the north from New York.

Counting Captain Tallmadge's squadron, Washington had about 260 light horse from the 1st, 2nd and 4th Dragoons under Colonel Bland at his disposal by 24 June 1777. The appearance of this new corps was variegated, to say the least. Some of Bland's Horse still wore the blue coats with red collars and cuffs that had been issued by the Virginia public store in 1776, but the whole regiment was converting to the short brown coats with yellow buttons and green facings that had been decreed by their colonel on 13 April 1777. There was little uniformity between the different troops of Sheldon's 2nd Dragoons, but eventually they all adopted the blue coats with buff facings worn by Seymour's troopers at Saratoga as the regimental standard. Baylor's 3rd Dragoons received white coats faced with blue. Since Moylan's officers went ahead and provided themselves with sparkling scarlet uniforms, Washington had his Clothier General issue the 4th red coats with blue facings that had been captured from the enemy. That proved to be a bad mistake. When some of Moylan's dragoons were fired on by their own infantry, who mistook them for the British 16th Light Dragoons, Washington ordered their colonel to dye the coats another color. Moylan selected green with red facings, although a few of his men were still seen in their old red coats as late as 15 September. The Continental cavalrymen were supposed to have waistcoats of their respective regiments' facing colors, and they preferred black half boots and leather or buckskin breeches when they were available. Initially they were issued black leather light dragoon caps – some with visors and some without – gaudily adorned with colored turbans, bearskin or horsehair crests, and feathers, as specified by the different regimental patterns. Sheldon's Horse later had brass helmets, presumably from France.

Lieutenant Colonel William Washington, originally a major in Moylan's 4th and later the commanding officer of the 3rd Continental Light Dragoons, spoke for nearly all his confrères when he called the sword the 'most destructive and almost only necessary weapon a Dragoon carries.' All the regimental commanders were most diligent in acquiring sabers or broadswords for their men. At first these were British or homemade models, and later fine blades were imported from France. On 9 February 1778, General Washington had one hundred and forty-nine of the heavy Brunswick broadswords taken from the Dragoon Regiment Prinz Ludwig at Bennington issued to the 2nd Dragoons at their winter quarters in Chatham, New Jersey. Despite such an imaginative use of sources, the Continental light horse did suffer an occasional shortage of swords. For instance, when Bland's Virginia Light Horse first turned out, many of the men carried spears and tomahawks. Handguns were even less readily available, although an American dragoon was seldom without at least one or two smoothbore pistols. Carbines and musketoons were the rarest weapons of all. Relatively few had been shipped from Great Britain to the Thirteen Colonies before the war, and evidently fewer were made in America once it started. Unless a Rebel dragoon was fortunate enough to capture one from a British or Loyalist cavalryman or received one that had been smuggled in from France, he had to make do with a slinged or converted musket – or else do without.

Instead of concentrating his four new cavalry regiments into a mobile strike force at the outset of what was to be his futile defense of Philadelphia, General Washington split them up among the divisions of his Main Army to serve as escorts and messengers for himself and his major subordinates, and as scouts and pickets for his infantry. This was to be the general pattern for most of the conflict, and it is debatable whether the Commander-in-Chief ever appreciated the full potential of mounted troops or whether the scarcity of forage prevented him from assembling them in any considerable body. Whatever the reasons, the British also failed to exploit their horsemen to their utmost, and the presence of American light dragoons did make a definite difference. At the Battle of Brandy-

Charles Willson Peale painted Lieutenant Colonel Henry 'Light Horse Harry' Lee in 1782 in the uniform of his renowned legion, with a buff coat and waistcoat, green facings, gilt buttons, gold epaulette and black leather swordbelt.

wine on 11 September 1777, Colonel Bland spotted Howe's flanking column in time for Washington to save the Continental Army by an orderly withdrawal.

On 13 September 1777, Congress named Count Casimir Pulaski, an exiled Polish revolutionary and professional soldier, as a brigadier general in command of the Corps of Continental Light Dragoons. It was a strange choice. Pulaski was a brave and able leader, and his devotion to the Rebel cause was never doubted, but he was a foreigner and his elevation generated a burning resentment among native American officers, especially Colonel Moylan, who was the senior field officer in Washington's cavalry. Furthermore, the thirty-year-old, Polish nobleman was abrupt, reserved and inclined to periods of melancholy. He and his Polish aides despised their American colleagues as bumbling amateurs. Friction was inevitable. Later Pulaski even subjected Moylan to an unsuccessful court martial for disobedience and striking an arrogant member of the Count's staff.

On 2 October, two days before the ill-fated Rebel attack at Germantown, Pulaski was instructed to muster all his dragoons near the Commander-in-Chief's headquarters, except those on detached duty, in preparation for the coming fight. The Count was barely able to round up 200 troopers, and as they tried to shield the American retreat they were overrun by the enemy cavalry and ignominiously driven back on their own infantry.

Following two more months of inconsequential maneuvering and skirmishing, Washington had his foot regiments throw up their pitiful winter huts at Valley Forge, but he kept his light dragoons out in the frost and snow well into January as an advanced corps of observation to monitor the British lines around Philadelphia and to intercept any shipments of food or supplies being sent to them by neighboring farmers. It was a grueling assignment, as Benjamin Tallmadge, by then a major commanding a squadron of the 2nd Dragoons, testified:

> My duties were very arduous, not being able to tarry long in a place, by reason of the British light horse, which continually patrolled this intermediate ground. Indeed, it was unsafe to permit the dragoons to unsaddle their horses for an hour, and very rarely did I tarry in the same place through the night.

As a result of their exertions, not one of the Continental light dragoon regiments had more than 150 officers and men fit for duty by February 1778, but Congress was about to institute measures that were intended to greatly enlarge the cavalry corps.

On 28 March 1778, Congress granted the wishes of Count Pulaski, who had grown weary of his administrative tasks and jealous subordinates, and authorized him to raise an independent corps of sixty-eight cavalrymen and 200 light infantry. Ignoring Washington's guidelines he filled his unit with German and British deserters. By the fall Pulaski's Legion consisted of three troops of cavalry, a rifle company, a grenadier company, two of infantry and one 'supernumerary' company, each numbering twenty-five to thirty men. Pulaski was allotted $130 to equip every soldier he enlisted, and he dressed his horsemen as Polish lancers.

PLATE 2: THE CORPS OF CONTINENTAL LIGHT DRAGOONS, 1777–8

4. Private, 4th Continental Light Dragoons, 1777: *Moylan's dragoons first fielded in British coats captured in Canada, but they switched to green regimentals with red facings to avoid being mistaken for the enemy.* **5. Sergeant, 3rd Continental Light Dragoons, 1778:** *A deserter-report on a runaway sergeant from Captain Lewis's Troop in June 1777 described his dress as 'a very nice uniform of white with blue facings and silver, also silver epaulettes and a nice headpiece.'* **6. Trumpeter, 1st Continental Light Dragoons, 1778:** *Musicians wore coats of reversed colors. Trumpeters in this regiment were further distinguished by brown shoulder fringe and hearts on their sleeves as specified by Colonel Bland on 13 April 1777.*

In a decision that pleased many more of its own people, on 7 April 1778, Congress promoted Captain Henry Lee of Bland's 1st Dragoons and made his 5th Troop the nucleus of a two-troop formation that was to be known as 'Lee's Partisan Corps'. From the very moment he went into combat, young 'Light Horse Harry' Lee had distinguished himself as a champion raider. His speciality became capturing British supply convoys, which made him nothing less than a living legend to the half-starved Continentals at Valley Forge, and he foiled every enemy effort to snuff out his glittering career. On one occasion Lee beat off 200 English cavalry that were attacking his lodgings with only seven officers and dragoons! On 28 May, Lee's Partisan Corps received its third troop of light horse, and on 13 July 1779, it became Lee's Legion with the addition of a splendid company of Delaware light infantry. The energetic Lee saw to it that his 200 officers and men were well dressed, armed and equipped and that they demonstrated their appreciation with a long list of daring exploits.

The four regular regiments of light horse underwent structural changes on 27 May 1778, when Congress reorganized the whole Continental Army. The regimental staff was streamlined down to the traditional three field officers, one surgeon and mate, a riding master, a saddler and a trumpet major. Each of the six troops was now supposed to contain a captain, two lieutenants, one cornet, one quartermaster sergeant, two sergeants, five corporals, one trumpeter, one farrier and fifty-four privates. This new table

PLATE 2: 1777–8

4. Private, 4th Continental Light Dragoons, 1777

5. Sergeant, 3rd Continental Light Dragoons, 1778

6. Trumpeter, 1st Continental Light Dragoons, 1778

A period print of the tragic death of Count Casimir Pulaski during the Franco-American assault on Savannah, 9 October 1779.

raised the recommended size of a Continental cavalry regiment from 280 to 416 effectives, but it was only achieved on paper. That June, Moylan's 4th Dragoons turned out with 120 mounted rank and file, and the peak strength Baylor's Horse achieved for the year was exactly 159 enlisted men. For the rest of the war the regiments of Continental light dragoons rarely counted more than 200 fit members on their rolls, and the average usually hovered down between 120 and 150.

The same day that Congress established its overly optimistic system of cavalry organization, it founded the Provost Company of Light Dragoons to serve as the military police of the Continental Army.

Commanded by Captain Bartholomew von Heer, a German, this 'Marchesie Corps', as it was popularly called, was supposed to consist of a captain, four lieutenants, one clerk, one quartermaster sergeant, two sergeants, five corporals, two trumpeters, forty-three provosts (privates) and four excarabineers (executioners) drafted from the brigades under Washington. They wore blue coats faced yellow, yellow waistcoats, leather breeches and typical dragoon helmets.

When Sir Henry Clinton, the new British commander who had succeeded Sir William Howe upon the latter's resignation, began his retreat across New Jersey from Philadelphia to New York in June 1778, the four Continental light dragoon regiments repeated the inglorious supporting roles they had played the previous summer – reconnoitering, running messages and protecting the brass. Once the war was centered back around New York City, however, the American horsemen got more action than they could handle.

Since it drew all its replacements and supplies from New England, Sheldon's 2nd Continental Light Dragoons was placed on the east side of the Hudson in Westchester County. This region was a no-man's-land between the lines, infested by roving bands of Whig and Tory foragers and desperadoes known respectively as 'Skinners' and 'Cowboys', who terrorized the local inhabitants and bushwhacked enemy patrols. This bleak and bloody 'Neutral Ground' was essentially to be the 2nd's home for the next four years, and its job was to keep watch over British positions, report any major troop movements and counter small raids, which grew alarmingly common. 'Our parties and those of the enemy had frequent interviews,' Major Tallmadge droly recalled, 'and sometimes not of the most friendly nature.' He described life in the Neutral Ground as an incessant round of 'marching, and counter-marching, skirmishing with the enemy, catching cow-boys, etc., etc . . .' It was as hazardous as it was exhausting. On 2 July 1779, some 200 British and Loyalist riders surprised Sheldon's Horse at dawn at Poundridge, inflicting a dozen casualties and spiriting off a regimental standard in a savage mêlée of clanging sabers and broadswords.

During this hectic period, Major Tallmadge acquired a reputation as a raider that came to rival that of Light Horse Harry Lee. By the summer of 1779, the remount situation had degenerated to such an extent that Sheldon converted two troops of his regiment to dismounted dragoons with Washington's full approval. Within two years they would contain two thirds of the unit's 200 personnel. Tallmadge, a minister's son and a Yale graduate, would occasionally take detachments of forty to fifty dismounted dragoons to do all kinds of mischief on British-occupied Long Island, where he had been born in 1754. He would generally move at night to avoid detection, load his troopers onto longboats manned by volunteer crews, row across Long Island Sound, strike at dawn and then disappear as quickly as he had come. In this manner he and the 2nd Dragoons destroyed a camp of Tory marauders at Lloyd's Neck on 5 September 1779, and Fort St George and 300 tons of hay gathered for the British cavalry at Corum on 23 November 1781, without losing a single man. Tallmadge also engineered the burning of Fort Slongo in October of the following year, and on 20 February 1783, forty-five of his sea-going dragoons overtook a British privateer in a swift American sloop and successfully boarded it with a wild

and unorthodox bayonet charge. In his spare time the amazing and multi-talented Tallmadge set up and managed an espionage network for Washington from 1778 until the close of the struggle.

Life was just as eventful and perilous for the Rebel horsemen serving between the lines west of the Hudson. In the early morning hours of 27 September 1778, four battalions of British infantry under Major General Charles Grey crept up noiselessly on four troops of the 3rd Continental Light Dragoons as they lay encamped near the village of Old Tappan. Using only their bayonets, the Redcoats hurled themselves on the 104 sleeping Virginia and Carolina troopers,

Lieutenant Colonel Charles Armand Tuffin, Marquis de la Rouerie, commanded a legion of foreign deserters and adventurers who frightened their American comrades more than the British. Charles Willson Peale painted him in the unit's blue coat with buff facings and blue waistcoat. Armand's neckstock is red, his buttons gilt and his epaulettes gold with silver stars. He is wearing a leather 'Tarleton' helmet with a black bearskin crest, a leopardskin turban and a white plume.

Lieutenant Colonel William Washington posed for Charles Willson Peale in the plain white coat with blue facings that he wore while leading the 3rd Continental Light Dragoons in the South. His buttons and epaulette are silver.

PLATE 3: IMPROVISATIONS FOR A LONG WAR, 1779–81
7. Sergeant, 2nd Continental Light Dragoons (dismounted troops), 1779–80: *This regiment retained its buff facings instead of adopting the white ones General Washington specified for Continental light dragoons in his 1779 regulations. Officers and men had brass helmets from France and captured Brunswick dragoon broadswords. Coarse linen overalls and French 1777 Charleville muskets with bayonets were issued for service on foot.* **8. Private, Lee's Legion, 1781:** *Based on Virginia state records and the Charles Willson Peale portrait of Light Horse Harry Lee. With their green facings, Lee's men were sometimes mistaken for the British Legion.* **9. Lancer, Pulaski's Legion, 1779:** *A Hessian captain described this corps as 'dressed in a Polish uniform ... and generally well-equipped.' Pulaski procured Model 1777 rifled carbines from France for his command. The men had both coats and sleeved waistcoats, the latter pictured here. The cap was decorated with a six-pointed star, a black turban, white feathers and a horsehair crest. The legion colors were carried on a lance.*

brutally killing or wounding thirty-six of the helpless wretches and taking thirty-seven prisoners. Colonel Baylor was shot through the lungs and captured, and his second-in-command died of his injuries. The Commander-in-Chief acted quickly to help the 3rd Dragoons recover from this devastating blow, promoting his cousin, Major William Washington of the 4th, to lieutenant colonel on 20 November, and putting him in charge of the regiment's ninety-two survivors. Even so, Baylor's Horse was not fit for active duty again until the following September.

With the sudden British capture of Savannah in December 1778, the decisive theater of the Revolutionary War was switched dramatically to the Southern Department. On 2 February 1779, Pulaski's Legion was sent to assist Major General Benjamin Lincoln in his attempted recovery of Georgia, and the 1st

Dragoons followed in its wake in July. Those two units were combined with the mounted militia of South Carolina for the poorly-coordinated Franco-American assault on Savannah that occurred on 9 October. There the valiant Pulaski was struck down at their head by a chunk of canister while recklessly trying to charge through an abatis that blocked his way between two British redoubts. He succumbed to his wounds two days later. When Congress learned of the Count's tragic death, it ordered his legion dissolved. The cavalry was absorbed by the 1st Continental Light Dragoons and Pulaski's infantry went to the 1st South Carolina Regiment.

Following the débâcle at Savannah, Lincoln retreated to Charleston, South Carolina, where he was besieged in his turn by the 10,000 Redcoats and Hessians under Sir Henry Clinton that came by sea between February and April 1780. The remnants of the 1st Continental Light Dragoons took up a post about twenty-four miles outside of Charleston, where they were joined by the 3rd Dragoons under Lieutenant Colonel William Washington. Washington's white-coated troopers arrived from the north just as Clinton started to disembark his army, and the combined Continental light horse numbered 379 officers and

7. Sergeant, 2nd Continental Light
Dragoons (dismounted troops), 1779–80

8. Private, Lee's Legion, 1781

9. Lancer, Pulaski's Legion, 1779

The 3rd Continental Light Dragoons rout the British 17th Light Dragoons at the Battle of Cowpens on 17 January 1781. Painting by Don Troiani.

men. A contingent of South Carolina militia dragoons brought the total number of Rebel cavalry at Charleston up to 500 effectives, and the whole was commanded by Brigadier General Issac Huger of the host state. His mission was to keep an avenue of communications and escape open between the Charleston garrison and the interior and to hinder the English as they tried to push forward their siege operations.

Sir Henry Clinton had cavalry of his own, the British Legion, a regiment of rapacious Loyalist light horse commanded by the ruthless Lieutenant Colonel Banastre Tarleton, plus an attached squadron of the 17th Light Dragoons. Their voyage from New York had been stormy. Many of their horses had died en route and those that survived were so weakened by the ordeal that Huger's men had an easy time of it – in the beginning. But the resourceful and relentless Tarleton quickly got his troopers adequately mounted, and at three o'clock on the morning of 14 April, they pounced on Huger's sleeping camp at Monck's Corner, about thirty miles above Charleston. Fifteen Rebels were killed, seventeen wounded and 100 men and eighty-three horses captured. The survivors fled through the swamps, and Washington and Lieutenant Colonel Anthony Walton White of the 1st Dragoons managed to rally nearly 250 effectives from their regiments.

After pausing to refit and recuperate, White and Washington gamely moved back toward Charleston, intent on harassing British foraging parties and causing as much havoc as possible. Tarleton caught them once again at Lenud's Ferry, with their backs to the swollen Santee River, on the afternoon of 6 May. Forty-one Americans were cut down and sixty-seven taken into captivity. Most of the rest managed to swim to safety without their horses, but no more than 125 regrouped to fight again. Colonel White and his officers returned to Virginia to recruit the 1st Dragoons from scratch, while Colonel Washington took the remaining stalwarts from the two shattered outfits under his wing and retired into North Carolina to procure new chargers. On 12 May 1780, Charleston's 5000 odd defenders surrendered, and with them fell South Carolina.

Congress swiftly dispatched an army of Delaware and Maryland Continentals and Virginia and North Carolina militia, led by Major General Horatio Gates, the victor of Saratoga, to reconquer the state. The only regular cavalry to accompany this doomed, 4100-man host was supplied by a legion commanded by Lieutenant Colonel Charles Armand Tuffin, Marquis de la Rouerie, a French adventurer and soldier-of-fortune. Officially composed of a dragoon troop, two fusilier companies and a rifle company, Armand's Legion mustered sixty horse and sixty foot for this campaign. A disproportionate amount of the rank and file was made up of untrustworthy German deserters, and the officers were all foreigners, including some who had been inherited from Pulaski's Legion. Discipline was lax, and Armand's independent corps earned no honors at the Battle of Camden, where Lord Cornwallis trounced and scattered Gates's larger force with 2200 Redcoats on 16 August 1780.

Following this fresh disaster, Congress finally heeded General Washington's advice and put Major General Nathanael Greene, a fighting Quaker, at the head of the Southern Department. The only reinforcements the new commander brought with him from the Main Army were the 250 members of Lieutenant Colonel Henry Lee's Legion which, according to an act of Congress passed on 1 November, was supposed to be reorganized into three mounted and three foot troops by the first of the new year. Greene found Gates's much reduced forces at Charlotte, North Carolina, on 2 December 1780. Of the 1000 or so Continentals present and fit for duty, eighty belonged to William Washington's combined 1st and 3rd Dragoons, divided into four puny troops led by ten officers.

Greene assigned Washington's horsemen to his light infantry and riflemen, under Brigadier General Daniel Morgan, and sent them to challenge British authority in western South Carolina. On 4 December, Washington and his troopers bluffed 112 Loyalists into surrendering at Rugeley's Farm and demolished a fort

The green-coated dragoons of Banastre Tarleton's British Legion under fire at Guilford Court House. One of the most feared and hated of the Loyalist regiments, the British Legion very nearly brought Virginia to her knees, during the summer of 1781, by applying Lord Cornwallis's nascent concept of total war. Painting by Don Troiani.

there. Twenty-five days later the 3rd Dragoons attacked 250 Tory raiders at Hammond's Store with the help of 200 mounted militia, inflicting 150 casualties and taking forty prisoners.

Busily preparing to invade North Carolina, Lord Cornwallis, the British commander in the South, sent Banastre Tarleton and 1000 regulars to eliminate this nuisance on his western flank. Morgan met Tarleton with a like number at a place called the Cowpens on 17 January 1781, where he deployed his militia as a lure to tempt the Redcoats into rushing pell-mell into the withering, measured volleys of his waiting Continentals. Washington held his troopers in concealment behind a hill until precisely the right moment, and then

An eye-witness sketch of a private in the 2nd Continental Light Dragoons during the Yorktown Campaign, from the journal of Sub Lieutenant Jean-Baptiste de Verger of the Royal Deux-Ponts Regiment in Rochambeau's French army. This crude watercolor accurately portrays the 2nd's uniform – a short blue coatee with buff facings and shoulder straps, gilt buttons, slashed cuffs and vertical pockets. A black leather helmet is decorated with a blue and buff turban, and white horsehair crest.

PLATE 4: THE YORKTOWN CAMPAIGN, 1781
10. Private, 1st Continental Light Dragoons, 1781: *Uniform and horse equipment based on a watercolor from the journal of Sub Lieutenant Jean-Baptiste-Antione de Verger, an officer of the French Royal Deux-Ponts Regiment, who served at Yorktown. This is the uniform Washington prescribed for all his light dragoons in the General Order of 2 October 1779.* **11. Private, Corps of Virginia Light Horse, 1781:** *A Virginia physician wrote of this motley outfit in his diary: 'Most of our Horse are Volunteers, in small bodies, & chiefly Gentlemen; most of them exceedingly well mounted, but some of them badly armed, & all under very little discipline, & hard to govern.' White canvas stable jackets and coveralls, as well as accoutrements intended for the 3rd Continental Light Dragoons, were issued from Virginia state stores. This fellow wears a simple jockey cap, a hunting sword and carries an aged firelock.* **12. Private, 2nd Continental Light Dragoons, 1781:** *From another sketch in the Verger journal. Figures 10 and 12 are both armed with Model 1763–66 French carbines and American-made broadswords.*

unleashed them in a furious charge that smashed the enemy line from the flank and rear and rolled it up. Dashing on, those eighty slashed right through Tarleton's reserve, the 200 green-coated dragoons of the British Legion. Wheeling sharply, the elated Virginians whirled through their old antagonists again. Washington caught a glimpse of the hated Tarleton in the swirling donnybrook, but his sword, a faulty weapon, broke in two near the hilt when he crossed blades with an enemy officer. Still he managed to close up to the English leader and nicked his right hand with the ruined saber. Tarleton drew a pistol, grazed the American's knee and wounded his horse with the ball, making good his escape in all the hubbub and confusion. Behind him the humbled British cavalier left 100 dead, 229 wounded and 600 prisoners. Monck's Corner and Lenud's Ferry had been amply avenged.

Washington's 3rd Continental Dragoons stuck faithfully with Greene during his celebrated retreat across North Carolina, and they were with him when he turned back to meet Lord Cornwallis at Guilford Courthouse. At the height of the battle on 15 March, Washington pounced on the 2nd Battalion of Foot Guards, which had just thrown the 5th Maryland Regiment in Greene's last line of resistance into a

PLATE 4: 1781

10. Private, 1st Continental Light Dragoons, 1781

11. Private, Corps of Virginia Light Horse, 1781

12. Private, 2nd Continental Light Dragoons, 1781

terror-stricken rout. With the aid of the bayonets of the 1st Maryland, the intrepid Virginia troopers broke that elite enemy unit and chased it back to the shelter of a battery of the Royal Artillery. According to legend, one of Washington's privates, Peter Francisco, killed a dozen guardsmen with his long broadsword in that encounter, and his equally enterprising commander nearly captured Cornwallis himself, but a freak accident permitted the British peer to get away.

Cornwallis lost a quarter of his army at Guilford Courthouse, and he decided he would strike at Greene in the future by wrecking his base of supply – so he marched his 1500 survivors north to join approximately 5000 British, German and Loyalist soldiers then

Lieutenant Roger Nelson, who joined the 3rd Continental Light Dragoons on 9 November 1782. This miniature by James Peale shows Nelson in a fashionable white coat with blue facings. Silver lace adorns the buttonholes and the edges of the collar and interrupted lapels. The epaulette on his right shoulder is also silver.

ravaging Virginia, the arsenal and granary for the Rebel war effort in the South. This fatal decision left the Carolinas open to Greene, who gambled that he could do more damage down there than if he followed the Earl. Dispatching Lee's Legion behind English lines to cooperate with the guerrilla band of Francis 'Swamp Fox' Marion in attacking small posts, Greene kept Washington with his own army as he tackled larger detachments. At Hobkirk's Hill on 25 April, the 3rd Dragoons once again outflanked the foe and carried off fifty captives while covering the American retreat. Colonel Washington's luck ran out, however, on 8 September 1781, at Eutaw Springs when he charged the grenadier and light infantry companies from three British regiments that were protected by a blackjack thicket on the right end of the enemy line. The dragoons' horses became snarled in the dense brush, and they were subjected to a rapid succession of rolling volleys. Washington's horse went down, and its rider, entangled in the stirrups, was bayoneted and captured. All but two of his officers and half his squadron were killed or wounded before the fight ended.

Ironically, Cornwallis's doomed invasion of Virginia set the stage for the most imaginative application of mounted forces during the entire Revolution by reuniting the 400 crack light dragoons and hussars of the British Legion and Queen's Rangers. This was the largest concentration of mounted might ever achieved by the British in the South, and Cornwallis sent those hardy Loyalist troopers to confiscate every charger they could find on the nearby horse-rich Tidewater plantations. He also drew 12,000 to 30,000 black slaves to his banner by promising them their freedom, and when they came in they usually brought the steeds their naïve masters had commanded to their care. With this help, the Earl was not only able to assure his regular cavalry of an endless supply of superb thoroughbreds, but was also able to mount 1200 of his infantry. For the first time in the war, the British were able to consistently outrun their opponents. This paralyzed the state militia, which feared swift reprisals if it offered resistance, and it prevented the few Continentals on the scene from engaging in the same hit-and-run tactics that Greene had employed so successfully in the Carolinas. The only horsemen the Rebels had to oppose Cornwallis's hard-riding soldiers were sixty raw recruits from the 1st Dragoons, the remnants of Armand's Legion, and 200 to 300 citizen soldiers of the Corps of Virginia Light Horse, which did not turn out in any appreciable force until the campaign had practically run its course. Thus Cornwallis was free to accord the Old Dominion the same treatment Sherman was to mete out to Georgia more than eighty years in the future, and Virginia was nearing the verge of submission when Sir Henry Clinton stupidly directed his noble subordinate to establish and fortify a naval base on Chesapeake Bay with all his troops. The Earl chose Yorktown and began to dig in on 2 August 1781. That was the one break the wizardly George Washington needed to once again change the course of the war.

Learning that a powerful French fleet was about to

General George Washington awards the Badge of Military Merit on 3 May 1783, to two Connecticut sergeants. At right is Elijah Churchill of the 2nd Continental Light Dragoons, who was cited for his bravery in a raid on Long Island. He is dressed according to the uniform regulations of 1779, with a pair of white epaulettes to mark his rank and the white facings assigned to the four dragoon regiments. Churchill's badge and French broadsword are preserved today at the New Windsor Cantonment. Painting by H. Charles McBarron, Jr.

seal off the Chesapeake, the American Commander-in-Chief marched south on 21 August, with half the Continentals of the Main Army and the French Expeditionary Force of the Comte de Rochambeau, which had been in the northern United States since the preceding year. Ninety-five of Moylan's 4th Dragoons and a draft of eighteen men from Sheldon's Horse accompanied them. Moving quickly, the two allied leaders concentrated nearly 16,000 regulars and militia against Yorktown by 30 September, and on 19 October 1781, Cornwallis and his 8000 soldiers and seamen surrendered.

Yorktown may have decided the outcome of the War of Independence, but it did not mark an end to the fighting. The 4th Dragoons were transferred to Greene's army, which had cleared the whole of South Carolina of British troops except for their last bastion, the port of Charleston. The wily Quaker sent Moylan's Horse on to Brigadier General Anthony Wayne in Georgia, where the Pennsylvanians and Marylanders assisted the 1st Dragoons in keeping the British hemmed in around Savannah and in pacifying the Creek Indians, who remained staunch in their loyalty to George III. When the enemy evacuated Savannah on 11 July 1782, Moylan's Horse returned to Charleston. There Greene consolidated the 1st and 3rd Continental Light Dragoons into a single battalion of five troops on 9 November. Colonel George Baylor, recently released from a British prison, headed the composite command for a brief while. When the last Redcoats boarded their ships and sailed out of Charleston on 14 December, Greene stationed all his cavalry at Combahee to check any possible sorties from British East Florida. Unwilling to endure any more hardships with peace so close at hand, about 100 of those weary troopers deserted in a body in the spring of 1783.

By July 1783, all of the Continental light horse had been furloughed and sent home, except for Armand's Legion, which did not cease to serve until 29 October. A sergeant, a corporal and eight privates of the Provost Company of Light Dragoons stayed at Washington's headquarters to carry messages as late as 3 October, and they may have been the very last American horsemen to personally serve the Commander-in-Chief. By 25 November 1783, the day the Continental Army was reduced to a skeletal 1000 infantry, every regular American mounted regiment had been officially discharged. For a brief interval, the United States Cavalry ceased to exist.

2 Experiments, Expedients and Half-Measures

1784-1815

As the founding fathers of the United States viewed the matter, the Continental Army was never more than a temporary expedient created to cope with a specific problem, and once the British were driven from American soil, it lost its *raison d'être* and was quickly disbanded. On 2 June 1784, Congress peremptorily discharged the last 700 members of the Continental Line, retaining only eighty regulars to guard the military stores deposited at West Point and Fort Pitt. The very next day, 3 June, Congress asked the states of New York, New Jersey, Connecticut and Pennsylvania to furnish 700 men for one year to serve in a regiment of eight infantry and two artillery companies that would protect the western frontier. Less than a year later, the legislators voted that the soldiers comprising this 1st American Regiment be thereafter signed on for terms of three years.

To the modern mind, the meagerness of these military preparations may seem to border on the criminally negligent, but they were not at all shocking to eighteenth century Americans. Many of them saw a large standing army as the instrument of tyranny. The Revolution had been fought, in part, to rid the Thirteen Colonies of just such an institution. Besides, thanks to the weak Articles of Confederation, under which the new nation was governed until 1789, Congress had little power to do more. Indeed, only Pennsylvania filled its quota of enlistments for the 1st American Regiment, and the unit never achieved full strength.

Nevertheless, the young republic was beset on all sides by enemies who were determined to make its continued existence extremely difficult – if not downright impossible. Spain controlled Florida, the Gulf Coast and the vast expanses beyond the Mississippi, and she was doing all she could to retard the spread of American influence in their direction. Great Britain, still smarting over her defeat in the War of Independence, was firmly entrenched in Canada, where some royal officials were convinced that with the right

advice and proper material assistance, the Indians west of the Appalachians might be formed into a buffer state that would halt American expansion. To lend them moral support, the British violated the treaty that ended the Revolution by retaining their garrisons at Detroit and other posts throughout the Northwest Territory. Not that the Indians needed much encouragement to defend their homes and hunting grounds. In the decade following the Revolution, any American settler who ventured north of the Ohio River was taking his life into his own hands. From 1783 to 1790 hostile braves killed 1500 white people, stole 20,000 horses and destroyed £15,000 worth of property along the Kentucky frontier. Without any troops of cavalry, the 1st American Regiment lacked the mobility and the manpower needed to intercept the war parties or adequately defend the settlements.

It was not until nearly 2000 distressed debtor farmers rose in revolt in western Massachusetts in 1786 that serious thought was given to enlarging the American military establishment. On 20 October, Congress authorized the raising of an additional 1340 regulars. This new force, including two sixty-man troops of cavalry, was to be combined with the 1st American Regiment in a legionary corps of 2040 rank and file. The return of domestic peace to Massachusetts by the spring of 1787 caused Congress to renege on its decision, and the army was cut back to its original size.

With the ratification of the Constitution, the United States received the foundations for a strong central government, and the inauguration of George Washington as its first president brought into office an administration determined to bring peace to the Northwest Territory. In preparation for an offensive against the Miami tribes, the number of regulars was increased from 700 to 1216, and a full battalion of artillery took its place beside the 1st American Regiment.

On 3 October 1790, Brigadier General Josiah Harmer led 353 members of his 1st American Regiment and

1133 militia north from Fort Washington (present day Cincinnati) and set out to smash the Indian centers of resistance. The militiamen, who were divided into four battalions of infantry and one of cavalry, proved to be poor campaigners, and the column barely covered ten miles a day. Two weeks after setting out, Harmar's troops burned five deserted Indian villages, but on 19 and 21 October, the Indians ambushed two of his advanced detachments. On both occasions the militia bolted, leaving a total of seventy-five regulars to be massacred. With 108 citizen soldiers dead and twenty-eight wounded, Harmar had no other choice than to beat a precipitate retreat, and his chastised army struggled into Fort Washington on 3 November.

The mounted militia had performed reasonably well as flank guards, but they lacked the staying power for a tough fire fight. Harmar believed no western campaign could be successful unless the government instituted, 'a body of regular horses on the frontiers – Cavalry have emphatically been styled the eyes and the feet of an army.' On another occasion he wrote, 'Without a regular cavalry, I know not how the Indians can ever be effectually checked.'

While the Washington Administration was eager to avenge Harmar's humiliating repulse, it was not receptive to his recommendations. On 3 March 1791, Congress added a second regular infantry regiment of 912 men and 2000 six month volunteers called 'levies' to the Army. Major General Arthur St Clair was entrusted with taking this force, along with whatever militia he required, to crush the Indians once and for all. While St Clair's expedition was being assembled, Secretary of War Henry Knox sought permission to send mounted frontiersmen from Kentucky across the Ohio to raid Indian villages. 'By carrying the war into the enemy's country,' Knox assured President Washington, the Kentuckians would 'prevent in a great degree their invading the frontiers.'

On 23 May 1791, Brigadier General Charles Scott plunged into Indian territory at the head of 750 hand-picked and well-mounted riflemen. Travelling 150 miles in eight days, they then proceeded to burn five Indian towns, kill thirty-two warriors, take fifty-eight prisoners and return safely home at a cost of only five wounded. On 1 August, Lieutenant Colonel James Wilkinson, a regular officer, galloped out of Fort Washington with 500 mounted Kentuckians. Wilkinson got his men lost in rough country and lamed 270 of their horses, but he managed to destroy two villages, kill six

braves, two squaws and a child, and capture thirty-four Indians, losing only two dead and one wounded. His exhausted men completed their grueling 451-mile circuit on 21 August.

The Scott-Wilkinson raids demonstrated the superiority of well-led horsemen over the braves, but St Clair and his superiors did not perceive this clear message. On 17 September 1791, St Clair commenced his campaign with roughly 2000 dispirited and ill-provided troops – most of them still green. The army made lethargic progress through the wilderness, going into camp on 3 November at a spot just ninety-seven miles north of Fort Washington. Half an hour before dawn the next day, 1000 fierce Miami, Delaware and Shawnee braves crept up to within musket range and subjected the drowsy soldiers to a galling fusilade. They slew 657 whites and wounded 271 more before the panic-stricken survivors could burst clear of the murderous trap.

The St Clair disaster shocked the Federal government into adopting drastic measures. On 5 March 1792, Congress passed an 'Act for making further and more effectual provision for the protection of the Frontiers', which increased the regular army to five 960-man regiments enlisted for three years and organized in any manner the President deemed 'expedient'.

Following a suggestion from Baron von Steuben, Washington and Knox formed their new force into the 'Legion of the United States' to better facilitate woodland campaigning. The 5120 soldiers to be raised were to be divided into four sub-legions, complete mini-armies of 1280 men apiece, combining within themselves the three traditional combat arms. Each sub-legion was to be composed of eight companies of infantry, four companies of riflemen, one company of artillery and one company of dragoons. At full strength, a dragoon company was supposed to number one captain, one lieutenant, one cornet, six sergeants, six corporals, one farrier, one saddler, one trumpeter and sixty-five privates. Because recruiting was to be confined only to 'brave, robust, faithful soldiers', the Legion never counted more than 3300 effectives on its rolls at any one time. As a result, the rifle battalions of the 3rd and 4th Sub-Legions were not formed, but that did not detract appreciably from the Legion's effectiveness.

Major General Anthony Wayne, one of Washington's most energetic and aggressive field commanders during the Revolution, was picked to command the Legion of the United States. A strict disciplinarian who imposed high standards on his officers and men, 'Old Tony', as they were to call him, molded the Legion into a superb offensive machine. Assembling his recruits at Legionville, a camp he established twenty-two miles down the Ohio from Pittsburgh on 30 November, Wayne began the long, hard job of turning them into real soldiers.

The training of the Legion cavalry was handed over to Lieutenant Robert Mis Campbell, a jovial and popular fellow who only needed 'health of Body, Peace of Mind, a Pretty girl, a clean shirt, and a guinea' to feel rich and perfectly happy. The men practiced their riding on cold winter mornings under his affable tutelage, and those unlucky enough to slip and crash to the frozen ground soon learned to keep their seats. In the spring, Secretary Knox directed Wayne's Legion to move further down the Ohio to Fort Washington. Old Tony had most of his soldiers bivouac near the fort at Hobson's Choice, but his four troops of horse received a separate camp across the Ohio, named 'Bellerophontia' with classical aplomb. There they spent the summer riding, riding and riding some more. One militiaman wrote admiringly that the Legion dragoons were a joy to behold, cavorting across the country-side at breakneck speed, sailing over the worst obstacles with as much grace as if they were no more than hurdles on a racetrack.

On 4 September 1793, Wayne issued a set of tactical orders to his cavalry, decreeing they were to always 'charge in very open Order, to move easy.' He instructed them to act in close concert with their own light infantry until the Indians were put to flight, and then advance swiftly, 'every Man Charging Twenty Indians. In other Words,' he elaborated, 'they must Adopt that kind of Maneuvers suitable to the Country and Service for which they were intended,' and forget the stylized nonsense they may have read in 'Blinn, Dalrymple and others for Charging Squadrons of Dragoons or Battalions of Infantry on the Plains of Jumatry.'

Mad Anthony Wayne orders his dragoons to charge at the Battle of Fallen Timbers, 20 August 1794. This primitive painting is one of the few contemporary depictions of the cavalry of the Legion of the United States.

Little more than a week later, Wayne was forced to realize it would take more than brave words to make courageous cavalrymen. On 15 September, while guarding one of the Legion's horse herds near Fort Jefferson, a cornet and thirty dragoons spotted two Indians at the far end of a clearing. The Americans instantly gave chase and thundered straight into a well-laid ambush. The first Indian volley killed two sergeants, and as the cornet turned to urge his troopers forward, he was flabbergasted by the sight of them all scurrying back to camp. When Wayne heard the news, he fell into a passion, ordered the dragoons arrested and immediately court martialed, and drew up the entire Legion in formation to witness their punishment as soon as a verdict was rendered. 'While the trial was going on, the general had a grave dug for the dragoon who had led the retreat,' recalled one officer. 'The court found this man guilty and ordered him to be shot. The general, after haranguing the troops for half an hour, pardoned the prisoner and forgave the others.'

Old Tony had good reason for staging such a terrifying ruse. Only four days before he had learned that an eleventh hour effort to negotiate a peace with the hostile tribes had ended in failure. It was now up to him to win it by force of arms, and there was no room for faint hearts in his army. Anticipating this eventuality, he had already requested that Kentucky supply him with 1500 mounted riflemen, but when Charles Scott, now a militia major general, arrived at Fort Jefferson on 1 October with no more than 400 volunteers, Wayne realized he would not be able to deliver any decisive blows until the next summer. Undaunted, he boldly put his Legion into winter quarters at Fort Greenville, built right on the edge of hostile country, and on the day before Christmas he established Fort Recovery at the site of St Clair's defeat.

With the spring, the Indians took up Wayne's challenge by harassing his outposts and lines of communication. The dragoons were run ragged by patrolling incessantly between the forts, escorting officers and supply trains, pursuing deserters and riding to the rescue of beleaguered parties. Old Tony doggedly ignored these minor irritations, pushing ahead with the preparations for his grand offensive. On 26 July 1794, General Scott rode into Fort Greenville with 1500 mounted Kentucky riflemen. They were divided into two brigades under Robert Todd and Joshua Barbee, and what a Legion officer called 'a sort of Independent partizan corps' commanded by Major

PLATE 5: SPAWNED BY CRISES, 1792–1810

13. Dragoon Private, Legion of the United States, 1792–6: *Dragoons of the 1st Sub-Legion were denoted by white turbans; those of the 2nd had red; the 3rd wore yellow; and the 4th sported green. The Ohio wilderness was a cruel locale for cavalry operations. William Clark, an officer in Wayne's Legion destined for fame as an explorer, told his diary: 'The Dragoons ... Sust'd considerable fatigue & Injury from the thickness of the Woods and Brush thro which they Passed on the Flanks.' It is unknown if Wayne's dragoons received any carbines. At Fallen Timbers, they did all their fighting with broadswords.* **14. Dragoon Private, United States Army, 1799:** *The regulations of January 1799 decreed green coats with white facings for the eight authorized troops of light dragoons, but Major General Alexander Hamilton had the facings changed to black.* **15. Private, United States Light Dragoons (dismounted service), 1808–10:** *This regiment served without horses for the first few years of its existence. The men were given muskets, bayonets, shoes and gaiters, and functioned as light infantry. The jacket fastened down the front with seven pairs of hooks and eyes. It was decorated with narrow white binding and seventy-eight bullet buttons.*

William Price. Two days later Wayne led them and 2000 regulars into the dark forest in search of a showdown with the Indians.

Wayne found 500 to 1000 braves and a company of Canadian militia waiting for him on 20 August 1794, at a spot on the northwest bank of the Maumee River known as Fallen Timbers – so called because a tornado had struck down so many trees there. The Legion advanced with the Maumee on its right. Major Price's select battalion formed the advance guard, one brigade of mounted Kentuckians shielded the infantry's left and the other brought up the rear. The Americans marched five miles that morning in this formation, until at 10.00 a.m. an explosion of well-aimed musketry from warriors concealed behind the uprooted trees scattered Price's riders and hurled them back on the Legion.

Wayne coolly shook out his regular foot soldiers into two lines and sent them straight at the foe in a magnificently steady bayonet charge. Then emulating Hannibal's tactics at Cannae, he ordered Scott's Kentuckians to swing around the Indians' left and catch

PLATE 5: 1792–1810

13. Dragoon Private, Legion of the United States, 1792–6

14. Dragoon Private, United States Army, 1799

15. Private, United States Light Dragoons (dismounted service), 1808–10

A hard leather dragoon helmet typical of those issued to the four cavalry companies of the Legion of the United States. It has a bearskin comb and a red velvet turban, which means it may have belonged to a dragoon of the 2nd Sub-Legion.

them in a pincers. Scott's men were so slowed down by the timberland that the braves were able to outrun them, but the dragoons, dashing headlong across the fairly open plain along the Maumee, made one of the most memorable cavalry charges in American history. Their commander, Captain Robert Mis Campbell, was shot out of the saddle at the outset, but brandishing his broadsword overhead, Lieutenant Leonard Covington took his place and led the troopers on to avenge their beloved chief. Covington himself killed two braves, while his dragoons, hurtling over the fallen trees like jockeys in a steeplechase, hacked down or routed all who opposed them. The Battle of Fallen Timbers lasted for more than an hour until the Indians, broken and beaten, melted into the forest.

The Americans had lost thirty-three dead and 100 wounded, the natives twenty to forty killed, but the exact number for either side was of minor importance. Fallen Timbers had proven that the Legion of the United States and its commander were invincible. Within a year, the tribes had come to terms in the Treaty of Greenville, ceding most of present day Ohio and a small section of Indiana to the victors. No sooner had peace come to the Northwest Territory than the mercantilistic trade policies laid down by Spanish officials at New Orleans provoked the ire of Americans living along the Mississippi. To prevent an armed clash, Wayne shifted elements of the Legion south-

ward. By the beginning of 1796, two troops of dragoons were in Georgia and a third stationed in Tennessee.

Initially, Congress was so pleased with the results of Fallen Timbers that it voted to renew Wayne's Legion for another three years, but then on 30 May 1796, it reverted to true form, abolished the legionary structure and cut the authorized number of regulars by 60 per cent to 2000. On 31 October, the United States Army was accordingly reduced to four regiments of infantry, a corps of artillerists and engineers, and two companies of light dragoons. When Anthony Wayne died a month and a half later, a promising era came to a premature end.

Congress soon had cause to regret its hasty espousal of military frugality. In 1792 Great Britain and France had commenced a series of costly and bloody wars that would not run their vicious course until Napoleon's final defeat at Waterloo in the summer of 1815. As the possessor of the world's largest neutral merchant marine, the United States found herself caught in the middle when the navies of the two belligerents took up economic warfare. Jay's Treaty of 1795 brought a temporary rapprochement with the English, but it only goaded the French into increasing their depredations against American shipping. The rulers of revolutionary France were mindful of how their country had helped the Americans win their War of Independence, and now they expected their sister republic to aid them in their struggle for survival. When President John Adams sent a special mission across the Atlantic to iron out these differences, the French demanded a lavish bribe before they would even consent to negotiate.

The details of this humiliating 'XYZ Affair', once they were disclosed, sparked a fire of indignation that blazed across the United States. As American frigates, privateers and armed merchantmen exchanged shots with French corsairs, Congress dramatically beefed up the nation's land defenses. On 28 May 1798, it created a three-year 'Provisional Army' of 10,000 men and empowered the President to call it into service as soon as war was declared. Twelve regiments of infantry and six troops of dragoons amounting to 12,000 men were added to the regular establishment when the 'New Army' was authorized on 16 July. Finally on 2 March 1799, Congress gave conditional permission for the mobilization of a 30,000-man 'Eventual Army', twenty-four regiments of infantry, three of cavalry and a battalion of riflemen, but only if there were a war or the danger of an imminent French invasion. To prepare for that contingency, equipment for 3000 cavalrymen was to be purchased and stored at places where it could be conveniently issued to the newly-formed squadrons.

The six companies of light dragoons attached to the New Army were intended to serve together as a single regiment run by a lieutenant colonel-commandant, a major, a surgeon, a surgeon's mate, an adjutant and a paymaster. Each troop was to consist of one captain, two lieutenants, one cornet, four sergeants, four cor-

porals, one farrier, one saddler, one trumpeter and fifty-two dragoons.

Fortunately for his country, President Adams ignored bitter criticism within his own party and persevered in seeking a negotiated settlement to the quasi-war with France. Peace was achieved by 1800, but American public opinion had turned against the expansion of the military long before that. Because of it,

Captain Jacinth Laval of the Regiment of U.S. Light Dragoons. An engraved portrait published by Favret de St Memmin in 1809. Officers of this regiment wore blue coats with silver epaulettes, buttons and lace and silver binding entwined about the buttons on the lapels. Note the silver scale shoulder strap attached to Laval's epaulette.

Wade Hampton, the first colonel of the Regiment of U.S. Light Dragoons. Another St Memmin portrait. Hampton and his officers wore a black leather cap inspired by the British light dragoon pattern of the day. The crown was reinforced by a pair of metal strips, and a third edged the visor. A broad leopardskin turban was wrapped around the base of the crown. From these engravings it is impossible to determine whether the cap's black leather cockade, with its white embossed center, and the long blue-tipped white plume were mounted on the left or right side. The top of the crown was covered by a flowing bearskin crest. A metal chain, looped around the front of the helmet, could be fastened under the wearer's chin for mounted duty.

The leather cap that was issued to enlisted men of the Regiment of U.S. Light Dragoons in 1808. Originally the round 'front' was decorated with the brass letters $\frac{US}{LD}$. This specimen bears the pewter frontplate that was prescribed for the 1st and 2nd Regiments of U.S. Light Dragoons in 1812. It was converted to meet the new regulations. Note the worn leopardskin turban in the rear, the faded black crest, and the remnant of a blue feathery ten-inch plume, which originally had a white tip.

the Provisional and Eventual Armies were never activated, and only four foot regiments in the New Army attracted enough recruits to top half strength. None of the cavalry troops were raised due to a scarcity of horses. On 14 May 1800, Congress instructed President Adams to discharge the entire New Army within thirty-one days.

Early in March 1801, Thomas Jefferson was inaugurated as President, and his Democratic-Republican party swept into power in the new capital of Washington City. As the opposition party under Adams, the Democratic-Republicans rightly concluded that the recent troop increases had been meant to intimidate them as much as the French, and they were equally suspicious of the regular units that remained. On 16 March 1802, Congress abruptly shrank the U.S. Army down to a skeletal twenty companies of infantry and twenty of artillery, completely abolishing the two troops of dragoons. This last cut was more an act of mercy, however, as the cavalry had lacked horses for some time. Nevertheless, the United States was to be without any regular mounted soldiers for the next six years.

During that time, Great Britain, still engaged in her epic life-or-death struggle with France, wrested away control of the seas, and then, growing arrogant, intensified her blockade of Napoleon's Europe. The Anglophobic Democratic-Republicans deeply resented the increasing restraints placed upon American commerce, and a war scare that blew up in the summer of 1807 inspired grave concern over the reduced state of the armed forces.

Responding to the President's well-reasoned plea, on 12 April 1808, Congress added five infantry regiments, one of riflemen, one of light artillery and one of light cavalry – all to be recruited for five years – to the regular army. The Regiment of United States Light Dragoons was commanded by a colonel, a lieutenant colonel and a major, assisted by one adjutant, one paymaster, one quartermaster, a sergeant major, a surgeon, a surgeon's mate, one quartermaster sergeant, one riding master and two principal musicians. The strength of each of its eight companies was fixed at one captain, two lieutenants, one cornet, four sergeants, four corporals, two trumpeters, one saddler, one farrier and thirty-eight privates. The company officers for the regiment were appointed between May and July, and the field officers were named in October – their sole qualifications seeming to be that they were all good Jeffersonians. Unwilling to purchase horses for the unit until there was an actual shooting war, the Federal government armed and accoutred the smart new dragoons as light infantry.

Despite these timely preparations, the next major trial of strength the United States faced was with its own Indians – rather than the British. A great surge of emigration into the Old Northwest alarmed the native Americans there, especially as white homesteads began to spread beyond the lands ceded in the Treaty of Greenville. A great new leader, the Shawnee war chief Tecumseh, rose among the scattered tribes preaching Indian unity – a powerful confederation that would check the expansion of the whites. In the spring of 1808, Tecumseh founded a village at the juncture of the Wabash and Tippecanoe Rivers. It was called Prophet's Town after his brother, a soothsayer, whose preaching lent an air of mystical legitimacy to the whole enterprise. Within two years around 1000 young Chippewa, Miami, Kickapoo, Ottawa, Potawatomie, Sac and Fox, Wyandot, Winnebago and Shawnee braves had joined them there.

William Henry Harrison, the governor of Indiana Territory and a former aide to General Wayne at Fallen Timbers, was quick to perceive Tecumseh's power and the danger he posed to government interests. In the summer of 1811 he began to assemble a small army of regulars and militia to destroy Tecumseh's confederation at its roots – before it could really blossom. On 26 September 1811, Harrison left Vincennes with a force of 970, consisting of nine companies of the 4th U.S. Infantry, six companies of

Indiana militia, three companies of Indiana mounted riflemen, two companies of Indiana dragoons, two companies of Kentucky mounted riflemen, one company of Indiana riflemen and a platoon of scouts and guides.

Mounted men made up a sizeable part of the column, totalling 270 in all, and they got plenty of work scouting and flanking. The 100-odd Light Dragoons of the Indiana Militia were commanded by fiery Major Joseph Hamilton Daviess, an eccentric United States attorney from Kentucky with an ardent thirst for glory. Daviess dressed his troopers smartly in blue coatees and pantaloons, and gave them sage advice on Indian fighting, but he was a man who tended to let his impulses get the better of his judgment.

Moving with due caution, Harrison arrived at his destination on 6 November 1811, pitching his camp nearly within musket shot of Prophet's Town – as if he was deliberately daring the Indians to come out and fight. Luckily for the governor's plans, Tecumseh was far away to the south, trying to persuade the Creeks and Cherokees to join his alliance, and his unstable brother was too excitable not to snap at the bait. At 4.00 a.m. on Thursday, 7 November, some 550 to 700 grim warriors worked their way noiselessly toward Harrison's position. An alert sentry gave the alarm in time, and the Americans swiftly fell into a predesignated, rectangular perimeter, which they held against several savage onrushes.

As the Battle of Tippecanoe degenerated into a sniper's engagement, Major Daviess, tired of waiting in reserve with his dragoons, bombarded Harrison with three urgent demands that he be allowed to charge on foot and scatter some braves shooting at his comrades from behind a big log. His commander turned him down twice, but on the third time, he snapped testily to an aide, 'Tell Major Daviess he has heard my opinion twice; he may use his own discretion.' Elated, Daviess called to twenty of his men to follow him, but before they could form into line, he strode recklessly into the open, a conspicuous target in a white blanket coat. Before he had taken many steps, a bullet, possibly fired in the confusion from his own lines, buried itself between his right hip and ribs and brought him down, mortally wounded.

At first light, Harrison flung his dragoons and mounted riflemen at his stubborn antagonists in horseback charges launched from both flanks. The troopers boldly chased the Indians across the prairie, herding them into marshy ground, where their steeds could no longer pursue. William Henry Harrison had triumphed, but he paid a high price for the right to burn Prophet's Town. Sixty-two of his followers were dead and 126 wounded – a casualty rate of 20 to 24 per cent. The bodies of thirty-six Indians were found on the battlefield, but their total losses may have been as many as 200.

Tippecanoe was a severe blow to Tecumseh's hopes, but it did not put an end to Indian troubles in the Old Northwest. To counter the expected influx of raids, in January 1812 Congress authorized the formation of seven companies of United States Rangers. Two of these mounted units were to be raised in Ohio, and the rest in Kentucky, Indiana and Illinois. The Ohio companies of Captain James Manary and William Perry were the first to mobilize in April 1812, and the others fielded soon thereafter. Colonel William Russell was put in charge of these seven understrength companies and entrusted with the near impossible task of guarding a frontier 500 miles long. Part regulars and part woodsmen, the U.S. Rangers were supposed to patrol between the blockhouses erected by the state and territorial governors, and cooperate with the local militia in punitive strikes against marauding bands. The idea proved so well-advised that Congress formed ten more companies in February 1813: four in Indiana Territory, three in Illinois and three in Missouri. They would all find their services much in demand.

By the beginning of 1812, Anglo-American relations had reached the breaking point. The mounting strangulation of American trade, the impressment of Yankee seamen into the Royal Navy, a growing conviction that the British were behind Tecumseh's confederation and a strong desire to add Canada to the Union all conspired to push the young republic into open war with the world's mightiest empire. Facing up to the inevitable, on 11 January 1812, Congress increased the U.S. Army by ten infantry regiments, two artillery regiments and an additional regiment of light cavalry. The 2nd U.S. Light Dragoon Regiment was given a whopping twelve companies, each consisting of four officers, ten non-commissioned officers, two musicians, a master of the sword, a saddler, a farrier, a blacksmith and sixty-four privates. On 30 April 1812,

James Burn of South Carolina, who had entered the Charleston Volunteer Light Dragoons as a boy cornet around 1790, accepted the colonelcy of the regiment. His officers were accordingly appointed, and recruiting parties were sent out among the several states, meeting with the most success in Virginia, Maryland, Pennsylvania and Kentucky – although the scattered companies were really not strong enough to start forming up until the end of the summer.

When the United States finally declared war on Great Britain on 18 June 1812, most Americans, like former President Jefferson, confidently believed that the conquest of Canada would be merely a matter of marching. By the late spring Congress had called up a total land force of 35,925 regulars, 50,000 volunteers and 100,000 militia. The entire number of men enrolled in the state militias was 695,000 – a vast reserve – and 20,000 of them belonged to cavalry troops. To oppose them were just 6000 Redcoats and 2100 Canadian auxiliaries. But America's military might looked impressive only on paper. The regular army could barely field 4000 to 6500 trained effectives for the first year of the conflict, and the militia often could not be relied on to muster or fight. To top it all off, the quality of United States leadership was all but bankrupt in the initial months of the War of 1812. While the generals commanding on the Niagara and Lake Champlain fronts fiddled, fumbled and achieved nothing positive, complete disaster swallowed the whole 'Army of the North West'.

On 17 July 1812, Fort Michlimackinac on the northern tip of Michigan Territory timidly surrendered to a mixed force of British and Indians. On 15 August, Fort Dearborn at present day Chicago was given up without a fight, and the victorious Indians massacred many of the garrison. The very next day, Brigadier General William Hull surrendered the main American field army in the Northwest, 450 regulars, 1450 Ohio militia and 200 Michigan militia, to an inferior British force at

A primitive portrait of Colonel Jacinth Laval, circa 1812, when he was the commander of the 1st Regiment of U.S. Light Dragoons. His coat here is similar to the one he wore when he sat for St Memmin, except for a differently decorated collar. Laval sports a severe round hat instead of the sturdy regulation leather cap. The left side is decorated with a black cockade bearing a silver star, which is linked by a cord or chain of the same metal to a silver button.

Detroit. Two squadrons of Ohio and Michigan cavalry belonged to the conquered army, and they saw some action in this curious campaign before its ignominious finale.

The beginning of the end for Hull came on 4 August 1812, when Indians led by Tecumseh, who had thrown in his lot with the British, cut the road to Detroit at Frenchtown on the River Raisin. The following morning Hull dispatched 150 Ohio riflemen and Captain. G. W. Barreres' horsemen to reopen the vital lifeline, but Tecumseh ambushed them at Brownstown Creek. The riflemen fled at the first volley, but the mounted troops held their ground a bit longer, only retiring after they had received orders to do so following a second exchange of fire. Upon learning of this repulse, Hull next sent 300 regulars and 300 militia to do the job correctly. On 9 August, they ran into 410 Redcoats and Indians at Monguagon, fourteen miles south of Detroit. The 4th U.S. Infantry promptly pushed the British back a mile with true professional poise, but when the enemy rallied the American commander ordered the forty Ohio dragoons of Captain James Sloan's Light Cavalry and Captain Richard Smyth's Troop of Michigan Cavalry to charge. The horsemen refused, the British got away and the Americans left the site of their empty victory to participate in the crowning débâcle at Detroit.

Hull's surrender greatly inspired the Indians of the Northwest and called forth a flurry of raids against isolated forts, settlements and individual cabins. Frontier soldiers and officials responded vigorously, launching minor punitive expeditions to force the braves back on the defensive. On 14 October 1812, Brigadier General Stephen Hopkins sallied out of Fort Harrison with 2000 mounted Kentucky riflemen bound for some hostile villages on the Illinois River 100 miles away. Unseen warriors met them with a prairie fire, which so frightened this hardy host that it instantly turned tail and returned to base without accomplishing a thing. In the meantime, Colonel Russell took three companies of his U.S. Rangers, Governor Ninian Edwards of Illinois and four companies of mounted territorial militia and levelled a Kickapoo town on 18 October 1812.

Screened by all this commendable activity, Brigadier General William Henry Harrison was laboring hurriedly to rebuild the Army of the North West and launch a winter offensive against the British at Detroit. Determined not to let the Indians interfere with his

PLATE 6: THE WAR OF 1812, THE REGULARS, 1812–5

16. Sergeant, 2nd Regiment of U.S. Light Dragoons, Undress Uniform, 1813: *The undress coat had long turned back skirts and was laced and braided on the chest and collar just like the dress jacket. Sergeants had two white epaulettes; corporals wore one on the right shoulder.* **17. Major (James V. Ball), 2nd Regiment of U.S. Light Dragoons, Dress Uniform, 1813:** *All ranks wore a short 'hussar-jacket' for their dress uniform. Officers had silver lace on their collars and sleeves, and ornate silver wings. Braided blue pantaloons were worn on active duty. The major's mount is outfitted with a privately purchased hussar saddle, housing and surcingle of European extraction, and an unusually elaborate bridle.* **18. Private, 2nd Regiment of U.S. Light Dragoons, Dress Uniform, 1813:** *Enlisted men wore dark blue braid across their chests – just like officers – but the lace on their collars and sleeves was white silk ferret. Braided pantaloons of white cassimere or buckskin were donned for parade. Some men had converted Model 1808 light dragoon helmets. American cavalrymen carried Model 1805 Harpers Ferry flintlock pistols and Starr 1812-contract sabers.*

All based on the description of the uniform of the 2nd Regiment, U.S. Light Dragoons, which Colonel James Burn submitted to the War Department in June 1812. That uniform was approved for both the 1st and 2nd Regiments.

lines of communication, on 25 November he detailed Lieutenant Colonel John B. Campbell of the 19th Infantry and 600 troops to go and ravage a cluster of Miami towns on the Mississinewa River. Campbell's expedition was composed of one company from his own regiment, Major James V. Ball's squadron of regular dragoons, Lieutenant Colonel James Simrall's Kentucky Volunteer Light Dragoons, a company of Pennsylvania riflemen, the Pittsburgh Blues and some Ohio scouts. James Ball, whom Harrison called 'my friend and associate in Gen. Wayne's Army,' was the junior major in the newly-formed 2nd U.S. Light Dragoons and Campbell's second-in-command. He had reported to Harrison with Captain Hopkin's troop from his own regiment and two troops of '12 Months United States Volunteer Dragoons', from Pennsylvania and Kentucky. Volunteers were a special breed of regular. It was believed their one-year enlistments

16. Sergeant, 2nd Regiment of U.S. Light
Dragoons, Undress Uniform, 1813

17. Major, 2nd Regiment of U.S. Light
Dragoons, Dress Uniform, 1813

18. Private, 2nd Regiment of U.S. Light
Dragoons, Dress Uniform, 1813

would draw more men than the Army's standard five.

Assembling his soldiers at Greenville, Campbell moved them out on 14 December 1812. Campbell pushed his men so hard they made forty miles in two days, and then they marched all day and all night on the third to cover the last forty to their objective – an incredible feat over snow-covered wastes! Without resting, the column was formed into ten files and charged the principal village on the Mississinewa. Campbell's surprise was so complete he was able to kill eight braves, capture eight more and take thirty-four women and children prisoner. The Americans burned three villages that day and their commander had them encamp amid the smouldering ashes at the site of their first success.

At four o'clock on the morning of 18 December, the Indians struck the American camp in a frenzied attempt to exact bloody vengeance. Major Ball had wisely doubled the guard at midnight, and though hard-pressed, Campbell's troopers held their defensive square. After about an hour of bitter fighting, Campbell managed to disengage three companies of Simrall's regiment and had them charge and scatter the attacking warriors. The Indians had at least fifteen killed. Campbell lost ten dead and forty-eight wounded, and with the rest of his expedition suffering severely from the cold, he decided to hasten back to Greenville, arriving there on Christmas Day. It was not a festive occasion for his followers. One hundred and seven of their horses had died on the raid, increasing their hardships, and 303 of the men were rendered unfit for service by frostbite. One hundred and seven of Major Ball's squadron were temporarily or permanently incapacitated, and Simrall's Kentucky Volunteer Light Dragoons were so crippled by the loss of 138 troopers that Harrison immediately discharged all five troops.

Whatever the cost, the Battle of the Mississinewa did eliminate the Miamis and Delawares as a threat to Harrison's flanks, and it brought peace to the frontier until the spring of 1813. Harrison's hopes for a winter offensive were dashed, however, on 22 January 1813, when Brigadier General James Winchester and his entire brigade of 1000 Kentuckians were either killed or captured by 500 British troops and 600 braves under Colonel Henry Procter at Frenchtown. The murder of thirty-three wounded prisoners by the Indians inflamed Kentucky and gave the grieving state a new battle cry, 'Remember the River Raisin!'

On 28 April 1813, Procter and Tecumseh besieged

Colonel James Burn appears in an 1815 portrait by J. W. Jarvis in the uniform approved for the officers of the 2nd Regiment of U.S. Light Dragoons in the summer of 1812. Note the elaborate design of the silver lace on his collar and shoulder wings, which were worn in lieu of epaulettes.

Harrison's reduced Army of the North West at Fort Meigs, near the old Fallen Timbers battlefield. This time the Americans did not falter, compelling the enemy to abandon the siege by 9 May. Part of the garrison was Major Ball's squadron of dragoons. It had been quickly resuscitated with new recruits, and entered the post on 9 April. As Harrison wrote, however, the horses of Ball's troopers 'suffered considerably' from the British bombardment: 'Many were killed and the whole so reduced it is with difficulty they were gotten in. They will however be soon and cheaply recruited in the Rich pastures which this Country affords.'

Harrison spent the rest of the spring and summer gathering strength, defending what remained of American territory and waiting for Master Commandant Oliver Hazard Perry to take control of Lake Erie from the British. These were tense and hectic times for the lieutenants of the newly-commissioned major general. On 11 June, Lieutenant Colonel Joseph Bartholomew, 137 U.S. Rangers and a few militiamen trotted out of Fort Vallonia, Indiana, and travelled 100 miles to ravage some Delaware towns, killing one Indian and despoiling 1000 bushels of corn. At the beginning of July, Colonel Russell took elements of six Ranger companies and some Kentucky and Indiana volunteers – 573 men in all – on a four-week, 500-mile circuit through the Delaware towns, the Mississinewa area, down the Wabash to Tippecanoe, and on to Fort Harrison and Vincennes. They destroyed several vacant towns and ended the threat of Indian raids in Indiana for that summer. Major Ball rejoined Harrison at the end of July with 150 officers and men of his 2nd U.S. Light Dragoons. They were sent to patrol along the Lower Sandusky River, and on 31 July, they ran across twelve hostile braves, slaying all but one.

Perry's victory of 10 September 1813, off Put-in Bay gave the United States complete naval mastery on Lake Erie and freed Harrison for his invasion of Canada. Eleven regiments of Kentucky volunteers under Governor Issac Shelby arrived at the middle of the month. That provided Harrison with a formidable 3000 citizen soldiers from that state, 2500 regulars and 150 Pennsylvania militia. Procter had only a measly 800 Redcoats and Canadians and the 500 to 1500 warriors still loyal to Tecumseh. On 24 September, Procter evacuated Detroit and two days later commenced his retreat to the River Thames. Hot on his heels, Harrison landed his army on the Canadian shore at Amhertsburg on 27 September. Compelled to leave their horses behind by a lack of transport, Lieutenant Colonel James Ball and his dragoons still kept their spot in the American van, seizing a bridge over the Aux Canards River from the British rearguard on the very day of the landing.

Only one unit in Harrison's host was allowed to bring its chargers into Canada, Colonel Richard Mentor Johnson's Regiment of Kentucky Mounted Volunteers, the largest and perhaps the most effective outfit to enter Federal service in the Old Northwest. Johnson, an ambitious United States Congressman, had commanded a short-term, six-company battalion of mounted riflemen under Harrison in the fall of 1812, proving himself a capable and popular leader. Having resumed his seat in Congress upon their discharge, he waited for the spring campaign in Washington. On 26 February 1813, Johnson was authorized by Secretary

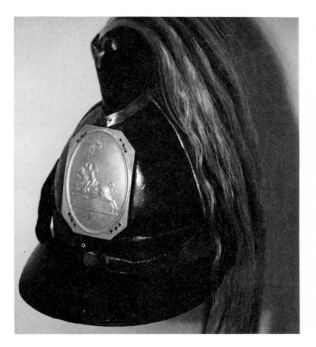

An enlisted man's helmet of the 2nd Regiment of U.S. Light Dragoons, circa 1812. The jacked black leather cap was reinforced by iron straps. The long flowing crest was made of white horsehair. The chinstrap consisted of pewter scales sewn onto two leather strips joined by a pewter button. This specimen is missing the prescribed blue plume with a white tip.

of War John Armstrong to raise a whole new regiment of two battalions 'to serve four months ... and six months if required.' Hastening back to his native Kentucky, Johnson issued an advertisement on 22 March for 'a regiment of Mounted Volunteers, consisting of 1000 men rank and file.' So great was the magic of his name and the sense of outrage over the River Raisin Massacre that 1200 enthusiastic young men flooded into the regiment's ten companies within sixty days. Indeed, the rush to enlist was so considerable that fourteen companies had to be created to accommodate all the applicants, although it appears that no more than ten served together at any one time. The first five companies of the regiment rendezvoused at their colonel's house on 20 May, and the second five mustered at Newport, Kentucky, two days later. Then the whole band, distinctively dressed in black hunting frocks and round hats, and armed with long rifles, tomahawks and butcher knives, rode off to join Harrison.

For the first few months of its existence, Johnson's Regiment scouted and patrolled. With the help of his brother and second-in-command, Lieutenant Colonel James Johnson, a thorough disciplinarian and solid soldier, the colonel whipped his riflemen into finely-tuned fighters. In between missions he would dismount a portion of his troops and supply them with blank cartridges. Then he would charge this line with the rest of his command as it blazed away. This little exercise accustomed the horses to gunfire and taught the Kentuckians to have no fear of volleying infantry. Johnson drilled his men on horseback so often and so long that they were able to fall into combat formation without thinking. It was only natural that Harrison should pick this large and splendid organization to ramrod his advance into Canada.

On 5 October 1813, with his harried forces fast disintegrating, Colonel Procter turned to face his nemesis on the River Thames, more than eighty-five miles east of Detroit. The British commander drew his 830 Redcoats up in a double line at extended order on a plain with the Thames on their left and a big swamp on their right. A small marsh in the middle of the plain divided the British into two wings. Tecumseh and his braves took up a position in the swamp to enfilade anyone approaching Procter's right.

Reconnoitering ahead of Harrison's oncoming brigades, Colonel Johnson must have whooped for joy when he made out the British dispositions. This was exactly the kind of situation for which he had been training his regiment. With the Redcoats standing three feet apart, they would be unable to withstand a mounted charge. He asked for permission to launch one. No fool, Harrison readily consented.

Forming the 500 men of one battalion into four columns under his brother, Johnson directed them to attack the left of Procter's line, between the river and the marsh. As Lieutenant Colonel Johnson bawled, 'Forward, Charge!' 500 voices thundered, 'Remember the River Raisin!' and bounded toward the foe. The Redcoats got off two volleys and possibly a third, then the Kentuckians came ripping through them, shooting men at point-blank range and maiming others with knives and tomahawks. Sweeping clear of the shattered line, the riflemen wheeled, dismounted and opened up a sweeping fire. Beleaguered front and rear, the British on that part of the field rapidly surrendered.

PLATE 7: THE WAR OF 1812, VOLUNTEERS AND MILITIA, 1812–5

19. Private, Colonel Richard M. Johnson's Regiment, Kentucky Mounted Volunteers, 1813: *A recruiting advertisement for this unit stated, 'The black hunting shirt ... to be the uniform of the respective companies ... one pair of overalls lined with leather ... two shirts, a pair of socks, one good pair of shoes and one pair of Mocasons and black neck-handkerchief, are recommended ... The arms, a rifle or musket, a tomahawk and butcher knife — those who do not furnish their own arms will be furnished.'* **20. Supernumerary, Colonel Richard M. Johnson's Regiment, Kentucky Mounted Volunteers, 1813:** *Colonel Johnson formed 'a corps of reserve out of the supernumeraries of the Regiment', arming them with rifles, pistols and swords. They probably comprised the 'Forlorn Hope' that rode by his side at the Battle of the Thames. Note how the black linen hunting shirt has faded to a dark grey.* **21. Private, 7th New York Dragoon Regiment, 1814:** *The New York militia cavalry adopted red coatees in 1809, and a troop of 7th Dragoons caused near panic during operations around Plattsburg, New York, in September 1814, when it was mistaken for British cavalry.*

Pushing on above the marsh, Colonel Johnson and his remaining six companies had a harder time of it, encountering thick underbrush and stubborn resistance from Tecumseh's warriors in the swamp. The 550 Kentuckians fought like tigers, and made gradual headway. Conspicuous on a white mare, Johnson had twenty-five bullets strike his person, his horse or riddle his clothing. At the height of the struggle, an Indian in pale buckskins leaped into the open and fired a rifle at the congressman turned colonel, the ball scraping along Johnson's arm from the hand to the elbow. Johnson nearly fainted from the pain, but as the brave came toward him with an upraised tomahawk, he drew and cocked a pistol, firing a bullet and three buckshot into his assailant's face when he was just four feet away. Legend has it that the man Johnson killed was Tecumseh. Whether he was or not, it is true that the great chief was killed around that time, and his surviving followers crept away into the forest.

Richard Johnson's courage and judgment had won the Battle of the Thames for William Henry Harrison at a surprisingly low cost — twelve dead and twenty-two wounded. British casualties were nearly the same,

19. Private, Colonel Richard M. Johnson's Regiment, Kentucky Mounted Volunteers, 1813

20. Supernumerary, Colonel Richard M. Johnson's Regiment, Kentucky Mounted Volunteers, 1813

21. Private, 7th New York Dragoon Regiment, 1814

but 600 Redcoats were captured. Their defeat was so decisive that the U.S. Rangers and local volunteers were sufficient to keep the peace in the country west of the Thames and the Northwest Territory to the end of the war. Elsewhere and much further to the south, other frontier cavalrymen demonstrated their mettle against an equally serious Indian uprising.

Inspired by Tecumseh's earlier successes, 100 Creek warriors massacred 400 white men, women and children at Fort Mims on 30 August 1813. The state of Tennessee mobilized instantly, mustering 2500 militia under Major General Andrew Jackson to punish the Creeks. The largest and most valuable component in Jackson's army consisted of the 1500 mounted riflemen raised by Brigadier General John Coffee. At 3.00 a.m. on 3 November, these backwoods cavalrymen fell on the Creek town of Tallushatchee in one of the most devastating blows delivered during the War of 1812. Drawing up his riflemen in a long line, Coffee sent the center tearing straight at the village while the two ends looped around, encircling the periphery with a living wall of shouting men, neighing horses and blazing flintlocks. Of all the 186 braves present at Tallushatchee, not one escaped alive. Coffee took eighty-four women and children prisoner and lost five dead and forty-one wounded.

Jackson copied Coffee's tactics six days later at Talledega, using foot soldiers to rush the town and mounted units on both flanks to surround it. Twelve hundred Creeks made their final stand against Jackson and an army of 4000 at Horseshoe Bend on the Tallapoosa River on 27 March 1814. While his infantry went for the Indian earthworks head-on, Coffee's cavalry came in from the rear, swimming the river on horseback or crossing in stolen canoes. About 700 warriors were cut down, to Jackson's twenty-six dead and 111 wounded.

The year 1813 brought considerable action to regular cavalry squadrons serving with other American armies, but their deeds, however valiant, were hardly as spectacular as those of Johnson's and Coffee's enthusiastic volunteers. On 27 May 1813, forces under Major General Henry Dearborn took Fort George away from the British on the Niagara frontier. But the operation was conducted in such a slip-shod manner that 1500 of the garrison escaped. The subsequent pursuit was carried on with so little vigor that 700 Redcoats were able to turn around and strike at a contingent of 1300 American regulars as they slept in battle formation on the banks of Stoney Creek.

Pouncing at three o'clock on the morning of 5 June, the British drove back the 5th, 16th, 23rd and 25th U.S. Infantry in fine style. Just as their comrades' line broke, a squadron of the 2nd U.S. Light Dragoons charged, riding right through an extremely surprised 49th Foot. Amid all the havoc, hubbub and darkness, however, the 16th Infantry mistook the intrepid troopers for enemy cavalry and fired into them. Then the two senior American generals stumbled into some British units and were captured, leaving the command of the column to James Burn, the next officer in rank and the colonel of the shaken dragoons. Conferring hurriedly with his subordinates, Burn ordered a withdrawal.

Elsewhere on the Niagara front, American cavalrymen behaved with a bit more dash. A British landing party of 1200 men tried to take Sackett's Harbor, the only decent harbor on the American side of Lake Ontario, on 29 May 1813. They were opposed by only Brigadier General Jacob Brown, 400 regulars and 250 volunteers. But Brown was stubborn, and 250 of his regulars belonged to the 1st and 2nd U.S. Dragoons. Together with some local militia, whom the troopers repeatedly had to rally, they fought the enemy to a standstill and saved the port.

A squadron of the 2nd U.S. Light Dragoons accompanied Major General James Wilkinson's half-hearted thrust against Montreal in the fall. This detachment opened the Battle of Chrysler's Farm on 11 November 1813, charging pell-mell at the 89th Foot. But the Redcoats held firm. With the help of the Royal Artillery and Mother Nature, who pelted the oncoming horsemen with sleet and snow, they blasted the Americans back across the muddy field to a stretch of trees. There the dragoons stayed for the rest of the battle, wasting their carbine ammunition on distant targets, despite the pleas of their officers to remount and attack again. The rest of Wilkinson's army made as little impression on the inferior British blocking force, and yet another American campaign ended in abject and humiliating failure.

There was to be humiliation a plenty in the year to follow, when the British burned Washington, D. C., in the late summer. A party of Maryland militia cavalry was present at the futile effort made at Bladensburg on 24 August 1814 to halt the enemy's drive on the capital, but its troopers refused to obey an order to charge and abandoned their position without a fight.

Lieutenant Matthew M. Standish's troop of the 7th

Lieutenant Colonel James Johnson, with his battalion of Richard M. Johnson's Regiment of Kentucky Mounted Volunteers, overrunning the British 41st Foot in the rip-roaring charge that won the Battle of the Thames, 5 October 1813.

New York Dragoon Regiment helped Major General Alexander Macomb's 1200 regulars and some militia to hold Plattsburg against 10,000 enemy veterans, fresh from victories over Napoleon's finest in Spain. The only trouble was that the New York troopers had red uniforms, and when they went to support some New England irregulars during a delaying action on 6 September 1814, their jumpy comrades panicked, thinking the British had gotten in their rear.

One hundred and fifty Mississippi Dragoons, a battalion led by Thomas Hinds, played a major role in the initial stages of the final campaign of the war, which was conducted around New Orleans at the end of the year. The Mississippians were so thorough and heartless on their patrols that the British did not get a good look at Andrew Jackson's lines until their army was right on top of them. On 29 December 1814, the Mississippi Dragoons blithely practiced their evolutions in the open for more than an hour within 200 yards of the foe. Despite all the British could do, they only managed to slightly wound three men and two horses. Jackson's watching troops gave those incredibly cool young bucks three rousing cheers as they came in, and the general complimented them. When Jackson's artillery and riflemen mowed down 2036 attacking Redcoats on 8 January 1815, Hinds's troopers stood by in reserve, ready to stem any enemy breakthroughs. None came.

American cavalrymen proved their worth time and time again during the War of 1812, but in the regular army their services and potential went largely unappreciated. The two regiments of U.S. Light Dragoons were kept apart, individual squadrons and troops being attached to separate commands. Even then their strength was further frittered away by short-sighted generals who detached troopers as escorts, couriers and scouts. On 10 February 1814, Congress voted to expand the army from 58,250 to 62,773 men, but the 1st and 2nd Dragoons were reduced to one 'Regiment of Light Dragoons'. This consolidation took place under Colonel Burn three months later. On 3 March 1815, Congress went so far as to abolish even this regiment, declaring cavalry was too expensive and not adept at fighting woodland Indians! Thus it was that a patent falsehood was invented to denude the young United States of a reliable mounted force for the third time in her short history.

3 The Birth of the U.S. Cavalry
1832-6

For seventeen long years the United States Army was without anything even remotely resembling a cavalry unit, and it was not until 1833 that a regular regiment of dragoons reappeared on its table of organization. The complete absence of any mounted troops was sorely felt, for American settlers were flooding into the Mississippi Valley, and friction with the surviving woodland Indians continued. And as settler towns and homesteads tumbled onto the edge of the Great Plains, they were confronted by a whole new race of mounted tribes, whom only cavalry could catch and control. Necessity alone, however, is always a weak argument in American politics, and it was not until the terror of Indian depredations was wedded to the irresistible allure of commercial gain that the Federal government in Washington City was persuaded to revive the mounted arm.

As long as hostile Spain ruled Mexico and the adjacent borderlands, Americans were barred from trading with their Hispanic neighbors in the Southwest. But then in 1821, the Mexicans overthrew their Spanish masters and the old mercantilist system. William Becknell, an enterprising merchant from Franklin, Missouri, was the first to take advantage of this change in attitude; in 1821 and 1822 he blazed a path to the capital of New Mexico that has been known ever since as the Santa Fe Trail. What Becknell found was a retailer's dream-come-true, 40,000 isolated New Mexicans eager to pay inflated prices in gold, silver and furs for manufactured goods their mother country could not provide. No one knows exactly how much Becknell made, but after his first trip one of his Franklin backers received a return of $900 on a sixty dollar investment.

With profits like that to be had, other frontier entrepreneurs were quick to get into the act, despite the fact the route that Becknell blazed stretched for hundreds of miles across vast, untamed prairies, over treacherous rivers, through the alkaline dust of the Cimarron Desert and up into the Rocky Mountains. There was one other danger, Indians. Comanche and Pawnee, intent on stealing horses and other booty, would often attack the trading parties as they crossed their territory. For their own protection, the merchants organized themselves into a caravan in 1824, and from that time onward they only crossed the Santa Fe Trail in large wagon trains, making the journey once or twice a summer. In Indian country, the wagons travelled in four parallel columns, which could be swiftly whipped into a hollow square at the slightest sign of trouble.

In 1828, however, the traders grew careless; some straggled and three were killed by the Comanches. A hue and a cry went up for government protection, and in May 1829, Captain Bennett Riley and four companies of the 6th U.S. Infantry set out from Fort Leavenworth to escort the caravan. Riley and his 170 hard-marching regulars saw the traders safely across the Arkansas River, then recognized as the boundary between the United States and Mexico, and set up a camp on the American side to await their return. From the end of July until 11 October, the troops were kept under constant siege by the Comanches, who were able to stay out of harm's way on their swift ponies. As one of Riley's subordinates, Lieutenant Philip St George Cooke, explained, the situation had a terribly demoralizing effect on the men:

> It was a humiliating condition to be surrounded by these rascally Indians, who, by means of their horses, could tantalize us with hopes of battle, and elude our efforts; who could annoy us by preventing all individual excursions for hunting, etc., and who could insult us with impunity.

The Santa Fe caravan made its way back to Riley with the help of five companies of Mexican cavalry, but it had been attacked twice by the Comanches.

Riley managed to get his troops and the traders home with no further complications of a major nature, but his expedition demonstrated that infantrymen could not cope with mobile, mounted war parties. Only cavalry could hope to meet the Plains Indians on anything like equal terms.

That lesson was not lost on Missourians or their representatives in Washington. In December 1831, Senator Thomas Hart Benton introduced an 'Act to authorize the President to raise mounted volunteers for the defense of the frontier.' Subsequent events provided that Benton's arguments would fall on receptive ears. In April 1832, Chief Black Hawk, the leader of a tribe whose lands east of the Mississippi had all been lost by treaty, recrossed the river with 400 Sac and Fox warriors and 600 women and children, guiding them straight toward their old haunts. Black Hawk's attempted homecoming set off a wild panic among the settlers that was far out of proportion to the cause. With the help of Governor John Reynolds, Brigadier General Henry Atkinson gathered together 400 regulars, 3000 mounted Illinois militia, 200 Illinois foot soldiers and 350 Michigan volunteer cavalry, unleashing them in June to annihilate the hapless natives. Coveting some of the credit for the suppression of this infamous 'Black Hawk War', Congress speedily passed Benton's bill into law, and on 15 June 1832, the United States Mounted Ranger Battalion came into being.

Not quite a bona fide cavalry regiment, this new outfit was a throwback to those semi-independent companies of regular irregulars who had patrolled the Northwest during the War of 1812. The U.S. Mounted Rangers were intended to be one-year volunteers who would furnish their own rifles and horses, and receive one dollar a day in compensation. They were organized into six companies each of 100 privates, commanded by a captain, three lieutenants and four non-commissioned officers. The battalion's first five captains were all appointed on 16 June, in the vain hope that they might recruit their companies in time to fight Black Hawk. Captain Jesse Bean of Tennessee had served with Jackson at the Battle of Horseshoe Bend in 1814, and Nathan Boone of Missouri, the youngest son of the great Daniel Boone, had been a ranger during the War of 1812. The other three captains, Benjamin V. Beekes, Lemuel Ford and Jesse B. Browne, lacked previous military experience.

President Andrew Jackson commissioned Henry Dodge as major and commander of the Battalion of U.S. Mounted Rangers on 22 June. A veteran militia colonel of long service who had seen some action during the last war with Great Britain, Dodge was the epitome of a frontier soldier-politician. At the outbreak of the Black Hawk War, he galloped into the field at the head of 350 Michigan mounted volunteers, and he was doing yeoman service with Atkinson's army when word of his new position reached him.

Although Dodge decided to stay with his Michiganders until Black Hawk was hunted down, his ranger captains wasted no time in signing up volunteers. Secretary of War Lewis Cass told one of them only to accept fellows 'capable of enduring all the fatigues of arduous service'. Captain Ford's Company, which was composed of Indiana men, entered Federal service on 20 July 1832, and Beekes's Company, also recruited from among the 'Hoosiers', was mustered in at Vincennes eight days later. Boone's Missourians and Browne's rangers from Illinois were officially incorporated into the battalion around the middle of August. Captain Bean raised his troop from among the villages around Batesville, Arkansas, and they became United States Mounted Rangers after they rode into Fort Gibson on 14 September. The battalion's sixth company, Captain Matthew Duncan's from Illinois, did not take the field until 5 November.

Dodge had originally intended to base his rangers at Fort Armstrong, Illinois, but a virulent epidemic of Asiatic cholera was raging there. So on 31 August 1832, he sent the four companies he had assembled to healthier locations. Browne and Beekes were to keep an eye on the Indians along the Illinois-Wisconsin frontier. Ford and Boone were directed to join Bean at Fort Gibson, a stockade on the Arkansas River that stood as the southernmost post on America's thin line of western defenses.

Colonel Matthew Arbuckle, the commander at Fort Gibson, had standing orders to 'keep the Rangers in active service,' and he entrusted Captain Bean's company with a delicate assignment. With the approval of President Jackson, Congress had passed the Indian Removal Act of 1830, under which the eastern tribes were transported from their ancient lands within the established states and resettled in new homes across the Mississippi and beyond the pale of white settlements. Once there, these uprooted and civilized people fell victim to the Plains Indians who had no love for their new neighbors. Arbuckle wanted Bean to steer a wide arc through the treaty lands, make contact with the

original inhabitants and try to entice them into coming to Fort Gibson for a peace parley with their less wild brethren.

Leaving thirty-three rangers behind sick or on detached service, Bean set out with about eighty men on 6 October 1832. A week later he was overtaken by an officer and fourteen rangers escorting Henry L. Ellsworth (a commissioner dispatched from Washington to negotiate a treaty with the warlike tribes), an English author named Charles J. Latrobe, and the famous American novelist, Washington Irving. Bean failed to accomplish his objective, and his followers made a very poor impression on his guests. All three of them left posterity extremely unflattering portraits of the U.S. Mounted Rangers. It was probably Ellsworth's opinion that pulled the most weight with the Federal government, and this brief excerpt goes a long way towards explaining the battalion's eventual fate:

> The Rangers generally, are smart active men at home, good farmers & respectable citizens. They enlisted only for one year, to explore the country and expect to return to their families again when their term is out – in the meantime, they seemed determined to keep up republican equality, by acknowledging no superior ... and let me here say, I consider the Rangers ... almost a failure – their dress in the first place is practically (leathern dress is the uniform) the poorest clothes they have or can get – their equipments are only one rifle – this often gets out of order, and then the Ranger has no weapon... Now, their appearance is that of so many poor hunters – they strike no awe.

The Mounted Rangers spent the winter at nearby Army posts and turned out for active duty in the spring. On 6 May 1833, Colonel Arbuckle ordered the rangers of Bean, Boone and Ford to accompany two companies of the 7th U.S. Infantry under Lieutenant Colonel James B. Many and intimidate whatever Comanche and Wichita bands they found between the Canadian and Red Rivers. In a tragic turnaround on 2 June, a war party cut off Private George B. Abbey of Boone's company. Many's entire command pursued

A lieutenant of the United States Dragoons gallops across a Philadelphia park in the dress uniform that was authorized for the Army's first permanent mounted regiment in 1833. This watercolor was done from life in 1840 by Augustus Koellner.

the marauders, but the infantry were too slow and they escaped. This futile chase left the rangers too drained and discouraged to go on, and four weeks later Many's disastrous expedition limped back into Fort Gibson.

A little further to the north at Fort Leavenworth, Bennett Riley, now a major, assigned Captain William N. Wickliffe, with twenty-six 6th Infantrymen, a field-piece and Captain Duncan's 115 rangers, to escort the annual caravan to Santa Fe. Wickliffe carried out his mission without a hitch, and he praised the mounted contingent for doing all he asked 'with cheerfulness, and considering the verry [sic] limited experience of Capt. Duncan's Company of Rangers, with much correctness . . . and in a manner that gave satisfaction.' Under the direct control of Major Dodge, the companies of Brown and Beekes provided the muscle at a council held on 22 June, where their commander persuaded the Winnebagos to surrender eight murderers, abandon their ancestral lands and retire across the Wisconsin River.

By the beginning of July, there arose a clamor among the various ranger companies as more and more men began to demand their discharge. On 7 July 1833, all of Beekes's men stacked their arms at Fort Winnebago and lit out for Indiana. The other companies slowly dissolved over the next few weeks, although Boone kept his troops together a full extra month until mid-September. With the disbanding of Duncan's company in November, the United States Mounted Ranger Battalion was no more.

There was no effort to raise a second ranger battalion. While not quite the total disaster that some historians have alleged, the U.S. Mounted Rangers did not live up to the government's expectations. The men had lacked discipline, and their short terms of enlistment limited their effectiveness and reliability. They looked so dirty in their greasy leather hunting shirts that they made their own countrymen feel ashamed, and to the Plains Indians, who were unable to distinguish them from ordinary mounted militia, they were objects of contempt. When Secretary of War Cass reported at the end of 1832 that it cost $150,000 more a year to maintain the Battalion of Mounted Rangers than a full regiment of dragoons, the unit's imminent demise was assured. Even so, the rangers had proved to the penny-pinching legislators at Washington that the Army could no longer do without a mounted corps of some sort. And so on 2 March 1833, acting on a measure originally presented, appropriately enough,

PLATE 8: THE BIRTH OF THE U.S. CAVALRY, 1832-4
22. Private, U.S. Mounted Ranger Battalion, 1832: *Frontiersmen who provided their own arms, clothing, horses and equipment, the Mounted Rangers were a seedy bunch. Dirty leather hunting shirts, blanket coats and greasy leather leggings were the norm.* **23. Sergeant ('Long Ned'), U.S. Regiment of Dragoons, Fatigue Order, 1833:** *Many shortages plagued the Regiment of Dragoons as its first battalion was mustered in the summer of 1833. Private James Hildreth said that Captain Edwin V. Sumner's Company B received Model 1833 shell jackets and white cotton pantaloons for drill and fatigue.* **24. Adjutant (Second Lieutenant Jefferson Davis), U.S. Regiment of Dragoons, Undress, 1833:** *A veteran dragoon remembered seeing the future Confederate President on the parade ground at Jefferson Barracks in 'white drill Pants, made quite narrow at the boot, and quite wide at the thigh, and undress coat.' An officer's collapsible leather forage cap was marked by a gilt, embroidered, six-pointed star. An enlisted man's bore his company's letter cast in brass.*

by Richard Mentor Johnson, Congress created the United States Regiment of Dragoons. This unit was destined to become a permanent part of the American Army, and its birth date is the real birthday of the U.S. Cavalry.

The U.S. Regiment of Dragoons was intended to meet a big need, and its authorized size was fixed at ten overstrength companies totalling thirty-four officers and 715 men. Henry Dodge was promoted to colonel and put in command. Commissions on the company level were offered to his officers from the Battalion of Mounted Rangers, and nine of them accepted. The rest of the officers were transferred in from the Army's seven infantry regiments. Dodge was highly pleased with this novel arrangement, commenting that 'taking a part of the officers from the regular army, who understand the first principles of their profession, and uniting them with the Ranging officers, who understand the woods' service, would promote the good of the service.' Dodge certainly had no cause for complaint about the caliber of the regular officers who entered his regiment. There were several among them destined for brilliant careers over the next three decades or so – Lieutenant Colonel Stephen Watts

PLATE 8: 1832–4

22. Private, U.S. Mounted Ranger
Battalion, 1832

23. Sergeant, U.S. Regiment of Dragoons,
Fatigue Order, 1833

24. Adjutant, U.S. Regiment of Dragoons,
Undress, 1833

Kearny, Captain Edwin V. Sumner, First Lieutenant Philip St George Cooke and Second Lieutenant Jefferson Davis.

Lieutenant Colonel Kearny, every inch a professional and a stickler for perfection, was fittingly empowered to supervise the new regiment's recruiting and training. He was warned to accept only 'healthy, respectable men, native citizens, not under twenty, nor over thirty-five years of age, whose size, figure and early pursuits may best qualify them for mounted soldiers.' Although some immigrants and ne'er-do-wells did get into the ranks, in most cases these stringent qualifications were observed. George Catlin, the famous painter of the American Indian who was to accompany the Regiment of Dragoons on its first expedition, declared that it was 'composed principally of young men of respectable families, who would act, on all occasions, from feelings of pride and honor, in addition to those of the common soldier.'

To dissipate possible sectional feeling within the regiment, recruiting parties were sent into nearly every part of the Union. This practice resulted in filling large sections of the command with raw tenderfeet from the East. Company E was raised in New York City, Company F consisted mostly of Bostonians, and Company B did its recruiting in western New York State. Other companies were formed in states closer to the frontier, such as Missouri, where Captain Nathan Boone permitted only 'enterprising and able bodied citizens' of good repute to join his Company H.

In order to replace the Battalion of Mounted Rangers before the expiration of its term of service, the first five companies of the Regiment of Dragoons were ordered to be raised and assembled at Jefferson Barracks, the organization's headquarters, by the fall of 1833. The second battalion was to be completed and to join them that following spring.

Jefferson Barracks was a pleasant post perched on a beautiful bluff overlooking the Mississippi River three miles south of St Louis, but its charms were wasted on

Artist George Catlin painted Colonel Henry Dodge when he accompanied the U.S. Regiment of Dragoons on its first expedition in the summer of 1834. Dodge favored the simple round hat and blue buckskins of his U.S. Mounted Ranger days for field wear, instead of a confining military uniform. He also carried a long rifle and a brace of pistols. His only badge of rank was a sword.

A print of Jefferson Barracks, Missouri, in the 1830s, when the first battalion of the U.S. Regiment of Dragoons was organized there. This post continued to serve the U.S. Cavalry as a recruit depot throughout the rest of the century.

the five companies of disgruntled dragoons who came straggling in between May and September 1833. In order to attract the best type of men to their companies, the recruiting sergeants told them monstrous lies. Some were promised they would rank with the cadets at West Point and would someday become officers. Others were assured they would be bothered with no menial duties and 'would have nothing to do but to ride on horseback over the country, to explore the western prairies and forests, and, indeed, spend their time continually in delightful and inspiring occupations.'

Upon their arrival at Jefferson Barracks, the new dragoons found they had committed themselves for a five-year stay in a fool's paradise. They received no privileges that were not accorded to the rest of the

Army, and the discipline was brutally harsh. The recruiters had made a big point of telling their victims about how the government would give them splendid uniforms, so many of the enlistees went to Jefferson Barracks with only the clothes on their backs. The Quartermaster General's office, however, failed to deliver on time, and only Captain Sumner and First Lieutenant David Perkins possessed the foresight or the deviousness to procure at least a full fatigue uniform for every one of their New Yorkers in Companies B and E. According to James Hildreth, a private in Sumner's Company B, the rest of the battalion resembled 'Jack Falstaff's ragged regiment'. Furthermore, those dragoons lucky enough to find quarters at Jefferson Barracks did not have bunks to sleep on, and they had to pay for their kitchen utensils out of their own pockets. Every day after morning drill they were issued tools and set to building their own barracks and stables, a task these men with such high expectations found particularly galling. To top it all off, the first weapons they received were condemned muskets that had been rotting in an arsenal since the War of 1812. Most of them could no longer fire, and it did not make a fellow feel soldierly drilling with an antiquated flintlock that Hildreth called 'as effectual . . . as a broomstick.' The Regiment of Dragoons did not even receive any horses until October, and even though they were fine beasts, there were only enough of them to mount three of the five companies.

Discontent festered in the ranks and grew rife as the autumn progressed. The guardhouse was soon jammed full to overflowing; courts martial were convened almost daily to mete out punishments for infractions great and small. In October the men began deserting five, six or eight a night. By May the regiment had lost at least 100 dragoons in this fashion, and Brigadier General Henry Leavenworth, the commander of the Army's Department of the West, had to implement strict penalties to keep the outfit from falling apart. He threatened deserters with the loss of their citizenship, and if apprehended, they would be given fifty lashes with a rawhide whip, chained to a cannonball for several months and forced to serve out the rest of their enlistment without pay.

Many of the officers were unable to win the respect or the affection of their troopers during this difficult preparatory period. They may have had considerable experience as rangers or with the infantry, but none of them possessed the slightest prior knowledge of formal

PLATE 9: A NEW REGIMENT'S GLITTERING FINERY, 1833–6
25. Lieutenant Colonel (Stephen Watts Kearny), U.S. Regiment of Dragoons, Dress Uniform, 1833–6: *Commissioned rank was indicated in a number of ways. Field officers rated four gold lace slashes on their cuffs; captains had three; lieutenants boasted two. The horsehair pompoms on the caps of officers above the rank of captain bore 'a small strip of red hair, to show in front.' Field officers wore dark blue trousers with gold stripes down the outer seams, while company officers had blue-grey trousers with yellow stripes. The regiment's colonel had a silver 'embroidered spread eagle' on the strap of each gold epaulette. The epaulettes of the other officers were without rank devices until 1839.* **26. Bugler, U.S. Regiment of Dragoons, Dress Uniform, 1833–6:** *Buglers wore coats 'of red cloth, yellow turnbacks and cuffs, yellow buttons.' Enlisted men had stamped brass shoulder knots in lieu of epaulettes. Musicians carried the Model 1833 dragoon saber with a browned-iron scabbard as did other troopers.* **27. Private, U.S. Regiment of Dragoons, Dress Uniform, 1833–6:** *Corporals and privates had one yellow stripe along the outer seams of their blue-grey trousers, and sergeants had two. The U.S. Model 1833 Hall carbine was manufactured at Harpers Ferry especially for the Regiment of Dragoons. Private James Hildreth wrote that while on the march, the men carried their carbines across their backs, as pictured here. All based on the regulations of 2 May 1833. American dragoons wore what was basically the same dress uniform until 1851.*

cavalry tactics or the intricate maneuvers associated with the mounted service. Still learning himself, Kearny had to drill his officers in squads before sending them out to teach the men. There was a gigantic sergeant in Sumner's company known familiarly as 'Long Ned'. Before some mysterious run of ill fortune prompted his immigration to America, he had been a cornet and riding master in an English regiment of dragoon guards. Every afternoon he was called upon to demonstrate the finer points of horsemanship and the saber manual to a class of ignorant but eager subalterns. It became a great joke among the other ranks to see their officers, with all their West Point airs and education, taking instruction from a common soldier, and this embarrassing spectacle did not instill much confidence in the regiment's leadership.

25. Lieutenant Colonel, U.S. Regiment of Drageons, Dress Uniform, 1833–6

26. Bugler, U.S. Regiment of Dragoons, Dress Uniform, 1833–6

27. Private, U.S. Regiment of Dragoons, Dress Uniform, 1833–6

Captain Nathan Boone of the 1st Regiment of U.S. Dragoons sits for one of the earliest photographs taken of an American soldier, dating from the first half of the 1840s. He is wearing the frock coat authorized for dragoon officers in 1839, with its distinctive shoulder straps and solid gilt crescents.

The officers as well began to grow short with one another, and factions formed among them. Lieutenant Jefferson Davis was named regimental adjutant on 30 August 1833, but he soon fell out with Colonel Dodge and relinquished that position the following February. On 18 April 1834, Dodge denounced both Davis and his third-in-command, Major Richard B. Mason, in a letter to a friend:

> I find More treachery and deception practised in the Army than I ever expected to find with a Body of Men who Call themselves Gentlemen   My Situation is unpleasant   Davis who I appointed my adjt was among the first to Stand against me   Major Mason and Davis are Now two of My Most inveterate enemies

the desire of these Gentlemen appears to be to Harrass ⟨me⟩ in Small Matters   they dont want to fight ... and indeed unless Harmony and good feeling exists in a Corps the public Service Cannot be promoted and to undertake an Expedition with Such Men I should run the risque of Loosing what Little reputation I have acquired ...

Dodge had only himself to blame for the loss of a considerable amount of the 'Harmony and good feeling' that yet remained in his unhappy command. Anxious lest the frontier be left devoid of cavalry with the discharge of the last of the Mounted Rangers, Dodge recommended to the War Department that his first battalion be permitted to winter at Fort Gibson, 500 miles to the southwest. The order was accordingly issued, and on 20 November 1833, the dragoons departed from Jefferson Barracks, three companies still short of clothing and two without horses. A severe snowstorm, common to the Plains, tore into the column on its third day out, and the rest of the trip through the frigid, uninhabited countryside was conducted under the most disadvantageous circumstances imaginable.

When the battalion reached Fort Gibson on 14 December, the shivering troopers were already as tough as the most hardy veterans. There were no barracks for them there, so they established their winter quarters a mile to the west at Camp Jackson, and they had to erect leaky, barnlike structures for themselves in below-zero weather. The horses had no stables and there was not enough corn to subsist them. To keep them from starving, Colonel Dodge was forced to turn them loose among the canebrakes that grew along the Arkansas River. Some strayed so far they were never recovered.

Somehow the Regiment of Dragoons survived that harrowing winter, and with the spring, preparations commenced with a bustle for a full summer of campaigning. As elements of the second battalion trickled into Camp Jackson, the men were put through the 'School of the Trooper'. On 10 June 1834, General Leavenworth reviewed the 7th Infantry and the dragoons who were present at Fort Gibson. It was a gala occasion, and 'the proud and manly deportment' of the Regiment of Dragoons thrilled George Catlin as he stood in the audience. 'Each company of horses has been selected of one color entire,' he observed. 'There is a company of blacks, one of whites, one of sorels, one of greys, one of cream color, &c. &c. &c. which render the companies distinct, and the effect pleasing.' Two days later the regiment's last three companies arrived, giving Dodge a rough aggregate of about thirty officers and 600 other ranks. The U.S. Cavalry was finally ready to go into business.

A portion of the Regiment of Dragoons was already out earning its spurs. On 13 May 1834, Captain Clifton Wharton and the fifty Tennesseans of his Company A rode out of Camp Jackson to offer themselves as an escort to the annual caravan to Santa Fe. They had a rough time of it at first, but they managed to link up with the traders on 18 June. Two days later a couple of merchants came rushing up frantically to Wharton, shouting hoarsely that they were being chased by Indians. Hoping to buy time while the wagons formed square, the captain galloped toward an oncoming dust cloud, and as a Comanche war party came into view, he ordered his forty effectives into line and charged.

When the dragoons closed to within sixty feet, they heard one of the Indians shouting '*Buenos amigos! Buenos amigos!*' while another kept chanting in broken English, 'How do you do? How do you do?' This band was friendly, as was every other the dragoons encountered on the journey. Wharton was able to see the caravan safely into Mexican territory by 28 June, without having to do any fighting at all. His biggest headache was restraining the panicky civilians from firing on every brave they saw. After Wharton had arranged a parley with the first Comanches he met, the traders dragged out a cannon they had brought along with the train and tried to discharge it at the Indians. It was only with a great deal of difficulty and no little danger to himself that a dragoon lieutenant was able to dissuade them from perpetrating such an atrocity. Then the crafty leader of the traders rode out and told the Comanches to go away or they would be fired on, thus ruining Wharton's chance for a peace conference.

In his own way, Wharton was trying to accomplish what the rest of the regiment had been ordered to do – locate the hostile tribes of the Southwest and talk their chiefs into coming back to Fort Gibson for a council with the whites and the resettled tribes of the East. Leaving Company K behind at Camp Jackson, Dodge set out on 15 June 1834, with his remaining eight companies – twenty-seven officers and 500 dragoons. General Leavenworth accompanied the expedition, and he brought along thirty-two Osages, Cherokees,

Delawares and Senecas to serve as scouts, interpreters and hunters, as well as a Kiowa and a Pawnee girl to be used as ransom for any white prisoners held by their people.

The enterprise began pleasantly enough, as the keen young troopers steered their way through vast golden prairie seas full of broad-blossomed prickly-pears, but the novelty of campaigning translated itself into tedium, and nature turned its wrath on the brash invaders of the wilderness. It was beastly hot from the very outset, with temperatures ranging between 103 deg. and 107 deg. – even in the shade! Under that blazing and merciless sun, the soldiers' blue wool shell jackets had them swimming in sweat, and their leather forage caps were converted into brain-baking pressure cookers. When rations grew short, the men had to hunt buffalo for their food, and the buffalo were not always around to be had. The column would travel whole days at a time without finding any creeks or streams, and often the only water available came from green stagnant pools that had been fouled by wallowing buffalo.

Under such conditions, typhus and dysentery were not long absent from the column, and with every sick call the toll mounted. Ten or twelve men, too ill to continue, dropped out of the line of march the very first day. An officer and twenty-seven more were left behind on 26 June, at an infantry camp on the Canadian River. Two days later General Leavenworth sustained a fall from his horse while chasing a buffalo calf, which left him too weak to resist the 'bilious fever' that was decimating the command. He died within a month.

At half past noon on 29 June, the ailing regiment rode into Camp Washita, a primitive post 200 miles from Fort Gibson manned by two companies of the 3rd Infantry. Over the next few days, while a platform was rigged on two canoes to ferry them over the deep, wide and miry Washita River, the dragoons got a well-deserved rest. Two whole days, 3 and 4 July, were occupied in getting the men and horses across. Once the Regiment of Dragoons was on the west bank, the dying Leavenworth authorized a general reorganization for the last leg of the journey. Colonel Dodge was to push on with seventeen officers and 250 troopers divided into six companies of about forty-two men apiece. They were each to be issued with eighty rounds and enough rations for ten days. Lieutenant Colonel Kearny stayed behind with 109 fit dragoons to guard the regiment's baggage wagons and eighty-six invalids.

Starting out on 9 July, Dodge's reduced battalion made slow, short marches to preserve the thinning mounts. Topping a hill on 14 July, the colonel made out a party of forty Comanches far to the right. Sending out a single lieutenant to greet them with a white flag, Dodge followed at a distance with his anxious soldiers. The Comanches sent out a brave of their own with a white cloth stuck to his lance, and when the two emissaries met, the warrior raced up to Colonel Dodge and the two men shook hands. That symbolic gesture of friendship acted like an electric signal to the other Indians, who came dashing down on the column, delighting the dragoons with their horsemanship and shaking hands with every trooper they saw.

The Comanches escorted the white soldiers to their village of 200 lodges, which was forty-eight hours away. The Indians treated their guests hospitably and offered to guide Dodge to the camp of the Pawnee Picts, their friends and allies. Constructing a rude shed for his thirty-nine sick and detailing a lieutenant and thirty-six men to look after them, Dodge rode out of the Comanche village on 19 July with 183 remaining stalwarts and started climbing up the foothills of the Rockies.

On 21 July 1834, the tired dragoons reached the Pawnee Pict camp, and the next day their colonel convened his grand council. It was to last three days, and it was attended by over 1500 Kiowa, Waco, Pawnee Pict and Comanche braves.

Dodge conducted himself well. He told the head men that President Jackson, 'the great American captain', wanted to make peace, and he invited them to accompany his dragoons back to Fort Gibson to sign treaties of friendship. Fifteen Kiowas, five Comanches and three Pawnees accepted. The colonel exchanged the two Indian girls he had brought for a nine-year-old white boy and a black slave held captive by the Pawnees. He also confirmed the death of Ranger Abbey from the previous summer.

For the sake of his tottering command, Dodge had his dragoons marching homeward by 25 July. Picking up his infirm at the Comanche camp, he wisely charted a more direct course for Fort Gibson, sending word to Kearny to make his way back with his detachment on his own. The return trip was as grueling as the one coming out. Forty-three men rode doubled over by cramps and fever, and seven had to be carried on litters. It was not until 15 August that Dodge's men caught sight of Fort Gibson, and Kearny's column did not get in for another nine days.

The dragoons looked more like scarecrows than their old swaggering selves. Their once-splendid uniforms, torn at by briars and thorns, now hung in tatters from their gaunt forms. Somewhere around 150 officers and men died from the hardships they suffered and the maladies they contracted. Still the regiment had much to be proud of. Even though they were reduced in strength and numbers, Dodge's dragoons boldly rode into the midst of four hostile Indian nations and brought their chiefs back for a successful powwow at Fort Gibson.

The survivors were not given much time to bask in their own glory or even to recuperate. On 2 September 1834, Major Mason and Companies E, F and K were sent twenty miles from Fort Gibson to winter at Camp Jones on the Creek reservation. The next day Lieutenant Colonel Kearny took Companies B, H and I to a location on the right bank of the Mississippi near the mouth of the Des Moines River. There they built Camp (later Fort) Des Moines, and for the next two years they put in long, frustrating hours smashing stills and arresting unscrupulous traders who ignored Federal law and tried to sell whiskey to the very susceptible Indians. Colonel Dodge moved his headquarters and Companies A, C, D and G to Fort Leavenworth to keep his dragoons closer to where the action was.

In the spring of 1835, Kearny's squadron advanced up the Des Moines River to Raccoon Fork and then proceeded to scout the Sioux. The Indians found Captain Boone's Company H alone one day in the upper Des Moines Valley and attacked. Boone was outnumbered three-to-one, but he held the Sioux off until nightfall and then escaped to the south. Except for that close brush with disaster, 1835 was a peaceful year for the Regiment of Dragoons. All ten companies spent the summer out in the field, confining their activities largely to exploring.

Little changed for the unit the following year. The dragoons continued to scout among the western tribes – especially on the Missouri border – and to keep white undesirables out of the Indian Territory. The regiment's biggest event of the year occurred on 4 July 1836, when Colonel Dodge resigned from the service to accept an appointment as governor of Wisconsin Territory. Stephen Watts Kearny took his place, with Major Mason and Captain Wharton each being moved up a notch on the totem pole.

Colonel Kearny was determined to make his troopers the elite of the Army. The men needed a leader like him, for they now faced stiff competition. A messy little war in Florida had prompted Congress to add a second regiment of dragoons to the U.S. Cavalry.

Friendly Comanche Indians drive a herd of buffalo through the famished ranks of the U.S. Regiment of Dragoons during its homeward march to Fort Gibson, August 1834. George Catlin, the famous artist, accompanied the dragoons on their expedition to make peace with the Southwestern Plains tribes, and he painted this scene from memory. Note the dragoons ride in a column of twos grasping their carbines.

4 In the Vanguard for Manifest Destiny

1836-48

The Seminole War was a direct consequence of Jacksonian America's heartless Indian removal policy, which the present generation may well regard as a fitting punishment for the burgeoning republic's cruel dispossession of the indigenous population. Almost immediately after Spain ceded Florida to the United States in 1821, the Seminoles were pressured into surrendering their claims to the whole of the territory and restricted to a wretched reservation, where they were largely dependent on the Federal government for food. In 1832–3, some Seminole chieftains were cajoled or coerced into signing two treaties that agreed to the deportation of their people and their resettlement in the Indian Territory alongside the other displaced tribes. The drive to exile the Seminoles for once did not spring from a ravenous land hunger, that perpetual American malady, or even an onward surge of the line of settlement, but from growing Southern anxiety about preserving the institution of slavery. For over a century, Florida Indians had granted a haven to runaway blacks from the Carolinas and Georgia. As the 'Cotton Kingdom' increased in size and influence and the number of runaways mounted, so did the demand to eliminate this threat to the fabric of Southern society.

Whatever assurances the white men thought they had on paper, the Seminoles were determined not to leave their homes without a fight. As small and scattered detachments of the U.S. Army were deployed lazily to shoo the Indians west, the war axe fell. On 28 December 1835, Osceola, the leader of the diehards, and a gang of warriors murdered the American agent who was supposed to superintend their departure. That same day fifty miles to the south, 180 Seminoles and their black allies ambushed and annihilated 107 regular artillerymen armed with muskets under Major Francis Dade, leaving only three badly wounded soldiers alive.

The Dade Massacre jolted the Army out of its complacency. Within a year, 23,530 militiamen had been called out from Florida and the adjoining states, and the number of regulars in the territory mushroomed from 405 to 1890, nearly a third of the standing army's total complement. Some of the troops entered Florida without proper authorization. Lieutenant James F. Izard of the Regiment of Dragoons was at Memphis, returning to duty after a leave, when he heard about what happened to Dade. He automatically turned south to New Orleans, where Brevet Major General Edmund P. Gaines was throwing together an expedition of 980 soldiers and Louisiana volunteers. Gaines made Izard his brigade major and put him in charge of his advance guard. On 28 February 1836, while trying to lead his troops over the Withlacoochee River under a heavy fire, the young dragoon officer was shot through the head by a Seminole brave. He died five days later. The U.S. Cavalry had made its first contribution to one of the longest and ugliest wars in American history.

That same month, First Lieutenant Thompson B. Wheelock and a party of recruits he had raised in New York for the Regiment of Dragoons were ordered to join the fighting in Florida. The rest of the regiment did not follow them there, for it was needed to police the Plains. Besides, Brevet Major General Winfield Scott, who was then readying a 4618-man force to hunt down the Seminoles, had declared on 29 January 1836, that additional mounted troops would not be required. Scott's three converging columns combed the Indian country without ferreting the hostiles out of their hiding places. To the baffled Americans, Florida's tangled swamps were about as inviting and familiar as lunar landscapes, while the Seminoles had been born and raised there. They had little trouble avoiding the ponderous lines of blue-coated 'Doughboys', striking instead at small, isolated detachments or undefended pioneers. Soon Scott was saying a company of regular cavalrymen would be worth two of infantry.

On 23 May 1836, Congress added the 2nd Regiment of Dragoons to the United States Army, appropriating $300,000 to get it on its feet. Recruiting depots were set up throughout the Eastern Department, meeting with their greatest initial success in New York and South Carolina. To provide the new regiment with a seasoned nucleus, Lieutenant Wheelock and his enlistees in Florida were incorporated into its ranks.

Forty-six-year-old David Emanuel Twiggs, an elegantly handsome man with a bull neck, broad shoulders and a powerful body, became the regiment's first colonel. His troopers called him 'Old Davy' or the 'Bengal Tiger,' and they bragged that he 'cursed them right out of their boots.' Lieutenant Colonel William Selby Harney, Twiggs's second-in-command, had a temper as fiery as the blaze of red hair that framed his fierce-looking face. Harney was an excellent physical specimen, a veritable iron man with a grip like steel, arms like pistons and an unshakable resolution that was to make him one of the Seminoles' most dangerous and relentless foes. There was much about Harney that personified sheer brutality, but he was a conscientious and imaginative officer. Twiggs took so many extended leaves during the Seminole War that it was Harney who actually commanded the 2nd Dragoons for most of its stay in Florida, and he shaped the regiment to his character. He was willing to adopt any measure that might promise success, including dressing his men as Indians to lure the foe within range. When enterprising Samuel Colt journeyed down to the war zone in February 1838 to demonstrate his new revolving carbine to the Army, Harney was among the few officers to be favorably impressed. That month of March he had enough Colt's rifles purchased to arm fifty picked dragoons, and he secured another fifty for his troopers in the succeeding year.

By December 1836, the first five companies of the 2nd Dragoons had been completed. They were immediately shipped down to Savannah, Georgia, given horses and marched half-trained into Florida. The remaining five companies went to Jefferson Barracks, where they were put through the School of the Trooper. They arrived in Florida in October 1837, after riding the 1200 miles from Missouri in fifty-five days.

Well before either battalion reached the territory, the 2nd Dragoons had already drawn their first blood against the Seminoles, and the regiment received one

Second Lieutenant Bezaleel Wells Armstrong, an 1845 graduate of West Point, sat for this portrait shortly before or after his service with the 1st and 2nd Dragoons in the Mexican War. He wears the dress uniform coat prescribed in 1833, along with an 1839 model officer's forage cap – a peculiar and very non-regulation combination. Note his orange sash and button-up gauntlets.

of its proudest battle honors. On 9 June 1836, some 250 warriors laid siege to Fort Defiance, near Micanopy. Major Julius F. Heilman's garrison consisted solely of seventy regulars, including Lieutenant Thompson Wheelock's platoon of recently converted 2nd Dragoons, but the major possessed the courage of a lion. Sending a company of artillerymen toting muskets to hit the Indians' right flank and Wheelock's cavalrymen around their left, Heilman advanced on them head-on with only a 6-pound howitzer and its crew! Wheelock and his troopers quickly swept behind their distracted opponents, and then the lieutenant ordered a cavalry charge. The dragoons lumbered forward, loading and firing their Hall carbines from the saddle, while the Seminoles broke and fled. It was a great victory, but Wheelock was not cheered by glory. Six days later he committed suicide.

Some said the lieutenant was deranged by fever, but it is just as probable that he had a glimpse of what the future held in store for him and his companions. The Second Seminole War was to last until August of 1842, more than six years of the bitterest kind of guerrilla fighting in a terrain that had been created for anything but campaigning armies. Florida in those days was a soldier's nightmare. Much of the territory's 58,560 square miles was as yet unknown to the whites, a semi-tropical wasteland of swamps, rivers and creeks, dark, dank and steamy. In the summer temperatures topped 102 deg., and the land abounded in disease, snakes and clouds of insects. If a soldier was not up to his ankles in water, he was up to his armpits, and when he did find passably dry ground, his shoes, trousers and skin were lacerated by sawgrass.

The Seminoles were perfectly adapted to this hellish environment, and they led the soldiers a merry chase over nearly every inch of it. Even when they did make a stand in some hummock, they only held their ground long enough to exact a few casualties from their impetuous attackers. Then they would melt into dense undergrowth, to live and fight another day. Some of the Army's brightest names, Scott, Gaines, Jesup, Taylor and Worth, tried their hands at subduing the hostiles, and none of them achieved total victory, no matter what tricks they pulled.

Whenever Americans have run into a thorny military problem, they have traditionally put their trust in the press of numbers, and the Second Seminole War was no exception. In the conflict's first year alone, 152 companies of mounted volunteers, 10,712 men and at least as many horses, entered Federal service to round up the measly 900 to 1400 braves who were on the war path. South Carolina supplied a regiment, and Tennessee sent a full brigade of 1200 militia cavalrymen. Even faraway Missouri was to raise a regiment of 600 men. Seven-hundred-and-fifty friendly Creek Indians were formed into another cavalry regiment. The warriors wore white turbans so they would not be fired on by American troops, and their colonel was John F. Lane, who had only been recently appointed as a captain in the 2nd Dragoons. Lane must have been cursed with the same kind of prescience as Wheelock, for shortly after he came to Florida, he retired to his

PLATE 10: A SECOND REGIMENT OF DRAGOONS, 1836–42

28. Private, 2nd Regiment of U.S. Dragoons, Summer Dress, 1838: *A fatigue uniform of plain white cotton was issued for campaigning in warm climates. It received extensive wear while the 2nd Dragoons tracked the Seminoles in Florida. In March 1838, Lieutenant Colonel William S. Harney armed fifty of his men with the Paterson Colt revolving carbine, an early six-shooter.* **29. Corporal, 2nd Regiment of U.S. Dragoons, Undress, 1836–9:** *The 1st Dragoons had the same campaign uniform. This dragoon defends his company's guidon with the S. North Model 1819 Army flintlock pistol. This pattern of guidon served the U.S. Cavalry, with very few changes, from 1833 to 1863.* **30. First Lieutenant, 2nd Regiment of U.S. Dragoons, Undress, 1839–42:** *The 1839 regulations altered the dress of dragoon officers. A single-breasted frock coat replaced the 1833 undress coat. Rank was designated by a pair of shoulder straps, officially described as, 'Formed like the strap of the epaulette, and made of blue cloth, edged with gold lace like an epaulette; solid gilt crescent, with the number of the regiment embroidered within. The strap of the colonel to have on it a silver embroidered eagle; that of the lieutenant colonel two gold leaves at the points, where the crescent joins it; that of the major two silver leaves; that of the captain two gold bars; that of the first lieutenant one bar; that of the second lieutenant plain.' Cloth forage caps were issued to all ranks, but dragoon officers retained the traditional gold star on their caps.*

tent on 19 October 1836, and plunged his own sword through his right eye.

Aside from the Creeks, who fought like demons and were not above torturing their prisoners to extract information, most regular officers were extremely ambivalent about the mounted volunteers. Their three, six or twelve-month enlistments were too short to make them a really stable resource, and Florida just did not possess an adequate logistical base to supply those many thousands of eager horsemen who came flocking to get a crack at the Indians. Some companies were not admitted to the territory at all. Others were kept in the north to serve as a mobile constabulary in the white areas. Those aspiring cavaliers who did see action, did not find any of the adventure or renown they had dreamed about.

The tragic tale of Colonel Richard Gentry's 1st

28. Private, 2nd Regiment of U.S. Dragoons, Summer Dress, 1838

29. Corporal, 2nd Regiment of U.S. Dragoons, Undress, 1836–9

30. First Lieutenant, 2nd Regiment of U.S. Dragoons, Undress, 1839–42

Regiment of Missouri Volunteers is typical. Raised in the autumn of 1837 amidst a flurry of popular frenzy, the regiment left Jefferson Barracks under a merry silk flag embroidered by patriotic ladies with this stirring motto; 'Gird, gird for the conflict, Our banners wave high; For our country we live; For our country we'll die.' When the regiment reached Tampa, 190 of its 600 men had to be discharged right away because their horses had been lost at sea. Then fever set in. By the time they entered their first real battle at Okeechobee under Colonel Zachary Taylor on Christmas Day, 1837, only 132 of the Missourians were left on their feet. Taylor put them in his front line and had them recklessly charge close to 400 warriors on foot. Colonel Gentry was mortally wounded in the initial volley, and his leaderless Missourians broke for the rear after the second volley, leaving it to the regular infantry to finish the job.

Frank B. Mayer sketched a first sergeant (left) and a private (right) of the 1st U.S. Dragoons at Fort Snelling when he toured Minnesota in 1851. Both of these swaggering fellows are in the full dress uniform that was designed in 1833.

The Seminoles were not to be beaten by battle, however; but by an unceasing, hydra-like operation of harassment and terror. The Army eventually learned to flood the enemy's country with a continuous stream of wide-ranging, mobile detachments that would sniff out the hidden Indian villages, and destroy the hostiles' property, personal effects and food. Impoverished and starving, the renegades would have to surrender. It was heartbreaking, frustrating work, and often brought the troops small returns for truly heroic efforts.

Loading fifty musketmen from the 3rd U.S. Artillery and fifty 2nd Dragoons with Colt's rifles into fifteen canoes, Lieutenant Colonel Harney led them on an extensive search through the murky swamps. They glided and sloshed over miles of water too foul to drink, and across a stretch of coral rock that sliced up their shoes like a bed of knives. Finally spotting a Seminole campfire on 24 April 1838, Harney promptly

formed his men into three attack columns and rushed the hostiles on the double. The fighting lasted two hours, much of it tree-to-tree skirmishing. When it was over the enemy had disappeared, leaving the exhausted Americans nothing more for their pains than one dead warrior and one prisoner.

It was often like that, but sometimes the soldiers got lucky. Early on 9 September 1837, three companies of the 2nd Dragoons and two of mounted Florida volunteers surrounded an unsuspecting village. They charged it at first light, taking its entire population intact, including an important chief named King Philip.

One by one, the Seminoles were shot down or rounded up to be transported west in sizable batches. But even after the Indians surrendered, there was no guarantee they would stay caught.

On the night of 2 June 1837, Osceola and 200 braves slipped into a detention camp at Tampa containing 700

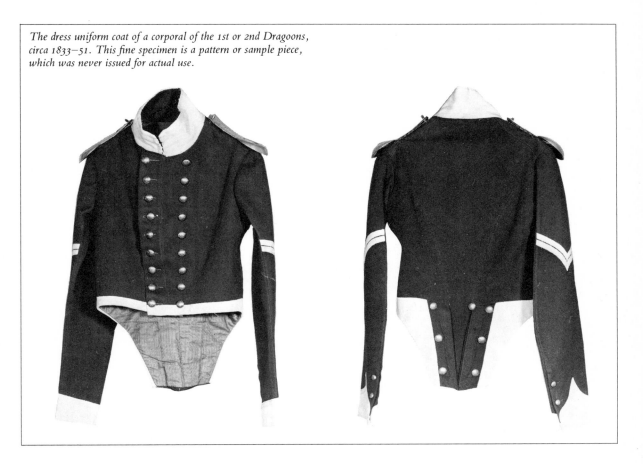

The dress uniform coat of a corporal of the 1st or 2nd Dragoons, circa 1833–51. This fine specimen is a pattern or sample piece, which was never issued for actual use.

Captain Samuel H. Walker, an indomitable Texas Ranger, who was rewarded for his gallantry under Zachary Taylor with a commission as captain of Company C, U.S. Regiment of Mounted Riflemen. He was killed at the age of thirty-five while hunting guerrillas in Humantla, Mexico, on 8 October 1847.

of their people. By morning the place was empty – its occupants spirited out from under the noses of Harney and the 2nd Dragoons, who had been forewarned against such an attempt. Brigadier General Thomas Sidney Jesup, Harney's commander, was determined to get them all back, and he wrote to the humiliated cavalryman, 'I will sanction all you may find it necessary to do in relation to the Indians.' Harney took those words quite literally, eventually employing ferocious bloodhounds to track renegades.

The 2nd Dragoons participated in other breaches against the rules of civilized warfare. In October 1837, Osceola and another chief came to confer with American officers at Fort Peyton under a flag of truce. As the talks commenced on the twenty-first, Brevet Major James A. Ashby of the 2nd Dragoons and 250 troopers from his regiment and the mounted Florida militia encircled the council area. At a pre-arranged signal they bounded forward, bagging seventy-three warriors, four Negroes and six women. A few months later General Jesup lured hundreds of trusting Seminoles to another parley, and then on 21 March 1838, he ordered Colonel Twiggs to disarm and arrest them. The scurrying dragoons trapped 504 to 513 Indians, including 151 warriors. It was the biggest catch of the war.

Treachery was not confined only to one side during the Seminole War. In May 1839, Major General Alexander Macomb, the Commanding General of the Army, arranged an honorable truce with the hostiles. That July he sent Lieutenant Colonel Harney and thirty-two 2nd Dragoons to escort a merchant who would set up a trading post within the fringes of the Seminole reservation. On the night of 23 July, 160 warriors fell upon the unsuspecting camp, killing or capturing eighteen troopers. Harney and the fourteen others managed to escape, learning later to their horror that many of the men left behind were tortured to death.

More than a year passed before the embittered Harney got his revenge. On 4 December 1840, he launched another one of his amphibious expeditions – twenty-one 2nd Dragoons with Colt's rifles, sixty-nine musketmen from the 3rd Artillery, a Negro guide captured from the Seminoles and sixteen canoes. They plunged into the Everglades, surprising some Seminole families in canoes. Harney hanged whatever warriors he overtook on the spot. Coming across an island harboring a hostile village, Harney had his men paint and dress themselves like Indians. Then he attacked, destroying the village and scattering its inhabitants. When Harney returned to Fort Dallas on 12 December, he could report his soldiers had killed four warriors in battle and hanged five, with the loss of only one man. One of the Indian dead was an important chief, and his band had been permanently broken. As a result of this exploit, Harney became known unfairly throughout the Army as the man who 'ravished young Indian girls at night, and then strung them up to the limb of a live oak in the morning.' Despite such an unwholesome reputation, Harney remained unrepentant, and a young officer who served with him afterwards in Mexico remembered:

He told me he hanged all of his prisoners, because the Indians had a great and superstitious horror of hanging; for they believe that no man's soul will be received into the happy hunting grounds that does not pass through the throat, which is impossible when that route is closed by a rope; it must seek another road of exit, and all such souls are rejected at the gates of Paradise. He said a fine moral effect was produced upon the Indians by this method of execution.

And so it went, year after endless year. By 1841, the Seminole War had become an embarrassing nuisance to the Army. There were no more than 400 hostile Indians left in Florida, and not even half of them were warriors. Notwithstanding all that, with 47,000 square miles of wild country still to hide in, no amount of troops could hope to catch them all. Some officers came to believe that if they de-escalated their war

A contemporary lithograph of the charge of Captain Charles A. May and the 2nd U.S. Dragoons at the Battle of Resaca de la Palma, 9 May 1846. This version incorrectly depicts the dragoons in their dress uniforms and portrays May as the captor of a Mexican general.

effort, the remaining renegades might be persuaded to reciprocate. It was in the pursuit of this hope that five companies of the 2nd U.S. Dragoons were withdrawn from Florida on 17 October 1841, and stationed either at Fort Jesup or in Arkansas Territory. The second battalion of the regiment fought its last battle in Florida near Lake Ahapopka on 19 April 1842. In the following month those five companies were sent to join their comrades out West.

For the next four years, the 2nd Dragoons were to know the varied joys of peacetime soldiering, but their days were not exactly uneventful. The two companies posted to Fort Jesup in 1841 were briefly armed with lances, but the men did not take very well to the new weapon, and this interesting experiment was dropped. Then on 23 August 1842, the House of Representatives, responding in its usual parsimonious fashion to the ending of the Seminole War, passed 'An Act to Perfect the Organization of the Army'. The bill called for the complete elimination of the 2nd Dragoons, but the Senate commuted the death sentence. Instead, the unit was dismounted and redesignated as the Rifle Regiment. To Twiggs, Harney and their troopers this transformation, which became effective on 4 March

An image of an American dragoon of the 1840s that poses more questions than it answers. While his dress cap, trousers, sword-belt and Model 1840 heavy dragoon saber are all regulation, his coatee is single-breasted and there are glaring irregularities about his epaulettes, collar and cuffs. Either he is a regular whose company tailor got the wrong patterns, or a volunteer who was raised to fight the Seminoles or Mexicans. This clever dragoon put his swordbelt on backwards so it would come out on the correct side in the daguerreotype, but a glance at his beltplate gives him away.

1843, was extremely galling. After intensive lobbying, Congress was shown the error of its ways, and the 2nd Regiment of United States Dragoons was reconstituted and remounted a year later. Once again those tempered cavalrymen were able to canter along with their characteristic devil-may-care swagger, proudly roaring the chorus of the regimental song, another veteran of Florida:

> Oh! the dragoon bold! he scorns all care,
> As he goes the rounds with uncropped hair;
> He spends no thought on the evil star
> That sent him away to the border war.

Brevet Lieutenant Colonel Charles A. May, the phony hero of Resaca de la Palma. He wears the double-breasted frock coat introduced by the Army's 1847 regulations, but unbuttoned at the collar to expose his shirt and tie. The gold leaf on his epaulette designates his rank, and the numeral inside the crescent identifies his regiment, the 2nd Dragoons.

While the 2nd Dragoons were chasing Seminoles, the Army's original dragoon regiment, now known as the 1st Dragoons, was going about its various and sundry duties on the Great Plains.

With Henry Dodge's resignation from the service and his own promotion to colonel, Stephen Watts Kearny set to work to make his command the best in the Army. A stern, hard-driving man, his two goals became efficiency and smartness. In March 1837, he redistributed the regiment's horses according to color. Companies A and K received blacks; B, F and H got sorrels; C, D, E and I were issued bays; and G had mounts of iron grey. That same year Kearny published a carbine manual for his regiment through the War Department. Later he had three of his lieutenants sent to France to study the mounted arm in that country and write the U.S. Cavalry's first comprehensive manual.

Kearny's sustained improvements bore immediate results. Before 1837 had come to an end, the 1st Dragoons were reviewed by General Gaines, the commander of the Western Department, who raved afterwards:

The First Regiment of Light Dragoons at Fort Leavenworth, recently inspected by the Commanding General, was found to be in a state of police and discipline reflecting the highest credit on Colonel Kearny – the exemplary commandant, – his captains and other officers, non-commissioned officers and soldiers, whose high health and vigilance, with the excellent condition of the horses, affords evidence of their talents, industry and steady habits.

Kearny's achievement seems all the more remarkable when it is remembered that the companies of the 1st Dragoons never all served together. They were usually parcelled out by ones, twos or threes among the posts that comprised America's frontier defense line, forts like Gibson, Towson, Des Moines, Wayne, Atkinson, Scott and Washita. The names and locations changed as the tide of settlement crept further west. Whatever the regiment's dispositions, Colonel Kearny almost always managed to keep a full battalion of five companies under his direct supervision at Fort Leavenworth, his headquarters. The companies were assigned there on a rotating basis, so Kearny was able to put his personal stamp on every one of his troopers over the cycle of a couple of years.

The 1st Dragoons had more to do during those years than merely look pretty. The Indian removal policy tremendously increased the red population on the prairies and added immeasurably to the regiment's duties. The dragoons had to keep the peace among the transplanted tribes, as well as prevent clashes between them and their neighbors – both Indian and white. Kearny whipped his five companies at Fort Leavenworth into a crack mobile reserve that was capable of reaching any trouble spot within a few days. Marching his battalion forty to fifty-seven miles a day, he was able to suddenly appear in the midst of any unruly tribe with 200 to 250 well-conditioned, heavily armed and splendidly accoutred troopers.

Usually a brief show of force was sufficient to cow the Eastern bands back into a posture of submission, although it had to be repeated every few years or so. Some of Kearny's more stubborn adversaries were the recently arrived Seminoles. In 1842, about 300 of them trespassed on the Cherokee reservation. Kearny rushed to the scene, but they refused to budge, so he ordered his troopers to draw their sabers and prod them along. In the ensuing confrontation, one pugnacious boy was badly cut, and a large number broke out of the circle of dragoons. Kearny sent Captain Philip St George Cooke and two companies to round up the fugitives. They led the soldiers on a merry chase across the Illinois River, but Cooke caught every one of the malcontents, and they were returned to their own reservation.

The wilder tribes on the unsettled Great Plains were treated in much the same fashion. Small expeditions of the 1st Dragoons traversed their territory in the warmer months, showing the flag, performing drills and firing off small brass mountain howitzers or Congreve rockets to dazzle the supposed savages with the white man's might.

Wherever possible, any bloodshed was scrupulously avoided, even if this meant taking tremendous risks. On 5 September 1839, Kearny led two companies, considerably less than 200 men, from Fort Leavenworth and headed for the country of the Otos, the warlike allies of the Pawnees, to try to get them to adopt a more placid mode of behavior. In a council held on the sixteenth, he faced 1000 warriors, all of them armed to the teeth and many of them dangerously drunk, and by the sheer force of his personality

31. Captain (Charles A. May), 2nd Regiment of U.S. Dragoons, Undress, 1846: *Dragoon officers wore a rather plain shell jacket for 'ordinary stable duty, marches, or active service' from 1833 to 1851. Some had collars adorned with gold borders and laced blind buttonholes. Others, as shown here, had plain collars. Officers wore no stripes on their undress trousers.* **32. Private, 2nd Regiment of U.S. Dragoons, Undress, 1846:** *The memoirs of Samuel Chamberlain, an enlisted 1st Dragoon with Taylor's army in northern Mexico, recount that the 2nd Dragoons wore orange bands on their forage caps. This spirited steed is outfitted with the Ringgold saddle and horse equipment, which were adopted in 1844.* **33. Sergeant, 1st Regiment of U.S. Dragoons, Undress, 1847:** *Company C was on Kearny's arduous march from New Mexico to California in late 1846, virtually dismounting itself in the process. The men took the field against California rebels in January 1847 on foot. This sergeant has donned a pair of 'breed' leggings to protect his lower legs. He is armed with the U.S. Model 1843 Hall carbine and the Model 1840 heavy dragoon saber.*

compelled their chiefs to hand over three wrong-doers for punishment.

Occasionally, sterner measures were required. When the Otos proved recalcitrant, Major Clifton Wharton visited them again in September 1844 with a large squadron, a pair of howitzers and a rocket battery, vowing total destruction should they persist on their wayward path. 'Such conduct will not be suffered,' he simply announced, 'and I tell you, that if thus your hand be raised against every man every man's hand will be raised against you.' In the summer of 1845, Captain Edwin V. Sumner and two companies rode north into Sioux lands and arrested three braves guilty of murdering a party of whites.

The 1st Regiment of U.S. Dragoons had been founded originally, in part, to protect the traffic along the Santa Fe Trail. In 1834, however, Wharton's expedition proved that if the traders kept together and were vigilant, they had little to fear from the Indians. The 1st Dragoons provided the Santa Fe caravans with no further escorts until May 1839, when Lieutenant James M. Bowman and his forty-man company met the wagons at Cross Timbers and accompanied them to the international boundary. Once again the train passed through unmolested, and the 1st Dragoons

PLATE 11: 1846–8

31. Captain, 2nd Regiment of U.S. Dragoons, Undress, 1846

32. Private, 2nd Regiment of U.S. Dragoons, Undress, 1846

33. Sergeant, 1st Regiment of U.S. Dragoons, Undress, 1847

were not concerned with the Santa Fe trade until 1843.

In February of that year, the Republic of Texas commissioned a certain Jacob Snively to take a force of no more than 300 men to prey upon Mexican merchants along the Santa Fe Trail. Ever since the Texas Revolution back in 1836, Mexico had maintained a sporadic border war with her former province, and the Texans sought to strike back any way they could. Snively and his followers were no more than free-

Major William H. Polk, President Polk's brother, wore this frock coat and sash while he served with the short-lived 3rd U.S. Dragoons in the Mexican War.

booters bent on plunder, and there were no guarantees that they would distinguish between American and Mexican property. The Mexican minister and the American business community appropriately exerted their influence at Washington, and the 1st Dragoons were ordered to protect that summer's caravan.

Kearny dispatched Captain Philip St George Cooke, two howitzers, Companies C, F and K from Leavenworth and Company A from Fort Scott, a total of 187 officers and men, to rendezvous with the traders at Council Grove. The whole party got moving on 6 June 1843, and the journey proceeded pleasantly and peacefully enough for the next twenty-four days. On 14 June, Cooke met up with Captain Nathan Boone and Companies D and H, who were out surveying the region between the Arkansas and Canadian Rivers. The two squadrons rode together for about a week, until Boone's mission caused him to veer off the trail.

It was 30 June 1843, that Cooke ran into 'Colonel' Snively and 107 of his Texans. Determining that they were on United States soil, Cooke met with Snively under a white flag, peremptorily demanded that the Texans lay down their arms, moved his men forward in line of battle, unlimbered his howitzers and disarmed the interlopers. The next day the defenseless bushwhackers were given the option of being escorted part of the way to the American settlements or returning to Texas. The majority chose the latter, and Cooke led the caravan to the Arkansas crossing without further incident, seeing the wagons safely over on 4 July.

Captain Cooke regarded Snively's party as interlopers and bandits, and he had acted accordingly. A court of inquiry presided over by Colonel Kearny endorsed his conduct in April 1844. As a prior sign of approval, the colonel had entrusted Cooke with 150 dragoons drawn from six different companies at the end of August 1843, and sent him to escort 140 wagons owned by Mexican merchants down the Santa Fe Trail. This time there were no Texans to discipline, and Cooke turned his charges over to a squadron of Mexican lancers on 4 October.

Around this time, Great Britain and the United States began to press their conflicting claims to Oregon Territory with nearly belligerent enthusiasm. With infinitely more settlers piling into the area, America's case was considerably stronger, but James K. Polk, the newly-elected President, was not the kind of man to leave things to chance – especially where the nation's territorial aggrandizement was concerned.

Brevet Major General Stephen Watts Kearny, painted shortly after his triumphs with the Army of the West. The first lieutenant colonel and the second commander of the 1st Dragoons, he retained cavalry yellow on the collar and cuffs of his general's coat.

Fort, and then headed up the Santa Fe Trail for home. Kearny halted his march for two days in the middle of June at Fort Laramie to hold a productive council with the Sioux. When the command trotted back into Fort Leavenworth ninety-nine days after its departure, it had covered 2200 miles. Kearny noted proudly that the men looked hale and hearty, and not a one had died. The 1st U.S. Dragoons had come a long way in eleven years, but their greatest days were about to begin.

When the United States annexed Texas in 1845, she embarked upon a collision course that would shortly involve her in a war with Mexico. The Mexicans had never recognized Texan independence, and they looked upon America's action as the most blatant kind of aggression. Even before a Texas convention could convene at Austin on 4 July to accept the American offer, President Polk directed Brigadier General Zachary Taylor to enter the future state with a 3900-man 'Army of Observation'. Taylor shipped his infantry and artillery from New Orleans to Corpus Christi Bay, but he had Colonel David Twiggs and the 2nd U.S. Dragoons ride overland from Fort Jesup. They joined their comrades on the Gulf Coast roughly 400 sabers strong, having lost three dead and fifty deserters in the process.

President Polk had more on his mind than merely adding one state to the Union. He fully intended to negotiate the peaceful acquisition of New Mexico and Upper California. Still fuming over Texas, however, the Mexicans refused to deal, and Polk resorted to more drastic means to get what he wanted. On 13 January 1846, he had his Secretary of War order Taylor's Army of Observation to the north bank of the Rio Grande, and on 8 March, 'Old Rough and Ready's' 3000 effectives ambled out of their winter camp, headed by Colonel Twiggs and his 378 2nd Dragoons. Texas audaciously claimed the Rio Grande as her southern boundary, but the Mexicans fixed the line much further north along the Nueces River. By occupying the disputed territory, Polk hoped to bully Mexico City into parting with the provinces he coveted. Ironically, this unwarranted invasion brought him a full-fledged shooting war instead.

The Mexicans mobilized a large army at Matamoros to sweep the Yankee heretics from sacred soil. Receiving unsubstantiated reports that the Mexicans were crossing the Rio Grande in force on 24 April 1846,

Kearny was directed to outfit and lead an expedition up the Oregon Trail, to intimidate tribes along the way and dissuade them from attacking the emigrants and to show the British just how quickly American soldiers could reach the disputed country. Kearny left Fort Leavenworth on 18 May 1845, with Companies A, C, F, G and K (250 of his most seasoned and trustworthy 1st Dragoons). They met trains of pioneers nearly every day and passed through a massive migration, overtaking 850 men, 475 women, 1000 children, 7000 cattle, 400 horses and mules, and 460 wagons. Reaching the Platte, they turned up the river to Fort Laramie, briefly crossed the Continental Divide, skirted the walls of the Rocky Mountains down past Long's Peak and Pike's Peak until they got to Bent's

Taylor ordered Captain Seth Thornton and two companies of the 2nd Dragoons upriver to investigate. The next morning at Rancho de Carricitos, twenty miles away from Taylor's camp, Thornton's sixty-three troopers ran into 1600 angry Mexican cavalrymen. Eleven Americans were killed, six wounded and the rest captured, except for Thornton's Mexican guide, who brought Taylor word of the disaster on the twenty-sixth. With his wonderful gift for understatement, Old Rough and Ready sent Polk a message that read: 'Hostilities may now be considered as commenced.'

After the usual preliminary maneuvers, a Mexican army of 3709 men gave battle with Taylor's 2288 troops on 8 May 1846, at Palo Alto, Texas. The affair was largely an artillery duel, but a squadron of the 2nd Dragoons was posted on either end of the American line to guard Taylor's flanks. When 800 enemy cavalrymen tried to turn the Yankee right, Captain Samuel H. Walker and his company of twenty Texas Rangers pounced on their flank, sweeping their ranks with a devastating fusillade from their rifles and Colt's revolvers. As the harried lancers reeled back, a squadron of the 2nd Dragoons joined in and helped push the enemy left beyond its starting point. The fight ended largely in a draw, but the Mexicans sustained 257 casualties to Taylor's fifty-five.

The next day, the Mexicans retired to a deep, dried-out river bed sheltered by a dense tangle of trees and chaparral known as Resaca de la Palma.

Following somewhat lackadaisically, Taylor sent Company C, 3rd U.S. Artillery, right up the Matamoros Road to tussle with the batteries at the Mexican center, while his infantry thrashed doggedly through the prickly undergrowth on either side. When his light artillerymen failed to silence the Mexican guns, old Rough and Ready directed Captain Charles A. May and his company of the 2nd U.S. Dragoons to charge them.

Over six feet tall and as straight as an Indian, dapper Charley May looked the very image of a 'dragoon bold', and he had the bluster and panache to match. He was instantly recognizable with his striking, full beard and flowing, dark brown curls. As he approached the American 6-pounders, he hollered gaily to their commander, Lieutenant Randolph Ridgely, 'Hello, Ridgely, where is that battery? I am ordered to charge it.'

'Hold on, Charley,' the gunner replied, 'till I draw their fire and you will see where they are.'

Ridgely's fieldpieces then barked their challenge, the Mexicans answered, and before they could reload, May's company sailed down the Matamoros Road in a column of fours. The enemy crews left their cannon and fled from the Americans' waving sabers, but May and his cheering dragoons, caught up in the exhilaration of their first real cavalry charge, failed to check their foaming steeds for another quarter of a mile. The company ground to a quick stop, like an accordion, with the rear ranks slamming into those in front and turning the whole column into a mishmash of shouting men and rearing animals. Mexican infantrymen alongside the road fired their muskets into the milling Yankees, hitting nineteen dragoons and eighteen horses. May just got back to the battery, with six troopers still beside him, too few to hold it, and he scurried shamefacedly back to Taylor, only to hear the general bellow sarcastically at the 5th and 8th Infantry, 'Take those guns, and by God, keep them!'

The doughboys went on to seize eight cannon and win the day, inflicting 515 to 1500 losses on the Mexicans at a cost of 122 Americans. Fortunately for May, his bugler, a Private Winchell, had possessed enough presence of mind to carry off a prisoner, who turned out to be no other than General Rómolo Díaz de la Vega, the commander of the enemy battle line. Hoping to assuage Taylor's wrath over his bungled charge, May claimed to be the general's captor. The American press hailed him as a national hero, and he was twice breveted up to the rank of lieutenant colonel. His peers and subordinates who knew the real story, especially the 2nd Dragoons' buglers, hated May and looked on him with contempt. A trooper who later served under him called the headline hero 'the cowardly humbug of the war'.

Two days later, acting on Taylor's report of the Thornton débâcle, President Polk asked the Congress to acknowledge that a state of war existed, alleging falsely that the Mexicans had invaded the country and 'shed American blood upon American soil'. Both houses quickly passed a war bill that permitted the President to raise 50,000 volunteers and appropriated $10,000,000 for the prosecution of the conflict. Polk signed the legislation on 13 May and issued an immediate call for troops.

Fittingly enough, a large number of the volunteers were to be cavalrymen, who could more easily traverse the great western expanses over which the war would be fought. Between May and July 1846, the Federal government called on various states to supply mounted regiments: one from Kentucky; one from Tennessee; two from Missouri; one from Arkansas; one from Texas. They were organized on the regular model, with ten companies apiece. But the companies were supposed to be smaller, with sixty-four men in each. Enthusiasm for the war, however, often caused such limitations to be ignored. Company C, 1st Regiment of Mounted Missouri Volunteers, reported to its regimental rendezvous with 119 rank and file. Polk left it up to the states whether their sons would serve for one year or the duration of the hostilities, and they invariably chose the shorter enlistment period.

The regular army was also temporarily augmented. In 1847, Congress authorized the creation of nine infantry regiments and the 3rd Regiment of United States Dragoons – to serve until the end of the war. At the same time all regular cavalry regiments received a second major, a move inspired, no doubt, by the desire to extend field officer grade to the President's brother, William H. Polk of the 3rd Dragoons.

The Mexican War was America's first real cavalry war since the Revolution. The Mexican Army had at least fourteen regular mounted regiments and six active militia cavalry regiments. The 1st and 2nd U.S. Dragoons, toughened by ten years of fighting Indians or Herculean rides on the Plains, made light of such odds. The story is told of Sergeant Jack Miller of the 2nd, who was leading a small patrol that stumbled across five times its number of enemy guerrillas near Monclova that November. As his men grabbed instinctively for their carbines, Miller roared, 'No firing, men! If twenty dragoons can't whip a hundred greasers with the saber, I'll join the Doughboys and carry a fence rail all my life.' The Americans charged and bowled the Mexicans over with their heavier horses, killing six guerrillas, wounding thirteen and taking seventy prisoners. Only one of Miller's men and three mounts were lightly scratched.

The prevailing prejudice in America against the life of a common soldier and the titanic immigration from Europe that swept over the country in the 1840s ensured that the regular infantry and artillery regiments were composed largely of what an English visitor called a 'rag-tag-and-bob-tail herd' and 'either of the scum of the population of the older states, or the worthless German, English, or Irish emigrants.' Fully one half of Taylor's troops were foreign-born. The dragoons were still drawn primarily from older stock

Richard Barnes Mason was the first major of the 1st U.S. Dragoons, and he became the regiment's colonel in 1846 when Stephen Kearny was promoted to brigadier general. This photograph was made then, and it offers a close view of the gold lace on the collar of Mason's dress coat.

Americans, and they considered themselves to be a far cut above their fellow soldiers. As Samuel E. Chamberlain, a teenaged private in Company E, 1st U.S. Dragoons, boasted:

> I came to the conclusion that the Dragoons were far superior in materials to any other arm of the service. No man of any spirit and ambition would join the 'Doughboys' and go afoot, when he could ride a fine horse and wear spurs like a gentleman. In our squadron were broken down Lawyers, Actors and men of the world, Soldiers who had served under Napoleon, Polish Lancers, French Cuirassiers, Hungarian Hussars, Irishmen who had left the Queen's service to swear allegiance to Uncle Sam and wear the blue.

Our officers were all graduates of West Point, and at the worst, were gentlemen of intelligence and education, often harsh and tyrannical, yet they took pride in having their men well clothed, and fed, in making them contented and reconciled to their lot . . .

The volunteer cavalrymen, in their ebullient and ignorant fashion, considered themselves as good as any regulars and the match of any Mexicans – and some of them lived up to their own bravado. One of the first such organizations to get into the field was Colonel Jack Hays's Texas Regiment of Mounted Volunteers, whose various elements linked up with Taylor's army through the spring and summer of 1846. Hays's outfit was an amalgamation of several companies of the famed Texas Rangers, led by such legendary Indian fighters as Captains Ben McCulloch and Samuel Walker. The appearance of their 500 men was nothing short of formidable, each one carrying a rifle and one or two Colt revolvers. Commencing his advance on Monterrey, the capital of Nuevo León, on 19 August, Taylor was soon impressed with the rangers' skill as scouts and exterminators of the guerrillas who infested his lines of communication.

The trouble with the Texans was that they were too prone to kill Mexicans on any pretext – including unarmed and unoffending men, women and children. Many of them nursed grudges as old as a decade against the 'greasers', and they were motivated as much by private vendettas as patriotism. Samuel Chamberlain called them 'packs of human bloodhounds', and any regular who tried to restrain their outrages found himself just as apt to become the victim of Texan fury. However uncontrollable they were at other times, Hays's Rangers were magnificent in a fight. When Taylor battered his way into Monterrey in a terrific four-day fracas that began on 20 September, the Texans were ever in the forefront. Following Colonel Hays's standing orders to 'Give 'em hell!' – they smashed an enemy cavalry charge to pieces, and then slid off their ponies to fight beside the infantry, storming redoubts, palaces and the thick-walled adobe houses where the Mexicans took shelter.

Taylor owed Hays and his Texans quite a debt for

A primitive watercolor of the Battle of San Pascual on 6 December 1846, by an American sailor who served alongside Kearny's 1st Dragoons in California.

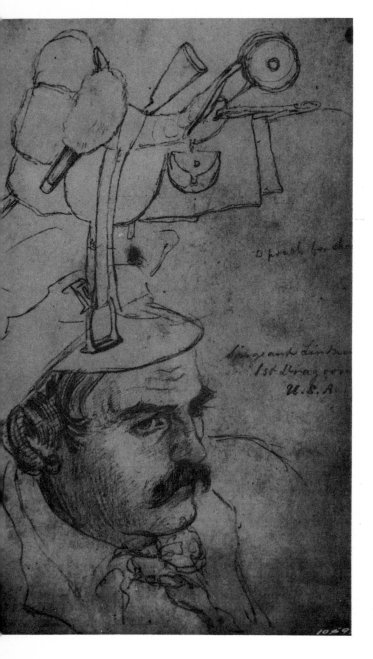

While in California, Kearny's 1st Dragoons were exposed to Spanish influences, and they readily succumbed. This charming 1851 pencil sketch by Frank Mayer shows a dragoon sergeant sporting a gold earring!

the conquest of Monterrey, but he was not at all sorry to see them ride home when their six-month tour of duty expired on 2 October. 'On the day of battle,' he quipped, 'I am glad to have Texas soldiers with me, for they are brave and gallant; but I never want to see them before or afterward.'

Taylor's victories were to weave the charismatic mystique that would place him in the White House in two years, but much further to the north, relatively small bands of American cavalrymen were achieving something much more significant and lasting – without the same loss in blood.

From the end of June into the first week of July, the Army of the West issued out of Fort Leavenworth, in staggered detachments to preserve the forage along the Santa Fe Trail, and disappeared into the endless prairie grasslands. The man responsible for this odd assemblage of 1700 regulars and volunteers was Colonel Stephen Watts Kearny, and his mission was to incorporate the provinces of New Mexico and Upper California into the United States. To attempt so mammoth a task, he was given the following forces: nearly 400 of his own 1st Dragoons from Companies B, C, G, I and K; 100 volunteer infantrymen in a two-company battalion raised in Missouri; a company of 100 St Louis cavalrymen called the LaClede Rangers; fifty Delaware and Shawnee scouts; and about 1000 mounted riflemen in the nine companies of the 1st Regiment of Missouri Mounted Volunteers. The Army of the West was also burdened by the twelve 6-pounders and four 12-pound howitzers of Major Meriwether Lewis Clark's Battalion of Missouri Volunteer Artillery, 1556 wagons, 459 horses, 3658 draft mules, and 14,904 cattle and oxen. It required a good month for this host to cross the 537 miles to Bent's Fort, and as it entered enemy territory, Kearny was forced to put his men on half rations.

The governor of New Mexico mustered a motley army of 4000 to contest Kearny's progress, but his force fell to pieces and dispersed as the Americans drew near. On 18 August 1846, three days after he had been notified of his promotion to brigadier general, the slim old dragoon occupied Santa Fe without having to fire a shot. Kearny stayed in New Mexico only long enough to institute a civil government and win the inhabitants over with his courtesy and respect for their religion. On 25 September, he set out for California with the 300 of his regular troopers still fit to ride. The 1st Dragoons must have made an interesting sight, for every man was mounted on a mule. The general had kept them constantly on the move with an inexhaustible list of special assignments, and the pace wore their horses down. Before he rode out of courier-range, Kearny instructed Colonel Alexander William Doniphan, a towering, sandy-haired lawyer and the commander of the Missouri Mounted Volunteers, to pacify the Indians in the province and then go down and capture Chihuahua, Mexico's gateway to the northwest.

Kearny had embarked upon the most trying march of his long career. On 6 October, about ten miles below Socorro, he encountered twenty mounted Americans hurrying east. One of them was the renowned scout, Kit Carson, who was carrying dispatches from Commodore Robert Stockton marked for Washington announcing the fall of California to the U.S. Navy's Pacific Squadron and Major John C. Frémont's battalion of 234 mounted frontiersmen. Carson's news caused Kearny to alter his plans. The route ahead would be difficult, lacking water and forage, and since California was already occupied, he sent 200 dragoons back to Santa Fe and exchanged his wagons for pack mules. After this was done, Kearny resumed his journey, retaining Kit Carson as a guide.

The closer the 1st Dragoons came to California, the more arduous the going – especially after they entered the Gila Desert. Men and animals reached and passed their breaking point many times, but somehow Kearny kept the column closed up and plodding on. To make matters worse, on 22 November, he met some Mexican horse traders who informed him that the Californians had risen in revolt against their insufferably arrogant American masters. Struggling out of the Gila and into the verdant San Felipe Valley on 2 December, Kearny sent a courier to San Diego to request an escort from Commodore Stockton for his small and weakened force. On 5 December, he was joined by Captain Archibald Gillespie, twelve 'Horse Marines' and twenty-six mounted riflemen.

Gillespie told Kearny that there were seventy-five Californian lancers blocking the road to San Diego at San Pascual. Urged on by Carson and the rash Gillespie, Kearny decided to attack the insurgents after a lieutenant and nine dragoons scouted their camp that night. Unfortunately, the mules and half-broken horses the dragoons were riding were still jaded from their long trek. When the Yankees charged their waiting opponents on 6 December 1846, the poor beasts were unable to keep together, and they carried the

Lieutenant Cave Johnson Couts of the 1st U.S. Dragoons came to help occupy California in 1848, married the daughter of a local grandee and spent the rest of his prosperous life there. Note the casual way he wears his shell jacket, his shirt and gaudy cravat, the jutting epaulettes, riding whip and crumpled forage cap set at a rakish angle.

dragoons at varying speeds – singly or in small groups – into the enemy's line. A continuous rain had ruined the powder in the Americans' pistols and carbines, and they were unable to reach past the Californians' lances with their sabers. The results were truly tragic. Kearny was speared twice by a young gallant who then bowed and rode off when it was apparent the general was no longer capable of defending himself. His subordinates

This tough young man is typical of the mounted volunteers from Missouri who followed Doniphan and Price in New Mexico and Chihuahua.

but the dragoons drove their assailants off the rocky summit, killing five. Kearny then dug in right there and then, his troopers enduring a three-day siege and near starvation. The general's second-in-command, however, had wisely sent Stockton a plea for help after the Battle of San Pascual, and at two o'clock on the morning of 11 December, some 180 Marines and sailors relieved the much-reduced Army of the West.

When Commodore Stockton sallied out of San Diego at the end of the month with 607 men to finally quell the rebellion, the partially recovered Kearny and sixty dismounted troopers of Company C, 1st U.S. Dragoons, went with him. On 8 and 9 January 1847, the Californians gave battle on the San Gabriel River and at La Mesa, and their power was broken. Stockton and Kearny took Los Angeles on 10 January, and the last of the insurgents surrendered three days later. California was now indisputably American, thanks in no small part to Brigadier General Stephen Watts Kearny, but his intrepid devotion to duty hastened his untimely death in the following year.

Back in New Mexico, Doniphan and his Missourians completely cowed the Zunis and Navajos with a swift seven-week campaign punctuated by several fruitful councils. The arrival of Colonel Sterling Price and the 500 roughnecks of his 2nd Regiment of Mounted Missouri Volunteers on 2 October 1846, freed Doniphan to carry out the second half of Kearny's orders. In the middle of December he and 856 of his citizen-soldiers set out from Valverde and struck out for Chihuahua. On Christmas Day, 1300 Mexicans attacked the Missourians at El Brazito, thirty miles from El Paso. Doniphan, who was probably the greatest natural soldier of the war, made his men lie down and hold their fire until the enemy was 150 yards away. Then they blasted their opponents apart, as mounted sorties drove the braver Mexicans into joining the general retreat that began half an hour after the first shot was fired. On 27 December, Doniphan rode into El Paso.

Doniphan remained at El Paso until Major Clark could join him with six artillery pieces and 300 traders intent on exploiting the Chihuahua market. When he resumed his campaign on 8 February 1847, he had 924 fighting men in his charge, not counting his civilian guests. Twenty days later, the Missourians reached the Rio Sacramento and met the army raised by the governor of Chihuahua. The Mexicans had mustered 1200 cavalry, 1500 infantry, 1000 rancheros with machetes,

were not that lucky. Three officers and fifteen men were killed, and another twelve were wounded. One of Kearny's two mountain howitzers was captured when its mule bolted toward the foe. A dozen Californians suffered some sort of wound, and one was captured, but they were not driven off until Kearny's remaining gun went into action.

As the maimed column continued on its way on 7 December, the Californians tried to catch it in an ambush at Rancho San Bernardo. The fighting was fiercest on the slopes of an elevation called Mule Hill,

A recently discovered daguerreotype of Second Lieutenant George H. Gordon, Company I, U.S. Regiment of Mounted Riflemen, circa 1847–8. He is wearing a frock coat and the crimson sash peculiar to officers of his regiment. He is also holding an officer's model of the 1840 heavy dragoon saber.

This corrected close-up of the Gordon daguerreotype reveals the ornament authorized for the forage caps of officers of the Mounted Rifles, 'a gold embroidered spread Eagle with the letter R in silver on the shield.' Prior to the discovery of this picture, there was no evidence that this insignia had ever been produced or issued.

and 119 artillerymen manning twenty-one guns of various sizes. Doniphan simply crossed the river out of range of the enemy's artillery, outflanked their line and chewed the Mexicans up with mounted charges and sorties on foot. The Chihuahuans suffered 300 casualties and 300 captured – not to mention the fall of their city on 2 March. Doniphan's total losses were one dead and seven wounded.

Following the receipt of orders from General

Taylor, Doniphan left Chihuahua on 23 April 1847, and marched 547 miles to join Old Rough and Ready's army. It took the Missourians a month to do, and then they were almost immediately shipped up to New Orleans, where they were discharged. In one year the 1st Missouri Mounted Volunteers had ridden 3600 miles, receiving no pay from the time they left Fort Leavenworth. Not a man of them drew a full ration until they had joined Taylor in May, and even then they faced a voyage of 2000 miles by water until they could return home again. Theirs was an epic worthy of the greatest poet.

While Doniphan's heroes were making a niche for themselves in American history, Price's loud-mouthed roughnecks were egging on the New Mexicans to rise in revolt. Once things came to blows, however, Price moved expeditiously to restore American rule. Moving out of Santa Fe with 350 of his 2nd Missouri Mounted Volunteers on foot, he whipped 1500 rebels near the Rio Grande on 24 January. Four days later he joined up with Captain J. H. K. Burgwin's G Company of the 1st U.S. Dragoons. Together they defeated 500 New Mexicans at Embudo and then fought their way into Taos, the center of the uprising.

The year 1847 brought a pronounced shift in American strategy. General Taylor was ordered merely to hold his ground in northern Mexico, while most of his regulars were peeled away to join Major General Winfield Scott for an amphibious assault on Vera Cruz and a march on Mexico City. Learning of Taylor's predicament, General Antonio López de Santa Anna gathered together 21,553 troops and marched north gleefully to annihilate him. Forewarned by Ben McCulloch's Spy Company of Texas Rangers, twenty-seven men dressed as Mexicans, and his dragoon patrols, Old Rough and Ready withdrew the 4759 men left to him – 4000 of them untried volunteers – and took up a strong defensive position near a hacienda called Buena Vista on 22 February.

Taylor's only regular cavalry amounted to a squadron apiece from the 1st and 2nd Dragoons, and he placed them in reserve behind his thin line of infantry. His left was guarded by Colonel Archibald Yell's Arkansas Mounted Regiment and Colonel Humphrey Marshall's Kentucky Cavalry. Had there been other troops available, Taylor might have made another choice. Those volunteer horsemen were considered the weak link in his army, and with good reason. They were proud young blades, who felt a soldier's only job was to fight. 'Their impatience of all restraint, and egotism made them worse than useless on Picket, while in camp they were a perfect nuisance,' observed Private Chamberlain of the 1st Dragoons. 'They took no care of their arms – not one Carbine in fifty would go off – and most of their Sabres were rusted in their scabbards.'

PLATE 12: WAR WITH MEXICO, 1846–8
34. Corporal, U.S. Regiment of Mounted Riflemen, Undress, 1847: *Mounted Riflemen dressed much like dragoons except for their trousers. General Order No. 18, published by the Adjutant General's Office on 4 June 1846, spelled out the difference in these words: 'The TROUSERS of dark blue cloth, with a stripe of black cloth down the outer seam, edged with yellow cord.' The regiment was originally armed with U.S. Model 1841 ('Mississippi') rifles, Model 1840 sabers and flintlock pistols. The War Department purchased 1000 six-shot Whitneyville-Walker Colt revolvers for the Mounted Rifles, and 220 were delivered shortly after the fall of Mexico City in September 1847.* **35. Second Lieutenant, U.S. Regiment of Mounted Riflemen, Undress, 1847:** *Officers of this unit had a distinctive eagle device embroidered on their forage caps. Their trousers were identical to those of the enlisted men, and their sashes were crimson.* **36. Private, Colonel Hays's Regiment, Texas Mounted Volunteers, 1846–8:** *Texas Rangers wore civilian clothing, freely mixing American and Mexican items. An American officer who observed Hays's regiment in November 1847 wrote: 'Each man carried a rifle, a pair of pistols, and one or two of Colt's revolvers ... A hundred of them could discharge a thousand shots in two minutes.' Hays purchased 1000 Colt revolvers for his 500 rangers, and he later armed them with captured Mexican sabers. All shown engaging guerrillas in the plaza at Huamantla, Mexico, 8 October 1847.*

Colonels Marshall and Yell were amiable Southern gentlemen and personally very brave, but they cared more about their creature comforts than putting their commands in order. Between 23 and 27 January, two majors, two captains and eighty-six men from the two regiments were caught napping and snapped up by Santa Anna's outriders while they were supposed to be scouting themselves! Their comrades failed to learn from their fate, continued to voice their spite for all Mexicans, and strove to prove their manhood by committing atrocities. When one of their number was found murdered on 10 February, 100 of Yell's 'Rackensackers' chased some Mexican refugees into a cave, shooting and scalping twenty to thirty of them. Taylor was so enraged at this that he had the two companies involved sent to the mouth of the Rio Grande as punishment.

Surprisingly enough, both the Kentuckians and

34. Corporal, U.S. Regiment of Mounted Riflemen, Undress, 1847

35. Second Lieutenant, U.S. Regiment of Mounted Riflemen, Undress, 1847

36. Private, Colonel Hays's Regiment, Texas Mounted Volunteers, 1846–8

Arkansans stood up well the first day at Buena Vista, 22 February 1847, fighting dismounted and frustrating every Mexican effort to gain Taylor's left. During the night, however, Santa Anna concentrated 7000 soldiers opposite to them and sent them forward at 8.00 a.m. on the twenty-third. The volunteer cavalrymen were pushed back steadily. Colonel Marshall, commanding the skirmish line, tried to conduct an orderly withdrawal, but as soon as they gained their horses, the battered troopers rode back to Buena Vista. This unauthorized maneuver threw Taylor's entire left wing back at a right angle – just like a door on a hinge. At that critical moment, a brigade of Mexican lancers burst from the mass and swooped down on the lightly defended hacienda.

Captain Enoch Steen and his squadron of the 1st

A battalion of the combined 1st and 2nd U.S. Dragoons escorts Major General Winfield Scott into the Grand Plaza of Mexico City on 14 September 1847.

Dragoons were rushed to the spot to stop the enemy from cutting Taylor's only avenue of retreat. Steen found that Marshall and Yell had already drawn their regiments up in a mounted line facing the oncoming lancers, but they were wasting precious time as the Mexicans thundered down arguing over who possessed the edge in seniority. When their antagonists were 500 yards away, the jumpy Marshall bawled at his Kentuckians, 'Fire!'

'Hold!' howled Yell. 'Don't fire until they are nearer!'

Thoroughly confused, the men in both regiments could offer no effective resistance, and most of them turned tail before the Mexicans made contact. Only Yell and a few officers refused to run. The colonel had a lance rammed into his mouth, and another impaled his chest.

Fortunately for Taylor's cause, Captain Steen had swung his squadron clear of this imbroglio. Though he had barely more than a hundred dragoons at hand, he bravely thrust them where they would do the most

good. 'Our column gave a wild Hurrah and charged the foe in the flank, taking them by surprise, and at a disadvantage,' recalled Private Chamberlain. 'We passed through their column, dividing it in two; their advance swept by the ranch and on into the San Juan valley, and the rear retreated back to the base of the mountain.'

The Mexicans made other attempts to pierce Taylor's line, and each time they were miraculously repulsed. When the firing stopped, 659 Americans lay sprawled dead or wounded around Buena Vista. Santa Anna lost 591 killed, 1048 wounded and 1894 missing. And his problems were just beginning.

On 9 March 1847, General Scott's army made a successful landing at Vera Cruz, and the city capitulated twenty days later. 'Old Fuss and Feathers', as the troops called him, was fairly well supplied with cavalry for his stupendous drive on Mexico City. He had three companies of the 1st Dragoons and six of the 2nd, all grouped into a single battalion under Colonel William S. Harney. There was also an entirely new unit that went along, the United States Regiment of Mounted Riflemen.

Created by Congress on 19 May 1846, the Mounted Rifles had been originally intended to garrison outposts along the Oregon Trail, but the Mexican War changed all that. Initially, the strength of each of the regiment's ten companies was set at sixty-four privates, but the next year it was raised to seventy, just as in the dragoons. The companies were quickly recruited and organized at Fort McHenry, Columbus, Ohio, and Jefferson Barracks. Beginning in September 1846, they were shipped off from Baltimore and New Orleans to join Taylor in northern Mexico, and soon thereafter, they put to sea again to sail with Scott to Vera Cruz. The Mounted Riflemen found the Gulf voyage rough going both times, and most of their horses were lost in passage. In some cases, the animals were carelessly tethered in lumber sheds on the decks of small schooners and swept overboard in sudden storms off the Texas coast. The surviving mounts were turned over to the 2nd Dragoons, and the Mounted Riflemen first saw action dismounted. By the end of May, however, enough suitable horses were found to remount Companies C and I.

The senior officers of the Regiment of Mounted Riflemen had been appointed by President Polk – less for their professional merits than for their politics. 'The proposed [Regiment of Mounted] rifle men are in-tended by western men to give commissions or rather pay to western democrats,' fumed General Scott. 'Not an eastern man, not a graduate of the Military Academy and certainly not a Whig would obtain a place under such proscriptive circumstances or prospects.' Scott was exaggerating, but many of the officers came from civilian backgrounds, and they were utterly incompetent. One exception to this sorry story was the regiment's colonel, Persifor F. Smith, whose talents were so obvious that he was quickly upgraded to brigadier general. His place was taken by Edwin V. Sumner, one of the original captains of the Regiment of Dragoons, who rooted out the unfit and promoted more deserving subalterns to replace them.

Serving as light infantry, the Mounted Rifles distinguished themselves at nearly every step of the way on Scott's brilliant Mexico City campaign. When Old Fuss and Feathers rode into the Grand Plaza to take formal possession of the enemy capital on 14 September 1847, he discovered that they had beaten him to the punch. Glancing up at the roof of the National Palace, Scott saw a knot of Mounted Riflemen clustered around a flagpole on which they had hoisted the Stars and Stripes. The Commanding General of the Army doffed his plumed chapeau, bowed from the saddle, and addressed them warmly: 'Brave Rifles! Veterans! You have been baptized in fire and blood and come out steel.'

The Treaty of Guadalupe Hidalgo, which put an end to the hostilities, was not signed until 2 February 1848. In the meantime, Scott's cavalry was constantly occupied hunting guerrillas who infested the road between Vera Cruz and Mexico City. Colonel Jack Hays and a second regiment of Texas Rangers landed in Mexico late in September 1847, and his fierce riders took a heavy toll from the partisans. When at last Scott's army evacuated Mexico, one of the last units to sail from Vera Cruz was a company of dragoons.

The Mexican War added territory including the present states of California, Nevada and Utah, as well as substantial chunks of New Mexico, Arizona, Colorado and Wyoming, to the great North American republic. The United States had achieved her 'Manifest Destiny'; she now stretched from the Atlantic to the Pacific. And in every permanent territorial acquisition, American cavalrymen had played a prominent, if not a decisive, role. Never in modern history, had mounted troops accomplished anything of comparable lasting value.

5 Skirting the Whirlwind
1848-61

The war with Mexico not only made it possible for the U.S. Cavalry to win a large share of glory and establish an enviable tradition; it also added immeasurably to its responsibilities and sphere of operations. In 1846 the American frontier had been fairly compact and reasonably well defined. Less than a dozen forts were adequate to provide a satisfactory level of security. With the accession of Oregon Territory and the Mexican Cession, the nation's size mushroomed by a third. The United States received 400,000 new citizens requiring protection, and her Indian population was augmented by 200,000 souls. American soldiers were now charged with the task of subduing some of the most cunning and formidable tribes on the North American Continent – the Apaches, Navajos, Comanches, Kiowas, Yakimas, Spokanes, Utes and many more.

The Army's difficulties were sorely exacerbated by the massive migration that flowed into the new lands, especially after gold was discovered in California on 24 January 1848. The long and winding trains of emigrants tramped over the tribal hunting grounds, destroying the game and other resources upon which the Indians depended. Life for the natives became a matter of stealing to survive, and that made clashes with the whites upon whom they preyed inevitable. What had largely been a comfortable garrison army was transformed overnight into a harried and overextended constabulary that was frequently pulled in two or more directions at once. Between 1848 and 1861, regular troops were called out to quell twenty-two separate Indian wars, and they took part in 206 individual engagements. By 1854, these same overworked soldiers had increased the number of frontier outposts from eight to fifty-two. They were scattered over 2,000,000 square miles in country beyond the reach of navigable streams and the existing railroad lines, and situated in some of the most desolate and unapproachable spots on the face of the globe. To make matters even worse, the Army was never furnished with

PLATE 13: A NEW DRESS UNIFORM, 1851–4
37. First Sergeant, 1st U.S. Dragoons, 1853: *The new (1851) regulations authorized one uniform for all occasions. The frock coat displaced the shell jacket. Dragoons wore orange facings and trim on their caps, coats and trousers. Sergeants were denoted by their chevrons and a red worsted sash with bullion fringe ends tied behind the left hip. All enlisted men changed to black leather accoutrements, a practice that lasted until 1902. The arms shown here are the U.S. Model 1847 cavalry musketoon and the Model 1840 heavy dragoon saber.* **38. Trumpeter, 2nd U.S. Dragoons, 1853:** *Dragoon musicians had broad orange facings on their coats. Both officers and men wore sky blue trousers, which were adorned with welts of the proper facing color.* **39. Major, U.S. Regiment of Mounted Riflemen, 1851:** *The Mounted Rifles were assigned green facings, and their officers wore embroidered gold bugles (with a silver numeral One within the bottom valve) on their caps. Officers' caps did not have colored bands. Gold bullion epaulettes were worn for parade and other dress occasions, and simpler shoulder straps were permitted for drills, inspections, fatigues and campaign. All regimental officers wore silk crimson sashes tied behind the left hip. All based on the regulations of 1851, which lent a strong French flavor to Army dress.*

enough men to allow it to cope with its expanded duties.

Americans had been in an unholy hurry to achieve their 'Manifest Destiny', but they never quite got used to the idea of having to pay for it. Hardly had hostilities commenced, than on 6 July 1846, President Polk blithely assured Congress that 'the old army, as it existed before the war with Mexico,' would be equal to all the exigencies of peacetime. Polk was nothing if not a man of his word, and as soon as the ink was dry on the Treaty of Guadalupe Hidalgo, the 3rd

37. First Sergeant, 1st U.S. Dragoons, 1853   **38.** Trumpeter, 2nd U.S. Dragoons, 1853   **39.** Major, U.S. Regiment of Mounted Riflemen, 1851

Dragoons and the nine regular infantry regiments raised for the conflict were disbanded. The rest of the Army was reduced to its pre-war size of 10,000 officers and men. The twenty companies in the two surviving regiments of dragoons were now supposed to consist of one captain, one first lieutenant, one second lieutenant, four sergeants, four corporals, two buglers, one farrier/blacksmith and fifty privates apiece. The ten companies of the Mounted Rifles were similarly constructed, except that each was authorized to have sixty-four privates. The command structure for the three horse regiments was identical: one colonel, one lieutenant colonel, two majors, one adjutant, one quartermaster, one sergeant major, one quartermaster sergeant, one principal musician and two chief buglers.

The puny postwar Army strove manfully to surmount its new challenges. Three fourths of its troops were stationed on the frontier, but two thirds of them were fit for hardly more than mounting guard on parade grounds or escorting slow-moving wagon trains. Twelve of the Army's fifteen regiments were artillery or infantry, and General Scott recognized that order of battle hobbled his subordinates in the West. 'The great extent of our frontiers, and the peculiar character of the service devolving on our troops, render it indispensable that the *cavalry* element should enter largely into the composition of the army,' he wrote in 1850. 'No other description of troops will answer for the protection of our immense lines of emigration and frontier settlements.'

True to its frugal nature, the government tried to redress the imbalance with some inexpensive half-measures. Occasionally, detachments of regular infantry were mounted on mules and companies of Texas Rangers were sworn into Federal service. Neither expedient was particularly successful. Then on 17 June 1850, Congress took a big step and authorized President Zachary Taylor to raise the strength of each company on frontier service to seventy-four privates. This legislation should have enlarged the Army to 13,821 officers and men. But paper figures can achieve nothing by themselves. According to statistics compiled in June 1853, the Army's actual enrollment was 10,417 of all ranks. Eight thousand three hundred and forty-two regulars were supposed to be serving on the frontier, but only 6918 men were at their stations. According to the 1850 expansion, the two 652-man dragoon regiments and the 802-man Regiment of Mounted Riflemen were supposed to muster 900

Captain John Buford of the 2nd U.S. Dragoons, 1859. He wears the frock coat and large gold epaulettes that were developed by the Army in the 1850s. After 1851, dragoon officers wore crimson sashes tied on the left side. An order issued on 24 March 1858, decreed dark blue trousers for officers and enlisted men.

troopers, but the average was usually down around 300 to 400 per regiment.

With the demand for cavalry far exceeding the supply, the only answer was to spread the pony soldiers thin. The mounted regiments were split up and their companies strewn across the untamed country. At the end of 1848, the 1st Dragoons had three companies in New Mexico, three in California, and one each at Forts

Leavenworth, Scott, Washita and Snelling. The 2nd Dragoons had six companies in Texas, two in New Mexico, and two on their way to California. From time to time, these dispositions were altered and new posts were assigned, but the extent of the dispersal was never mitigated and the dragoons rarely served together as whole regiments. Their burdens became even more crushing during the two long intervals when the junior unit in the mounted service was unable to take the field.

During the Mexican War, Congress decreed that any regular who signed up would have his enlistment terminated with the cessation of hostilities. This was meant to encourage recruiting, but it had a most deleterious effect on the peacetime Army. So many Mounted Riflemen took advantage of this escape hatch that their officers and NCOs had to return to Jefferson Barracks and raise the regiment again practically from scratch. Nearly a year passed before the unit could take up its original mission of safeguarding the Oregon Trail. Finally, on 10 May 1849, one-armed Lieutenant Colonel William W. Loring led his born-again Regiment of Mounted Riflemen out on a 2000-mile trek to the Pacific, dropping his companies off singly or in pairs at selected stations from Forts Kearny to Vancouver.

The Mounted Rifles hit the West Coast just in time to be infected by the gold fever emanating from California. It proved to be too strong for many of them, and they joined the 'Forty-Niners' by the dozen. In February 1850, approximately 120 troopers deserted from Oregon City in a body. Although he was in another part of the territory, Colonel Loring pursued them for 1000 miles through storms and blizzards. He apprehended all but thirty-five of the runaways, and most of them froze to death in the snow-choked mountain passes that led to the gold fields. Despite their sorry fate and the vigilance of Loring and his officers, the desertions continued. With the return of fair weather it became like trying to dam a flood with a sieve. By the summer of 1851, the regiment was so reduced it was decided to send the officers back to Jefferson Barracks to recruit it again. Most of the remaining privates and horses were transferred to the companies of the 1st Dragoons serving in California. After its third birth, the Regiment of Mounted Riflemen was assigned to Texas.

Under such impoverished, shorthanded conditions, American cavalrymen were forced to pursue a ba-sically defensive strategy. Small patrols were sent out continuously to prevent marauding Indians from infiltrating into settled or semi-settled areas, but they were not much of a deterrent. Usually the pony soldiers would receive a call for help from some pioneer whose ranch had been looted or livestock run off. Then a platoon or company would be sent off after the culprits for a backbreaking and frequently futile chase. It was not uncommon for some commands to cover eighty miles in a day, or 300 miles in less than two weeks. During the summer campaign season of 1851, Company B, 1st U.S. Dragoons, traversed some 2240 miles back and forth across the central Plains. More often than not, the men had no more than saddle sores and tattered uniforms to show for their pains, but a few hard-driving leaders sometimes got lucky.

On 16 January 1855, Lieutenant Samuel D. Sturgis of the 1st Dragoons overtook a raiding party of Mescalero Apaches, with eighteen troopers and six civilians after a rollicking stern chase of three days and 175 miles. The terrible cold made the soldiers' hands too numb to reload their weapons, so they tore into the braves with the saber – killing three and wounding four. Sturgis had three men wounded, but he recovered seventy-five horses and mules the Indians had stolen from a ranch near Santa Fe.

Despite their superior firepower and discipline, the soldiers did not always have everything their own way. On 30 March 1854, about 240 Jicarilla Apaches ambushed Lieutenant John W. Davidson and sixty 1st Dragoons in the Embudo Mountains about fifteen miles south of Taos. The command was overrun, and twenty-two troopers went down. Though painfully wounded, Davidson demonstrated indefatigable combat leadership and pulled the rest of his dragoons clear, but only two of the thirty-eight survivors were not hit.

Some of the more chauvinistic old veterans in the cavalry may have ascribed such disasters to the changed composition of the three mounted regiments. From their earliest days, the Dragoons and Mounted Rifles had prided themselves on the fact that their enlisted men had been drawn largely from native American stock. The teeming throngs of immigrants who started to deluge the country in the 1840s, and who would continue to swarm into the New World well into the next century, steadily made their presence felt in the United States Cavalry. By 1850, 60 per cent. of the regular rank and file were foreign-born. About half of them were Irishmen, and a fifth were German. Many

Supply shortages plagued Army units on the frontier. This 1851 Mayer sketch of a dragoon at Fort Snelling shows him still in the old 1839 pattern uniform and Indian moccasins in place of his worn-out ankle boots.

PLATE 14: A RETURN TO MORE TRADITIONAL STYLES, 1854

40. Sergeant Major, 2nd U.S. Dragoons, 1854: *In 1854 the regulations were revised and the shell jacket restored for all mounted troops. The new model had a shorter collar and fuller sleeves than its predecessor. A 'diagonal half chevron' sewn on the lower sleeves was awarded to each man who completed a five-year enlistment. This sergeant major's service stripes attest to ten years with the colors. The red border on the bottom set of stripes was a privilege granted to war veterans. The band on the cap was shrunk to a narrow welt of the facing color. Sergeants were entitled to a double row of brass studs on top of their shoulder scales. The arms pictured here are the U.S. Model 1847 musketoon and Model 1840 dragoon saber.* **41. Private, 1st U.S. Dragoons, Campaign Dress, 1854:** *Based on the memoirs of Sergeant Percival Lowe, a member of this regiment from 1849 to 1854. Dragoons adopted hardy clothing for Indian hunting. They donned blue, red or grey flannel shirts and broad-brimmed hats. Trousers were either the issue sky blue or some shade of corduroy. Lowe made imaginative use of a silk yellow and red check handkerchief: 'I often tied it around my hat and brought it around so as to cover my neck and most of my face to keep off the sun and the pestiferous gnats.' The 1st Dragoons were armed with the Model 1848 Colt revolver, in addition to the Model 1847 musketoon and Model 1840 saber. The horse is decked out in the 1847 Grimsley saddle and equipment.* **42. Captain, 1st U.S. Dragoons, 1854:** *This overcoat with its detachable cape was prescribed by the 1851 regulations. Rank was indicated by the black silk knot on the lower sleeves. Colonels warranted five braids; lieutenant colonels four; majors three; captains two; and first lieutenants one. Second lieutenants had plain sleeves.*

could not speak English, and it took a great deal of training to make them good soldiers.

As the number of immigrants in uniform grew, so did the general prejudice against common soldiers. The so-called 'real Americans' often sneered at the ordinary troopers as ignorant, drunken good-for-nothings who consumed public funds without contributing anything positive in return. Sentenced to five-year stretches of drudgery, danger and fatigue, these ill-paid, misunderstood and ill-employed men found it hard to take much pride in themselves or their mission.

Contrary to the convictions of intolerant nativists, the pony soldiers' real debility was not to be found in the article behind the uniform, but in the way in which he was used. As the 1850s approached their mid-point, American cavalry officers came to realize that the established defensive policy did little more than tire

the men, break their spirit and ruin their mounts. Gradually they came to advocate a more offensive policy. Instead of chasing after isolated war parties, entire tribes were now to be held liable for any depredations and subjected to the most severe forms of retaliation.

This new approach was implemented in the summer of 1855 with devastating effect. On 19 August 1854, Brevet Second Lieutenant John L. Grattan of the 6th Infantry seized upon a minor altercation to fire two artillery pieces into a camp of Brule Sioux near Fort Laramie. The enraged Indians fell on the bullying

40. Sergeant Major, 2nd U.S. Dragoons, 1854

41. Private, 1st U.S. Dragoons, Campaign Dress, 1854

42. Captain, 1st U.S. Dragoons, 1854

officer and his twenty-nine men and cut them to shreds in the blink of an eye. Encouraged by the ease of their victory and now grown contemptuous of the soldiers and settlers, the Brules became increasingly aggressive and started preying on stagecoaches and pioneers. The Grattan 'Massacre' and these other outrages prodded the Army into taking decisive action.

On 24 August 1855, Brevet Brigadier General William S. Harney cantered out of Fort Kearny at the head of a 600-man expedition drawn from the 6th and 10th Infantry, the 4th Artillery and his own 2nd Dragoons. To the gentler souls who urged him to employ the velvet glove rather than the steel fist, the old Seminole War hangman roared, 'By God, I'm for battle – no peace.' Harney's mounted troops were commanded by Lieutenant Colonel Philip St George Cooke of the 2nd Dragoons, the Army's foremost expert on cavalry tactics.

By 2 September, Harney's guides had located a band of 250 defiant Brules waiting for him on Blue Water Creek near Ash Hollow. Marching all night, Cooke got his battalion, two companies of dragoons and two of mounted infantry, in a blocking position above the Indian camp. The next day, Harney struck the Brules from two sides. After a sharp skirmish the Sioux broke and fled, Cooke's howling troopers pursuing them for five to eight miles. Eighty-five of the braves were killed, five were wounded and seventy squaws and children were captured. Harney's total losses amounted to an even dozen, and the murderous efficiency of his operations so unnerved the Teton Sioux that they remained at peace for nearly a decade.

Even as Harney was shaking up the Great Plains, the Army was receiving reinforcements that would enable it to do more of the same. On 3 March 1855, Congress authorized the raising of two regiments of infantry and two of horse. The 1st and 2nd United States Cavalry were the first regular American military organizations to actually bear the title of 'cavalry'. Some disgruntled Dragoon and Mounted Rifle officers believed that Secretary of War Jefferson Davis saw to it that they received a distinctive designation so that he could appoint their officers from among his Southern favorites without regard to seniority in the older mounted regiments. Whether the rumors were true or not, a disproportionate number of commissions in the two new outfits were dealt out to candidates from south of the Mason/Dixon line. This was to leave a terrible void in that arm when they cast their lot with the Confederacy six years later.

The two cavalry regiments were organized in the same fashion as the Dragoons. The 1st Cavalry was assembled and trained at Fort Leavenworth. Its commander, Colonel Edwin V. Sumner, was a veteran dragoon whose distinguished service on horseback spanned all the eventful years following 1833. Five of his officers, Lieutenant Colonel Joseph E. Johnston, Major John Sedgwick, Major William H. Emory, Captain George B. McClellan and Lieutenant J. E. B. Stuart, were all destined for great fame in the impending conflict. The 2nd Cavalry was whipped into shape at Jefferson Barracks, and its roster of officers read like a veritable *Who's Who* of the future Confederacy: Colonel Albert Sidney Johnston, Lieutenant Colonel Robert E. Lee, Major William J. Hardee, Captains Earl Van Dorn and Edmund Kirby Smith, and Lieutenants John B. Hood and Fitzhugh Lee. Major George Thomas and Captain George Stoneman were to remain loyal to the Union, the former turning his sword against his native Virginia to become one of Lincoln's best generals.

The 2nd Cavalry was known enviously as 'Jeff Davis's Own' and 'Jeff Davis's Pet'. Not only were its officers of the highest quality, but the Secretary of War worked wonders to provide it with the very best in everything. The regiment's horses were purchased in Kentucky. They were wonderful animals, and each cost well above the usual price the Army was permitted to pay for its steeds. On 27 October 1855, the 2nd Cavalry rode out of Jefferson Barracks and headed overland for its new home, the state of Texas, then the bloody crossroads for Indian traffic between the United States and Mexico, and the nation's gravest trouble spot in the West. There were over 750 men and 800 spirited chargers in the glittering cavalcade, and the march was made with remarkably little straggling or desertion. The 2nd reached Fort Belknap late in December 1855, relieving the Regiment of Mounted Riflemen, which was shifted over to New Mexico.

Although the 2nd Cavalry was unable to put a stop to Kiowa and Comanche raids on Texas settlements, its able officers and willing troopers exacted a rising toll on those Indians foolhardy enough to trespass on their turf. Within a year of their arrival, an Indian agent living in the state wrote, 'Our frontier has, for the last three months, enjoyed a quiet never heretofore known.' Over the next four years, the 2nd Cavalry clashed with the hostiles on a small scale nearly forty times, and it almost always drew blood. The regi-

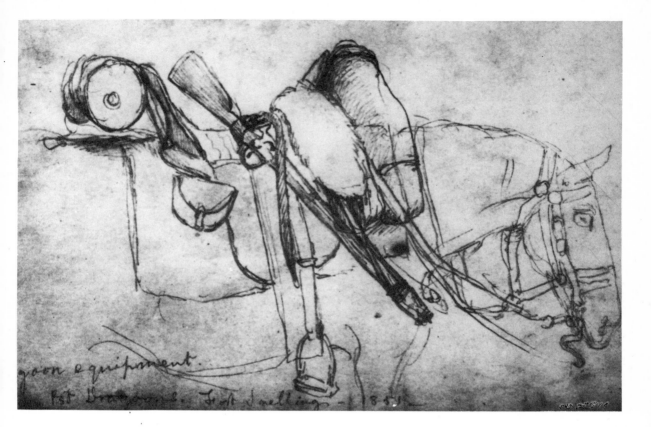

A Mayer sketch of the Grimsley dragoon horse equipment on a mount at Fort Snelling in 1851. This system was first adopted in 1847. The carbine is the U.S. Model 1847 smoothbore musketoon.

ment's most successful sorties were directed by its senior captain, Brevet Major Earl Van Dorn.

On 15 September 1858, Van Dorn, the 225 troopers of Companies A, F, H and K, 135 Indian auxiliaries and a camp guard from the 1st Infantry struck north from Fort Belknap for a campaign in the heart of Comanche country. Sneaking up through a low-lying morning fog on 1 October, Van Dorn charged an unsuspecting enemy camp of 120 lodges. In the prolonged and ferocious fighting, the 2nd Cavalry killed fifty-six Comanche warriors and two women, mortally wounded twenty-five more and utterly destroyed the village. Van Dorn lost one lieutenant and two cavalrymen dead, one private missing, one sergeant mortally wounded and nine soldiers seriously hurt. Van Dorn himself was hit badly, but he surprised many by recovering completely in five weeks.

With the following spring, Van Dorn was reinforced by two more companies of the 2nd Cavalry, bringing his battalion up to 500 mounted officers and men and fifty-eight friendly Indians. On 13 May 1859, he cornered 100 Comanches in a deep, bushy ravine near Crooked Creek. The troopers surrounded the depression and then swept in on foot to exterminate their quarry. In a ruthless, pointblank affair, the soldiers killed forty-nine warriors and wounded five. Five men and thirty-two women were taken prisoner. Not an Indian got away. Van Dorn's men had a captain shot in the thigh and a lieutenant got an arrow through his breast. Two enlisted men were killed and nine wounded. His Indian auxiliaries had two dead and one mortally wounded. It was a stunning victory, but by no means final.

Elsewhere in the West, the 1st Cavalry was earning

97

A company guidon of the 1st U.S. Dragoons, circa 1855 to 1860. The top half is red and the bottom white. This style was carried by both dragoon regiments from 1836 to 1863. When a guidon was issued, its company letter was added in white on the top half of the banner.

its spurs. All through the last half of 1856, the Cheyennes had been growing increasingly belligerent, and in the summer of 1857, Colonel Sumner was dispatched with six companies of his regiment and three of the 6th Infantry to make them behave. Pushing on with his 300 1st Cavalrymen, the old dragoon discovered an equal number of Cheyenne braves drawn up in line of battle on an open field beside the Solomon River. The Cheyennes had washed their hands in a supposedly magic lake, which their medicine men had assured them would ward off the white man's bullets, and they welcomed a chance to give battle.

As Sumner's troopers, their carbines held at the ready, approached the Cheyenne line, it lurched into action and lumbered forward. At that moment, the colonel surprised and delighted his men by shouting, 'Sling – carbine. Draw – saber.' With a metallic snap and whir, the cavalrymen produced a gleaming forest of cold steel. Then in the booming, bass voice that had won him the sobriquet, 'Bull o' the Woods', Sumner bellowed, 'Gallop – march!' and 'Charge!' Shrieking ecstatically, the pony soldiers levelled their long blades and dug in their spurs. That was too much for the befuddled Cheyennes. Their medicine was supposed to protect them from white guns, not white sabers. Confounded by their gods, they did the only sensible thing and ran for their lives.

The Battle of the Solomon River produced one of the U.S. Cavalry's few honest-to-goodness Hollywood-style saber charges during the Indian wars. Had Sumner had his men switch to their Colt's revolvers

A print by H. A. Ogden illustrating the uniforms of mounted troops in the 1850s. On the left are a private and a captain of the new 1st U.S. Cavalry, circa 1855. The mounted officer is a major of the 2nd U.S. Dragoons, wearing the French-style cap with orange welt and pompom that was authorized in 1854. Behind him are a private and first sergeant of his regiment in the 1854-regulation uniform.

Colonel Edwin V. Sumner, circa 1855. Sumner was a captain in the original Regiment of Dragoons, and in 1855 he became the first commander of the 1st U.S. Cavalry. He is seen here in the 1851-regulation frock coat.

Captain Thomas John Wood was with the 1st U.S. Cavalry from 1855 to 1861. He is wearing his shoulder straps fixed over his epaulettes, and the collar of his 1851-regulation frock coat is folded down. The Model 1855 officer's cavalry hat was supposed to have a gold cord drooping across the front and back of the crown, but Wood has pulled his so tight that it is very near to the top.

after the Cheyennes bolted, he might have won a greater victory. As it was, he could only report nine certain kills after a pursuit of seven miles. Two of his men were slain and Lieutenant J. E. B. Stuart and eight troopers wounded. What really counted, however, was the psychological impact of Sumner's tactics and the ease with which he humiliated his adversaries. For the next six years the Cheyennes would be peaceful.

The pony soldiers too had their share of reverses, although they usually managed to get in the last blow. On 6 May 1858, Brevet Lieutenant Colonel Edward J. Steptoe left Fort Walla Walla with three companies of

the 1st Dragoons and twenty-five infantry manning two mountain howitzers to investigate reports of Indian disturbances in the Pacific Northwest. Steptoe's mission was peaceful; his six officers and 158 men

carried a paltry forty rounds apiece. At eight o'clock on the morning of 17 May, 1000 frenzied warriors attacked the tiny command near Tohatonimme Creek. Shielding the flanks and rear of the embattled column, the dragoons held off the swarms of braves long enough for Steptoe to reach a hilltop and bring his guns into play, but they were shaken by the deaths of two popular officers. After a full day of desperate fighting, the troops had suffered six dead and twelve wounded, and they were down to three bullets per man. Burying their howitzers, the dragoons slipped out of the trap by cover of night and made their harrowing way back to Fort Walla Walla.

Captain George B. McClellan of the 1st U.S. Cavalry (far right) was part of the American military board sent to observe the Crimean War. As a result of his experiences, McClellan designed the famous saddle that was to serve the U.S. Cavalry well into the next century. From the left, the other gentlemen in this photograph are Major Alfred Mordecai of the Ordnance Department, a Russian officer and Major Richard Delafield of the Engineers.

Vengeance came quickly. Early in August, Colonel George Wright took the field with 600 regulars, six companies of foot soldiers, the crews for two 12-pound mountain howitzers and Brevet Major

William N. Grier's four companies of the 1st Dragoons, three of which had been mauled with Steptoe. At Four Lakes on 1 September 1858, Wright found a superior body of warriors positioned in rocky ravines and a pine forest blocking his line of march. Once the infantry and artillery had pushed the braves out onto the open expanses of the Great Spokane Plain, Major Grier howled, 'Charge the rascals!' The dragoons rode down the scattering tribesmen, sabering and shooting any fugitives with great relish. Sixty Indians were slain and others were wounded, but not one American was lost. At the Battle of Spokane Plains four days later, the same thing happened, and Grier's troopers fell

First Lieutenant Roger Jones of the Regiment of Mounted Riflemen, circa 1858–60. His Model 1858 officer's hat bears the regimental insignia, a gold embroidered trumpet with a silver numeral One 'within the bend'.

PLATE 15: NEW REGIMENTS AND NEW DUDS, 1855–60

43. Private, 2nd U.S. Cavalry, 1855: *The two new cavalry regiments were dressed much like dragoons, except their shell jackets were trimmed with yellow lace. General Order No. 13, issued by the Adjutant General's Office on 15 August 1855, authorized a black felt hat looped up on the right side for the cavalry. It came with a patent leather chinstrap that was often too short and had a tendency to break. The enlisted model was decorated with a black feather, a yellow worsted cord and the wearer's company letter. An officer's model had a gold cord and the regiment's number. Field officers wore three feathers and company officers two. Two companies of the 2nd Cavalry were armed with the Model 1855 Springfield pistol-carbine.* **44. Quartermaster Sergeant, 1st U.S. Dragoons, Dress Uniform, 1858:** *General Order No. 3 of 24 March 1858 had the entire Army switch to the 'Jeff Davis' or 'Hardee' hat. It also put all officers and men into dark blue trousers. After 24 June 1858, dragoons wore their regimental number above the brass crossed-saber badge – and their company letter below it. This arrangement was reversed for cavalry regiments. Both the 1st and 2nd Dragoons received a large issue of the Model 1848 Sharps carbine.* **45. Trumpeter, 2nd U.S. Dragoons, Dress Uniform, 1859:** *With the revival of the shell jacket in 1854, musicians received garments laced 'herring-bone' fashion.*

on the foe once the foe had been forced out onto clear ground. Wright concluded his brilliant campaign a month later, after securing the unconditional surrender of the bands he had so soundly whipped.

As intractable as the Indians may have been, the pony soldiers carried out their most difficult duties of the 1850s against their fellow Americans, and some of the most unpleasant episodes in their history were written in the territories of Utah and Kansas.

When President Franklin Pierce signed the Kansas-Nebraska Bill into law on 30 May 1854, he was attempting to defuse the great national controversy over the abolition of slavery that was, even then, threatening the preservation of the Union. Southerners had long resented that clause in the Missouri Compromise which forbade the formation of further slave states above the lower border of that state. To gain their support for legislation bearing on his personal am-

PLATE 15: 1855–60

43. Private, 2nd U.S. Cavalry, 1855   **44.** Quartermaster Sergeant, 1st U.S. Dragoons, Dress Uniform, 1858   **45.** Trumpeter, 2nd U.S. Dragoons, Dress Uniform, 1859

bitions, Senator Stephen A. Douglas of Illinois proposed that the citizens of Kansas be allowed to choose whether their state would be slave or free, and his view of popular sovereignty became the law of the land. Men of both persuasions settled in Kansas Territory, but each group was determined that its views should prevail. Neither side was above stooping to unethical practices, and the friction reached a dangerous level.

Captain Richard S. Ewell and three companies of the 1st Dragoons strike a camp of Coyotero Apaches in the shadow of Mount Graham on 27 June 1857, killing or wounding forty braves. This sketch is by a soldier who participated in the Gila Expedition of 1857.

When the Southerners illegally imported 'Border Ruffians' from adjacent Missouri to stuff ballot boxes and gain control of the legislature, the 'Free Staters' elected their own assembly and set up a rival capital in another town. As people started getting bushwhacked and burned out of their homes, the stage was set for a preview of the terrible civil war that would consume the entire nation within six short years.

The Federal officials in Kansas Territory initially favored the Slave Staters, and they tried to deploy the 1st Cavalry at Fort Leavenworth and the 2nd Dragoons at Fort Riley against the Free Staters. Colonel Sumner, a Massachusetts man, was not about to play the flunky for the 'Slavocracy', and he refused to act without specific instructions from the War

Department. Lieutenant Colonel Cooke of the 2nd Dragoons, though a Virginian, displayed the same commendable restraint. In May of 1856, open warfare erupted in Kansas, and the 1st Cavalry and 2nd Dragoons were run ragged in their constant efforts to maintain the public peace. Sumner and Cooke placed their troopers between opposing mobs and armies, protected free and slave settlements alike, and behaved with a fairness and tact that was highly commendable under the circumstances. They saved many lives and worked diplomatic wonders, but they received little thanks for their efforts.

Just as the wounds of 'Bleeding Kansas' were being closed, another brand of civil strife began to brew in Utah, which had been settled by Mormons during the preceding decade. The Mormons belonged to the only evangelical movement of wholly American origin that would blossom into a great religion in its own right. The Mormons had undergone sporadic persecutions from the time of their founding in central New York, largely due to their practice of polygamy and their abrasive clannishness. They were hounded from state to state until they took the plunge and crossed the Great Plains to the shores of the great Salt Lake. There by dint of their strong backs and stronger faith, they made the desert bloom and set up a thriving community of more than 40,000 souls. Once established in Utah, the Mormons refused to obey any Federal officials not of their own religion. Some of the more fanatical, no doubt remembering past injuries,

When Colonel Albert Sidney Johnston of the 2nd Cavalry was breveted to brigadier general for the Mormon Expedition, he merely removed his old shoulder straps from his 1851-regulation field officer's frock coat and had a pair of new ones sewn in their place.

helped their Indian friends massacre an entire wagon train of 'gentiles' from Arkansas. They were also wrongfully accused of debauchery and white slavery.

In July 1857, President James Buchanan ordered the Army to send 2500 troops to reassert Federal authority in the territory. No little difficulty was found in mobilizing the necessary men and in the selection of the commander for this 'Utah Expedition'. Brevet Brigadier General Albert Sidney Johnston, the colonel of the 2nd Cavalry, did not arrive at Fort Leavenworth to take charge until 11 September. However, Colonel Thomas L. Alexander had marched against

Lieutenant Colonel William J. Hardee, 1st U.S. Cavalry, in full dress uniform, circa 1860. Hardee, like many other cavalry officers, threw his lot in with the Confederacy when the Civil War began.

the Mormons two months earlier with the 5th and 10th Infantry and a battery of the 2nd Artillery. By 18 September, Johnston was hot on their trail, along with Lieutenant Colonel Cooke and six companies of the 2nd Dragoons.

Cooke's troopers were lashed for a dozen successive days by stinging rain. Then the weather turned cold and their world was transformed into a wilderness of ice and snow. The only fuel they had was buffalo chips, but these grew so sodden they would not burn. On 1 November, Cooke reached Fort Laramie, where he stripped his command down for the toughest leg of the journey. He directed his men 'to store all baggage and other things absolutely not necessary, to leave all camp women, and to grind the sabers, which were not to be drawn and not to be trailed, but hooked up whenever the trooper was afoot, so they might not be dulled by contact with the steel scabbard.'

Cooke set out again four days later, heading for South Pass in the Rockies. A five-day snowstorm piled up drifts fifteen feet high, and the temperature sank to 13 deg. below zero as the dragoons climbed upwards, but Cooke kept them floundering on. Eventually they made it to Bridger's Fort, a trading post seventy miles east of Salt Lake City, the Mormon capital, where Alexander's column had gone into winter quarters. Once there, the dragoons found little relief from the misery they had endured. Mormon militia had destroyed three of Johnston's supply trains and razed the surrounding countryside. The troopers suffered terribly from want and cold, and a third of Cooke's horses perished in Utah.

In the spring, events took a happier turn. A special emissary sent out from Washington convinced the Mormon leaders to accept Buchanan's Federal appointees, and what might have been a bloody insurrection was averted. Johnston staged a triumphal march through Salt Lake City, which the Mormons piously boycotted, and then set up a sizable garrison at Camp Floyd to the west. The rest of the Utah Expedition returned to their regular stations to resume fighting the Indians.

Twice in the 1850s, the officers of the U.S. Cavalry stared rebellion in the face, and though they never flinched, the sight sickened them. Nevertheless, when rebellion threatened the Union a third time in 1861, many of these same officers were in its forefront, and they were to preside over a conflict in which the American horse soldier was to enjoy his heyday.

6 A Terrible Golden Age
1861-5

For more than a century, historians have debated the exact causes of the American Civil War without arriving at a consensus of opinion. It seems clear, however, that as soon as the containment of slavery became a national issue around 1820, Southern leaders sought dominant positions in the Federal government to protect their 'peculiar institution' and to check its critics. The 'Slavocracy' openly tampered with the mails to halt the distribution of antislavery literature, and in Congress it temporarily denied abolitionists the rights of petition and debate. As the nineteenth century lengthened into middle age and the North took a pronounced lead in population growth, Southerners tried to make a bastion out of the Senate by adding more slave states to the Union. That was the primary reason why the South was so enthusiastic in its support of the annexation of Texas and the Mexican War.

Then in 1860, the Republican Party, a new and almost exclusively Northern political organization dedicated to the eventual eradication of slavery, elected Abraham Lincoln as its first President. Southerners were now painfully aware that the Federal government was a two-edged sword, and that it could be used against them! Starting with South Carolina in December 1860, eleven states from below the Mason-Dixon line voted for secession and dissolved their ties with the United States. Almost immediately, their militias began seizing Federal forts, arsenals, arms and naval yards, incarcerating or expelling their garrisons.

The U.S. Army was in no shape to stem the rushing tide of disunion. First of all, it was much too small to interfere with such a widespread popular movement. On paper, it was supposed to number 18,093 officers and men, but in January 1861, its actual strength ranged from 13,024 to 16,367. It was ludicrous to propose that such a handful could coerce 5,500,000 Southern whites into doing anything against their will. Furthermore, the Army was so badly dispersed and so far from the crisis area that its regiments could not be mobilized for

a timely show of force. Out of 198 infantry, cavalry and artillery companies, 183 of them were at posts on the frontier. The remaining fifteen were spread thin among twenty-three border and coastal forts and other installations in the East. Denied any firm directives from Washington, the commanders of those regular units unfortunate enough to be caught in the seceding states were hard-pressed to keep their men safe and still not rouse an already-inflamed local populace to acts of violence. After five arduous years of fighting Indians in Texas, the troopers of the 2nd Cavalry found themselves being jeered and threatened by the very folk whose lives and property they had done so much to protect. Shortly after Texas left the Union, the regiment concentrated at Green Lake, thirty miles from the Gulf of Mexico, and in March 1861, six companies boarded steamships at Indianola bound for New York City. Further to the north, the 1st Cavalry evacuated Forts Smith, Cobb, Gibson, Arbuckle and Washita, just barely evading a force of Texans sent to seize its arms and horses. The 3rd Infantry also made good its escape, but the whole 8th Infantry was caught (though later exchanged).

Even those outfits that managed to get out of the new Confederacy suffered serious losses. Out of the 1080 regular officers on active service in 1861, 460 were from the seceding states, and 297 of them, along with sixteen Northerners who shared Southern sympathies, resigned their commissions to offer their swords to the 'Lost Cause'. The Army's five mounted regiments were especially hard hit. One hundred-and-four of their 176 officers were Southerners, and most of them stood by their native states, including four of the five colonels. West Point did not graduate enough second lieutenants in 1861 to take up the slack, so many vacancies were filled with appointees from civil life. As a result, the U.S. Cavalry was saddled with a large proportion of green and untested subalterns who would have to learn their profession while practicing it

– a factor that was to seriously hamper its performance over the next two years.

Very few enlisted men deserted from the regular army to join the Confederate forces, but they must have been affected by the departure of trusted and beloved officers. There is a story told of Captain James McIntosh, a Floridian who resigned from the 1st U.S. Cavalry on 7 May 1861. Nearly three months later, McIntosh's old company had a skirmish with the Rebels at Dug Spring, Missouri. As they drew near the enemy in a column of fours, one of the troopers whistled and gasped, 'My God, boys, that's Captain McIntosh.' At that moment, the new captain commanded a set of fours to dismount and fire their new Sharps carbines at McIntosh's party. The order was

Captain Franklin Moore of the 1st Vermont Volunteer Cavalry, one of the 272 mounted regiments the North raised during the Civil War. Note the officer's emblem on his felt Model 1858 cavalry hat – an embroidered pair of gold crossed-sabers with the regimental number in silver on a black velvet ground.

instantly obeyed, but the bullets went whistling harmlessly through the tree limbs high above their intended targets. Taking off his hat, the popular McIntosh bowed low to his old command and galloped out of range.

Such gracious amenities were not observed in Charleston Harbor on 12 April 1861, after Major Robert Anderson declined to surrender Fort Sumter to Confederate troops. The thirty-four hour bombardment that commenced at four o'clock that morning produced the opening shots of the bloodiest and most wrenching war in American history. About 2,000,000 men and boys fought for the Union, and 1,000,000 for the Confederacy. According to the best records, 618,000 American soldiers gave their lives in the Civil War, 360,000 of them in Yankee blue and 258,000 in Rebel grey. That was more dead than the total lost in every other American war from the Revolution up through Korea.

The Civil War was unique in countless ways. It scourged and utterly transformed the adolescent republic. It also marked the highest position the pony soldier would ever hold in American military practice. More Americans fought from horseback during this war than in any struggle before or since. Between 1861 and 1865, 272 full regiments of cavalry were raised to preserve the Union, not to mention forty-five separate battalions and seventy-eight independent companies. The South mustered at least 137 mounted regiments, 143 distinct battalions and 101 unattached companies.

The War between the States marked both the apotheosis and the demise of the cavalier tradition that was so dear to Americans of the first half of the nineteenth century. In those early days, thousands of youngsters rode from their sheltered homes in plumed hats and tight, elegant uniforms, envisioning themselves as chivalrous knights errant, setting forth on the high road of honor to give battle with gleaming blades. By the end of the contest, those who survived had been converted to drab mounted infantry, who did their killing with revolvers and repeating carbines.

As far as General-in-Chief Winfield Scott and the other directors of the Union war effort were at first concerned, there would be little need for cavalry to settle what appeared to be no more than a domestic quarrel. On 15 April 1861, the day after the fall of Fort Sumter, President Lincoln called for 75,000 ninety-day volunteers to suppress the Southern rebellion. When the governors of Indiana, Minnesota, Iowa and

A young Confederate cavalryman in a homemade grey jacket. His bewildering array of arms reflects the all too chronic shortage of cavalry weapons that existed in the South. He is holding a double-barrelled shotgun, an enormous Bowie knife and has two revolvers stuffed in his belt.

A Federal cavalryman in a shell jacket with an 1860 Colt Army revolver.

Pennsylvania offered to send mounted regiments as part of their quotas, the War Department turned them down flat. American cavalry doctrine had been shamelessly copied from the French, and the French preached that it took two or three years to make an efficient cavalryman. Any mounted regiments formed under the President's summons would have to be discharged before they could be trained. And even if they did sign up for a more extended enlistment, the North's leaders confidently believed that the Confederacy would be crushed before any volunteer Federal horsemen could get into the field. Furthermore, General Scott was convinced that the crucial battles of this war would be fought in Virginia, and as he himself put it, 'the surface of Virginia was so cut up with fences and other ob-

structions as to make operations with large bodies of cavalry impracticable.' Seen in this light, cavalry was an extravagant and needless expense, to be stringently discouraged.

Nevertheless, the U.S. Army's mounted strength was grudgingly augmented. Coming to a more realistic appreciation of the trial he faced, on 3 May 1861, President Lincoln appealed for 42,034 men to serve for three years or the duration. These long-term volunteers were to be divided among thirty-nine regiments of infantry and one of cavalry, the 1st New York. This breach in General Scott's biases was the brainchild of Carl Schurz, a German-American politician who offered to raise a regiment composed wholly of German cavalry veterans from the New York City area. Since such men would already possess sufficient training and experience, they could be thrown at the Rebels with no appreciable delay. Lincoln saw to it that Schurz was permitted to go ahead with his project. Only enough German, Polish and Hungarian veterans were found to fill up four companies, but the incorrigible Schurz invited four unauthorized cavalry companies consisting of native Americans that had been privately raised in the city to join his regiment. He also absorbed the 'Philadelphia Light Cavalry' detachment, which was willing to take any step to reach the front. One company from Syracuse, New York, and another from Grand Rapids, Michigan, completed the unit. In this irregular and under-handed fashion, the 1st New York 'Lincoln' Cavalry became the first volunteer mounted regiment in the Union Army.

A similar streak of ingenuity was demonstrated in Illinois. After prolonged pleading with the War Department, Governor Richard Yates received authorization to raise five companies of cavalry. He got ten instead, and happily decided to keep them.

Even the regular army was not immune to the contagion. On 4 May 1861, General Order No. 16 was issued, creating the 3rd Regiment of U.S. Cavalry. Ten days later, David Hunter, a native of Illinois and a friend of Lincoln, was named as its colonel. Unlike its five sister mounted regiments, the 3rd Cavalry was organized with twelve companies instead of the customary ten.

These developments represented a compromise on the part of Scott and his cronies, rather than a conversion to a belief in the high value of mounted troops. When Brigadier General Irvin McDowell led his green army of 36,000 south from Washington in July 1861, on a vain and hasty campaign to capture the Confederate capital of Richmond, Virginia, he was accompanied solely by seven companies of cavalry. They were all regulars – two companies from the 1st Cavalry, four from the 2nd and one from the 2nd Dragoons, but there were not enough of them to make any difference. McDowell was defeated by 32,000 Rebels at the First Battle of Bull Run on 21 July 1861. The Rebels were supported by a full regiment of grey-clad cavalry, the 1st Virginia under Lieutenant Colonel James Ewell Brown ('Jeb') Stuart, the four-company mounted battalion of Colonel Wade Hampton's Legion and several independent companies. When the Federal troops were forced at length to retreat, the Confederate horsemen pursued them a short distance, and the sight of those oncoming centaurs, especially the Black Horse Cavalry of Fauquier County, with its dark, plunging steeds, threw the Yankees into a panic. The retreat

PLATE 16: THE CIVIL WAR, UNION REGULAR OFFICERS, 1861

46. Major, 4th U.S. Cavalry, Dress Uniform, 1861: *Officers wore the 1851-regulation frock coat until 1872. Field officers had a double-breasted version with two rows of seven buttons. A company officer's single-breasted coat had one row of nine buttons. For full dress, officers sported a pair of gold epaulettes adorned with the proper rank insignia. General Order No. 7 of 24 June 1858, authorized cavalry officers to wear a black velvet patch with a pair of embroidered gold crossed-sabers on their hats. The regimental number was embroidered in silver in the lower angle of the sabers.* **47. Second Lieutenant (George A. Custer), Company G, 2nd U.S. Cavalry, Undress, 1861:** *Custer appears here just as he did at the Battle of First Bull Run, 21 July 1861, just a few days after his graduation from West Point. He holds a Colt Root sidehammer pistol and a saber, which he purchased in New York City on his way to the front. His 1858 forage cap bears the same style of hat insignia described above. Custer's horse has the Model 1859 equipment.* **48. Lieutenant Colonel, 3rd U.S. Cavalry, Undress, 1861:** *General Order No. 108 of 16 December 1861, permitted officers and men to wear sky blue trousers. After the six mounted regiments were reorganized as cavalry in August 1861, all officers switched to detachable oval hat badges. Now the regimental number was seen in the upper angle above the crossed-sabers.*

became a rout, and by nightfall Washington was the refuge of a broken mob.

The performance of the Confederate cavalry at Bull Run, magnified by the hysterical ravings of the frightened youths who survived the catastrophe, radically altered the attitude of the Union high command toward its own mounted arm. The Confederate cavalry had not been created wholly from scratch. Some Southern horse companies had been in existence since 1857 or 1859, but most of them were organized following the secession of their respective states – and the Yankees decided anything the Rebels could do, they could do better.

The floodgates were opened and by 31 August 1861 thirty-one volunteer cavalry regiments had been raised for the Union Army. That same day the loyal states and Federal government took over the awesome responsibility of supplying these troopers with their

PLATE 16: 1861

46. Major, 4th U.S. Cavalry, Dress Uniform, 1861

47. Second Lieutenant, 2nd U.S. Cavalry, Undress, 1861

48. Lieutenant Colonel, 3rd U.S. Cavalry, Undress, 1861

A Confederate sergeant from an Alabama cavalry regiment.

horses. As the year drew to a close, the North possessed eighty-two newborn regiments of cavalry.

On 21 July 1861, the very day of the Bull Run débâcle, the U.S. Congress set up a table of organization for the volunteer cavalry regiments that was based on that of the regular 3rd Cavalry. The regiment was proportioned with twelve companies, each consisting of one captain, one first lieutenant, one second lieutenant, five sergeants, eight corporals, two musicians, two farriers, one saddler, one wagoner and seventy-two privates. That was a total of 104 officers and men per company. Two companies made a squadron, and there were two squadrons in a battalion. Each of the regiment's three battalions was commanded by a major, assisted by an adjutant, a quartermaster, a commissary and six sergeants; that gave a battalion a paper strength of 426. The regiment was run by a colonel

and a lieutenant colonel, and the regimental staff was composed of an adjutant, a quartermaster, a commissary, a surgeon, an assistant surgeon and two chief buglers. That made for a total complement of 1278.

On 3 August 1861, an Act of Congress directed that the six mounted regiments in the regular army be reorganized as one uniform arm – known thenceforth as 'Cavalry'. The old names were discarded and the regiments were rechristened and renumbered according to their seniority. Thus when the Adjutant General's Office issued General Order No. 55 on 10 August to carry out the legislative mandate, the 1st Dragoons became the 1st U.S. Cavalry; the 2nd Dragoons became the 2nd Cavalry; the Regiment of Mounted Riflemen became the 3rd Cavalry; the 1st Cavalry turned into the 4th Cavalry; the 2nd Cavalry became the 5th; and the young 3rd Cavalry became the 6th Cavalry. The abolition of their regimental titles did not set well with the former dragoons and mounted riflemen, who saw it as a snub to their deeds and traditions. The War Department allowed them to continue wearing their distinctive orange and green facings until their old uniforms wore out. These garments mysteriously assumed a remarkable dexterity, lasting as long as 1863, and some shell jackets with the old pipings were still to be seen as late as 1865.

On 17 July 1862, Congress further altered and streamlined cavalry organization. The permanent squadron and battalion structures were abandoned and the battalion staffs eliminated. The regimental staff was enlarged by the addition of a sergeant major, two hospital stewards, a saddler sergeant, a chief farrier and a chief trumpeter. The two chief buglers were dropped. Companies were renamed 'troops', and each received an additional sergeant, a commissary sergeant, two teamsters and six privates. The two troop buglers were discarded, leaving 112 officers and men. That added up to a grand sum of 1361 per regiment. At the same time, the five senior mounted regiments in the regular service were expanded from ten to twelve troops like the 6th Cavalry.

The Adjutant General's Office decreed a final organizational change with its General Order No. 110, issued on 29 April 1863. The rank of chief farrier was deleted, and the troop lost its two teamsters. Each company received two farriers or blacksmiths, two trumpeters and the number of privates was fixed between a maximum of seventy-eight and a minimum of sixty. With the inclusion of a veterinary surgeon on the regimental staff, that meant a Union cavalry regiment was to have a full strength of 1040 to 1156 officers and men.

Confederate cavalry regiments followed the old ten-company model. This was specified by a circular put out by their War Department in November 1861, which ruled that each company should possess a minimum of sixty rank and file. On 11 October 1862, the Confederate Congress ruled that cavalry companies were to have eighty enlisted men. These regulations were observed by some commanders and ignored by others. Lieutenant Colonel Nathan Bedford Forrest raised a battalion of Tennessee cavalry that boasted 650 troopers in eight large companies. By the end of April 1862, Colonel Turner Ashby had rallied 1400 cavaliers in twenty-two to twenty-six companies in the Shenandoah Valley. He refused to let them be divided into two or more regiments, preferring to keep the whole unmanageable mass under his personal leadership.

After just a few weeks of campaigning, a cavalry regiment's size dipped far below sanctioned levels. Union outfits usually counted 400 to 600 effectives. Even at the peak of their prowess in 1863, front line Rebel cavalry units averaged from 360 to 160 rank and file.

The major cause of such alarming attrition was what happened to the mounts. The cavalry service was extremely hard on its horses; it used them up at a rapid rate. During the first two years of the war, 284,000 chargers were delivered to Federal regiments, and yet no more than 60,000 troopers were mounted at any one time. The horse made an easy mark for even the poorest shot, and thousands were needlessly crippled by the inattention of inexperienced riders and the lengthy hare-brained raids that were so frequently sanctioned by commanders on both sides.

The United States government assumed the prickly problem of horse supply early on, but for nearly the entire conflict, the Confederacy had its cavalrymen provide their own steeds at a compensation of forty cents a day. This system meant that Rebel troopers were initially mounted on some of the best horseflesh in the South, but these beasts were as easily killed or lamed as the more common breeds. When that happened, the dismounted 'Johnny Reb' could either try stalking some Yankee picket, shoot him and steal his horse, or he could take a thirty-day furlough, go home and try to find or buy a new animal. Each alternative became increasingly unfeasible as time went

The guidon of Company E, 2nd Massachusetts Cavalry, a variation by a volunteer outfit on the regular pre-1863 model.

by. The devastation wrought on the Southern countryside by Federal armies exacerbated this increasingly precarious situation. As one Confederate captain recalled, 'As long as the country furnished an abundance of forage our cavalry was efficient. It was only when the horses could not be fed that the mounted arm deteriorated.'

Even in the more affluent Union Army, the remount shortage was not alleviated until the War Department established the Cavalry Bureau on 28 July 1863. This office was entrusted with the task of organizing, equipping and mounting all Yankee cavalrymen, and its officers worked wonders helping the Quartermaster's Department purchase suitable quantities of quality horses. In 1864 alone, the Cavalry Bureau expended $25,000,000 and delivered 180,000 steeds to its troopers.

Contrary to the popular conception, armament was a pressing problem for both sides. Due to the early Federal prejudice against mounted troops, the War Department did not start placing large-quantity orders for cavalry weapons until November 1861. At that time, the manufacturers had barely enough guns on reserve to outfit the regular regiments. In October 1861, there were 3163 partially armed cavalrymen with the Army of the Potomac at Washington, D.C., and 4268 more did not even possess a stick to defend themselves. Within the first couple of months of 1862, most Yankee cavalrymen were issued sabers and revolvers, but many regiments took the field with no more than ten to twelve carbines per company. It was not until 1863 that every Yankee trooper could be assured of being completely armed with the best in modern weapons. Early in 1864, the Cavalry Bureau, under the gifted management of Brigadier General James Harrison Wilson, initiated a program to provide every mounted regiment with the wondrous, seven-shot Spencer carbine. In spite of such commendable intentions, some units went into battle with a be-wildering variety of firearms. At the end of the war, the 2nd Ohio Cavalry was fighting with Spencer, Sharps and Burnside carbines. This diversity in weaponry complicated the supplying of ammunition to certain units, and this hampered their combat effectiveness.

Confederate commanders found it even more difficult to arm their followers. Often the men turned out with items they had brought from home – shotguns or hunting rifles, crudely fashioned sabers, Bowie knives and every kind of pistol. Confederate authorities also purchased arms from abroad and stripped United States arsenals in their territory of anything that would shoot. Rebel cavalrymen carried anything from the latest carbine or infantry rifle from England to flint-lock muskets left over from the Mexican War. More than any other source, the Johnny Rebs relied on the Yankee horsemen they defeated so regularly during the first two years of the contest for weapons and any other kind of gear they needed. As one cavalier from Virginia chortled, 'Everything but ourselves was branded U.S.'

Following the shock and humiliation of Bull Run, the Union issued strident calls for more troops. The recruits who came streaming into Washington were shaped by Major General George Brinton McClellan into the Army of the Potomac, a masterpiece of training, discipline and organization. McClellan had been a captain in the old 1st Cavalry, and he had designed the long-lived Army saddle that bore his name, but he had no flair for the employment of mounted troops. When he kicked off his amphibious expedition against Richmond via the James Peninsula in the spring of 1862, McClellan took along eight full cavalry regiments and sixteen companies from five others. Had they been brigaded together, they would have made a most potent strike force, but 'Little Mac', as McClellan was affectionately called, chose to parcel them out in inconsequential driblets to his four infantry corps.

PLATE 17: THE U.S. CAVALRY, 1862
49. Private, 4th U.S. Cavalry, Dress Uniform, 1862: *Companies A and E of the 4th served as escorts for Major General George B. McClellan when he commanded the Army of the Potomac. Then white gloves and shoulder scales were the rule. Note the brass insignia on the forage cap. The 4th was armed with the Model 1852 Sharps carbine, the Model 1860 Colt Army revolver and the U.S. Model 1860 light cavalry saber.* **50. Private, 5th U.S. Cavalry, Undress, 1862:** *Contrary to popular belief, the enlisted man's overcoat did not actually receive a yellow lining until the 1880s. This fellow wears a mashed up 'Hardee' hat and has tucked his trousers into his boots – an increasingly common practice. In 1862 the 5th Cavalry carried Sharps carbines, Colt Army revolvers and U.S. Model 1840 sabers.* **51. Corporal, 1st U.S. Cavalry, Undress, 1862:** *First introduced to the cavalry in 1858, the four-button sack coat (or fatigue blouse) saw extensive service in the Civil War and after. Forage caps were often worn without insignia. The 1st Cavalry fought with Smith carbines, Colt Army revolvers and U.S. Model 1860 sabers in 1862. Both regulars and volunteers turned out in an endless variety of enlisted dress.*
This cross-section of Yankee cavalry uniforms is based on contemporary records, photographs and sketches.

There they were further decimated by nearly every foot officer of general rank; these detached large numbers of horsemen to serve as escorts, orderlies and couriers.

For the first two years of the Civil War, the Confederate cavalry always seemed to be just one step ahead of its Yankee counterpart, organizationally speaking. Facing McClellan on the Peninsula along with Robert E. Lee's Army of Northern Virginia were Brigadier General Jeb Stuart and his cavalry brigade of five regiments and the Jeff Davis Legion. On 12 June 1862, Stuart undertook a reconnaissance at General Lee's request with 1000 troopers from four regiments and a section of horse artillery. He rode completely around the Army of the Potomac, losing only one man along the way. Even if McClellan's dispersed cavalry could have caught him, it would not have been in sufficient strength to halt his progress. Stuart returned to his own lines on 14 June, bringing in 165 prisoners and 260 horses and mules. He also ascertained that McClellan's right wing was in the air, which enabled

PLATE 17: 1862

49. Private, 4th U.S. Cavalry, Dress Uniform, 1862

50. Private, 5th U.S. Cavalry, Undress, 1862

51. Corporal, 1st U.S. Cavalry, Undress, 1862

Lee to launch a devastating series of attacks that nipped McClellan's lethargic invasion in the bud. Stuart was properly rewarded, over a month later, by being promoted to major general and given the command of a division of two brigades.

Stuart's spectacular ride around McClellan and the other flamboyant deeds he was to perform over the remainder of the year were to leave mounted leaders in both blue and grey obsessed with the idea of long horseback raids behind enemy lines. Stuart had dozens of imitators, but very few of their forays ever achieved the results hoped for. They normally accomplished little more than destroy their own men and animals, and rob the various armies of their eyes and ears. Even Stuart fell victim to this specter of his own devising, and his joyriding during Lee's second invasion of the North may have doomed the Army of Northern Virginia to defeat at Gettysburg.

To his everlasting credit, however, the dashing and reckless Stuart imbued the Southern cavalry with an aura of superiority that far exceeded its actual prowess. To this very day, scholars accept this bit of fatuous braggadocio that was published in the *Charleston Mercury* on 2 June 1861: 'Our people are used to arms. They are accustomed to the gun and the horse. The people of the North can neither shoot a rifle nor ride a horse, unless trained.'

According to the tired, overly-familiar myth, Yankee cavalrymen were largely recruited from the cities, and though they were richly provided with the best of everything, they needed two years of practice and experience before they could meet the Confederates on equal terms. Southerners, on the other hand, had been bred in the saddle, and as a rural people they possessed a natural edge over their adversaries. It was the North's industrial might that allowed her troopers to overcome their handicaps and ultimately triumph.

There may be some truth to this interpretation, but

A Yankee trooper holding a Savage revolver. He was obviously a stubborn individualist, as he wears his four-button sack coat civilian-fashion to show off his loud tie, and his Model 1858 felt hat is a calculated offense against regulations. The right side has been unbound and he has turned his brass crossed-sabers badge upside down and put it in the place that was supposed to be occupied by the regimental number. His company letter is also mislocated.

A private of the 12th Virginia Cavalry armed with a flintlock musket and a frail looking sword. He wears a 'militia' shirt, which served as the only uniform many Rebels had early in the war.

it is riddled with holes. Federal horsemen were often as badly armed as their opponents. While the North possessed more cities than the South, it was still predominantly rural, and at least half the Yankee cavalrymen came from the farm. The Confederacy did possess a pervasive cavalier culture, and though it produced superb fighters, such men made poor soldiers. 'Billy Yank' was no angel, but Southern horsemen excelled in insubordination, disregard for discipline and sheer disobedience of orders. This irreverent attitude was exhibited by the lowliest private and the most exalted officer. Even such legendary giants as Turner Ashby and Nathan Bedford Forrest refused to serve under superiors they pettily despised.

The trouble with the Union cavalry was not its composition, but its leadership. Northern generals were slow to appreciate the many vital uses of mounted troops, and they failed to assemble them in adequate numbers so they could have a decisive impact. Instead of being treated like an integral part of the army, Yankee cavalrymen were made to feel like unwanted pests, fit only to serve the brass as lackeys and messenger boys.

With McClellan stymied on the Peninsula, Major General John Pope was given the reins to the Army of Virginia to try his hand against the matchless Lee. Pope is largely remembered for his subsequent defeat at the Second Battle of Bull Run, but he deserved the everlasting gratitude of every Yankee pony soldier in the Eastern Theater for what he did at the start of his ill-fated campaign. He concentrated his cavalry into two brigades, one of five regiments and the other of four, commanded by two brigadier generals, George D. Bayard and John Buford respectively. These two brigades kept Pope extra-ordinarily well posted on enemy movements, but they could not overcome his incompetence enough to save the Army of Virginia from disaster. Nevertheless, they served notice to Jeb Stuart that his reign as king of the cavaliers was in peril. On 18 August 1862, Buford's 1st Michigan Cavalry surprised Stuart's headquarters at Verdiersville, Virginia. The resourceful Rebel chief just escaped capture, but one of the Yankees nabbed his famous plumed hat and carried it off as a trophy.

General Lee followed up his victory over Pope with an invasion of Maryland. On 13 September 1862, Thomas J. 'Stonewall' Jackson, his brilliant lieutenant, encircled 12,000 Yankee troops with six Confederate divisions at Harper's Ferry. Twenty-five hundred of the garrison were cavalrymen, practically useless for the defense of the town, but Colonel Benjamin F. 'Grimes' Davis of the 8th New York Cavalry was determined they should not end up rotting in some Southern prison pen. The next night he successfully guided the Union horsemen through Jackson's lines, and while leading them on toward McClellan's Army of the Potomac on 15 September, he fell on one of Lee's reserve ammunition trains near Williamsport. The gleeful Yankees seized ninety-seven wagons, a herd of beef cattle and 200 to 300 infantry. Davis's valiant coup compared favorably with anything Stuart had ever done, and it stood as an unrecognized omen for what was to come.

When McClellan failed to crush Lee at Antietam

PLATE 18: VOLUNTEERS FOR THE UNION, 1862–3

52. Private, 6th Pennsylvania Cavalry (Rush's Lancers), 1862: *In November 1861, General McClellan directed Colonel Richard Rush to arm his regiment with lances, making it the only Union horse unit to be so equipped. The lance Rush selected was an Austrian pattern, 'about nine feet long, with an eleven inch three-edged blade; the staff . . . of Norway fir, about one and a quarter inches in diameter, with ferrule and counterpoise at the heel; the whole weighing four pounds, thirteen ounces, with a scarlet swallow-tailed pennon.' Until the 6th discarded its lances in 1862, only twelve carbines were issued per company. This private's shell jacket is based on one belonging to a sergeant from Rush's Lancers, which is now part of the West Point Museum Collections.*

53. Quartermaster Sergeant, 7th Michigan Cavalry, 1863: *Members of Custer's Michigan Cavalry Brigade wore scarlet cravats in emulation of their adored 'Boy General'. The Stars and Stripes company guidon was used by the U.S. Cavalry from 1863 until 1885. The 7th Michigan carried .54-caliber Burnside breech-loading carbines and .44-caliber Remington Army revolvers. Both the Model 1840 and Model 1860 saber were issued; the latter is depicted here.* **54. Colonel (Alfred Napoléon Alexander Duffié), 1st Rhode Island Cavalry, 1862:** *An 1854 graduate of St Cyr and an officer with the French cavalry in Algiers, Senegal and the Crimea, Duffié came to the United States in 1859 and joined the Union Army at the outbreak of the Civil War. He designed his own uniform, which featured an embroidered chasseur cap and chasseur-pattern trousers.*

and Ambrose E. Burnside blundered at Fredericksburg, Major General Joseph Hooker was put in charge of the oft-beaten and thoroughly dejected Army of the Potomac. 'Fighting Joe' as he was called, reorganized the army and revived its morale. He also finally liberated the Union Cavalry and turned it into a force to be reckoned with.

On 5 February 1863, Hooker's headquarters released General Order No. 6, which created the Cavalry Corps of the Army of the Potomac and put it under the command of Brigadier General George Stoneman. Stoneman divided his 8943 troopers and 450 horse artillery gunners between three divisions. To preserve the integrity and efficiency of these new formations, the seven infantry corps of the army were permitted

PLATE 18: 1862–3

52. Private, 6th Pennsylvania Cavalry (Rush's Lancers), 1862

53. Quartermaster Sergeant, 7th Michigan Cavalry, 1863

54. Colonel, 1st Rhode Island Cavalry, 1862

to retain no more than a squadron apiece to furnish orderlies and escorts. Hooker's innovation was an immense step forward, and once his Cavalry Corps was properly trained, he put it to work.

On 12 April 1863, Fighting Joe directed Stoneman to leave one brigade behind with the Army of the Potomac and take the other six on a raid to tear up Lee's lines of communications between Fredericksburg and Richmond. Raging spring floods kept Stoneman's troopers waiting on the north bank of the Rappahannock River for two full weeks. Finally on 28 April, the Yankees struggled across the stream, and for ten anxious days they ranged unimpeded across central north Virginia, destroying twenty-two bridges, seven culverts, five ferries, three railroad trains, 122 wagons, five canal boats, four telegraph stations and three depots. They captured and paroled 500 Rebel soldiers, and took 356 horses and 104 mules. Stoneman lost no more than 100 men, but the damage done was soon repaired, and at least 1000 of his horses were ruined by their excessive exertions.

Hooker would have done better had he kept the Cavalry Corps with the Army of the Potomac, for on 2 May 1863, Stonewall Jackson was able to fall on Hooker's dangling right flank with 26,000 men in the Wilderness near Chancellorsville. Fortunately for Hooker, the commander of his lone cavalry brigade was an able and ambitious martinet named Alfred Pleasonton. As Jackson's screaming infantry came rolling up the line of the battered XI Corps, Pleasonton had the 8th Pennsylvania Cavalry charge the Rebs while he lined up twenty-three fieldpieces in a clearing. When Jackson's men burst through, Pleasonton's gunners sprayed them with double canister and blasted them to a standstill.

Fighting Joe ignobly blamed Stoneman for his own folly, and on 22 May, he made Pleasonton his new cavalry commander and saw to it that he was promoted to major general within a month. At the beginning of June, Hooker learned that Jeb Stuart had assembled his own corps of 9500 to 10,000 horsemen and twenty-four guns in the vicinity of Brandy Station. Fearing a Confederate raid, the Union general ordered his chief of cavalry to strike the first blow. Pleasonton had 8000 troopers divided into three divisions and 3000 infantry auxiliaries lent to him by Hooker. He set out to execute his instructions on 8 June.

Basking in his own supreme confidence and con-

Colonel Israel Garrard of the 7th Ohio Volunteer Cavalry, 1862–5. Many Northern cavaliers were as dashing as their Southern counterparts. Garrard affected the chasseur style, with his baggy sky blue trousers and the gold loops on the sleeves of his officer's shell jacket.

tempt for the Yankee riders, Jeb Stuart spent his time at Brandy Station planning gala cavalry reviews for Confederate bigwigs instead of tending to his picket lines. He was thoroughly chagrined, therefore, when the Federals thundered into his camps before dawn on 9 June. Pleasonton tried to catch the Johnny Rebs in a pincers, but his two prongs could not coordinate their movements, and the Battle of Brandy Station ended in a bloody draw, with the Bluecoats sustaining 856 casualties and the Rebels losing 483. Nevertheless, the Yankees knew they had surprised Stuart's vaunted 'Invincibles' and stood up to them manfully. That day the Federal cavalry shed forever its lingering inferiority complex. 'None of us thought anything of two to one odds as long as we had a chance to ride at them,' boasted one of Pleasonton's officers.

The day after Brandy Station, General Lee set the Army of Northern Virginia in motion down the Shenandoah Valley on his second invasion of the North. On 16 June, Hooker commanded Pleasonton to pierce Stuart's cavalry screen and find out exactly what the Rebels were up to. Consolidating his 7000 effectives into a pair of triple-brigade divisions, the natty Pleasonton went to work. Blue and grey horsemen clashed in furious little actions at Aldie, Middleburg and Upperville, but by 21 June, Pleasonton had divined Lee's intentions and reported them to Hooker. The Army of the Potomac began its fateful march north.

As one of his last acts before he was replaced by Major General George Gordon Meade, Hooker directed Pleasonton to advance his troopers ahead of the Union infantry into the region above the crossroads town of Gettysburg. That same day, 27 June 1863, Fighting Joe added a third division to the Cavalry Corps, transferring two fresh mounted brigades from the defenses of Washington.

When a division of Rebel infantry, looking for shoes, marched toward Gettysburg on the morning of 1 July, it ran into the barking carbines of two brigades from General John Buford's First Cavalry Division. Buford held the Rebs back for two hours, though outnumbered three-to-one. That was long enough for Federal foot soldiers to seize the high ground south of the town and set the stage for the climactic, three-day battle that would turn the tide of the Civil War in favor of the Union.

Lee had not intended to fight at Gettysburg, and had he kept Stuart on a tight leash, he might have avoided the cataclysm that was brewed there. But on 25 June, indulgent 'Marse Robert' let his irrepressible cavalier cut loose and make another one of his vainglorious rides around the Army of the Potomac. Stuart left

A Virginia trooper in a water-proofed jacket, and with a rain cover over his forage cap. He is armed with a Colt revolving rifle.

behind plenty of cavalry – he took only three brigades – but they were the best he had, and Lee had grown dependent on his personal reports. Depriving his chief of his eyes and ears, this misbegotten sortie netted Stuart a mere 125 wagons and 400 prisoners. On his return jaunt, he skirmished sharply with Pleasonton's new Third Cavalry Division, which delayed him from rejoining Lee until late on 2 July.

Marse Robert sent Stuart out at noon the next day with four brigades and three batteries to circle around Meade's right and stab him in the back, while 15,000 Confederate infantry pushed up Cemetery Ridge and assailed his center. At a cleared field three miles east of Gettysburg, Stuart found three brigades of Union cavalry blocking his way. There were 6000 Rebels pitted against 5000 Yanks, but after more than two hours of vicious, see-saw fighting, Stuart was stopped in his tracks and the rear of the Army of the Potomac was safe.

The brunt of that epic duel with Stuart, and the resulting losses to the Northern side, was borne by the 2nd Brigade of the Third Cavalry Division, four regiments from the same state soon to gain fame as the 'Michigan Cavalry Brigade'. The Michigan Brigade was commanded by Brigadier General George Armstrong Custer, a twenty-three-year-old West Pointer who up until four days before had been a mere captain on Pleasonton's staff. To those who scoffed at his favored aide's meteoric rise, Pleasonton retorted, 'Custer is the best cavalry general in the world and I have given him the best brigade to command.' His faith was amply justified on both counts that third day at Gettysburg. Three of Custer's regiments were utterly green, and yet they needed no two years' experience to whip Stuart and permanently lay to rest the myth of the innate superiority of Southern cavalry. And when the enemy sent two brigades in a mounted charge against the Federal center, Custer met them with the levelled sabers of his lone veteran regiment, the 1st Michigan Cavalry. To give his men courage in the face of such fearsome odds, Custer led the counter-attack himself, riding several horse lengths ahead of his followers and shrilling, 'Come on, you Wolverines!' Inspired by his example, the 1st Michigan stalled the Rebel column long enough for detachments from other outfits to pounce on its flanks and send it packing.

Custer represented the new breed of energetic and aggressive leadership that was emerging from the ranks of the Union cavalry. He possessed all the chivalric grace and swagger of Jeb Stuart – and the two were more alike than their contemporaries realized. Instantly recognizable in his broad-brimmed hat, long yellow curls, red cravat, blue wide-collared sailor shirt and a customized brigadier's uniform of black velveteen and exorbitant gold lace, Custer was idolized by the men and boys who served under him. 'We swear by him,' penned one of his officers. 'His name is our battle cry. He can get twice the fight out of this brigade than any other man can possibly do.' Custer's trademark was boundless courage and disregard for his own safety. A private in the 5th Michigan Cavalry, writing to his wife at the conclusion of the Gettysburg Campaign, explained how General Custer 'commanded in person and I saw him plunge his saber into the belly of a rebel who was trying to kill him. You can

PLATE 19: CONFEDERATE FINERY, 1861–2

55. Captain, 1st Virginia Cavalry, 1862: *Based on an eyewitness sketch by Alfred R. Waud. Confederate officers indicated their rank in two ways. The first was a gold badge attached to their collars: a colonel had three stars; a lieutenant colonel two stars; a major one star; a captain three horizontal bars; a first lieutenant two bars; and a second lieutenant one bar. The other insignia was the number of strands of gold lace embroidered on the képi (when worn in full dress) and in the 'Austrian knot' on the lower sleeves of the coat: field officers rated three braids; captains two; and lieutenants one.* **56. Major General (J. E. B. Stuart), Field Dress, 1862:** *Generals of all grades wore three stars surrounded by a laurel wreath on their collars and four braids of gold lace in the looped knots on their sleeves.* **57. Private, Sussex Light Dragoons, 1861:** *This independent militia company was eventually absorbed into the 13th Virginia Cavalry.* **58. Sergeant Major, Confederate Cavalry, Full Dress, 1862:** *Confederate uniform regulations prescribed a double-breasted frock coat with yellow facings for all ranks in the cavalry. Chevrons were similar to Union designs, but the Confederate Army only recognized the six primary grades of sergeant major, quartermaster sergeant, ordnance sergeant, first sergeant, sergeant and corporal.*

guess how bravely soldiers fight for such a general.' Custer's brand of valor was infectious; it was a prime ingredient in his spectacularly successful Civil War career. 'Under him a man is ashamed to be cowardly,' boasted a major in the 6th Michigan Cavalry. 'Under *him* our men can achieve wonders.' Young Custer not only had an abundance of guts, but plenty of brains, too. He possessed an uncanny tactical sense, an almost infallible intuition for locating enemy weak spots, and the resolve to slash through them.

Under Pleasonton's astute sponsorship, two other 'boy generals' came to the fore of the Cavalry Corps. Hugh Judson Kilpatrick was a waspish featherweight, an opportunistic roué whose daring matched Custer's. But Kilpatrick was flawed by a rash streak a mile wide. He gained a reputation for riding to renown and promotion over the corpses of his subordinates, and he was known through the ranks as 'Kill Cavalry'. Baby-faced Wesley Merritt wore a mild, almost scholarly demeanor, but that only served to disguise the fierce ambition that raged within him. He and Custer became

55. Captain, 1st Virginia Cavalry, 1862 **56.** Major General, Field Dress, 1862 **57.** Private, Sussex Light Dragoons, 1861 **58.** Sergeant Major, Confederate Cavalry, Full Dress, 1862

the most intense rivals, and Merritt always envied the latter his greater fame and accomplishments – even after death had ended their competition.

These three young firebrands, along with such stolid and much-tested colleagues as John Buford, David McMurtrie Gregg, Thomas Devin and Henry Davies, dogged Lee's tearful retreat from Gettysburg to Virginia. Fearing another bloodbath, Meade did not let them press their prey too severely, lest Lee feel cornered and turn around, but these strong-minded Yankee bloodhounds got their licks in. On 14 July 1863, for instance, Custer's Michigan Brigade piled into the Confederate rearguard at Falling Waters on the northern bank of the Potomac, sweeping off 1500 prisoners. Lee and Meade wound out the year with inconclusive maneuvering. Their cavalry spearheaded their advances and shielded their withdrawals, crossing sabers at such places as Culpepper Court House, Brandy Station and Buckland Mills.

With the spring of 1864, the winds of change rocked the Army of the Potomac. Lieutenant General Ulysses S. Grant, the conqueror of Vicksburg and the hero of Chattanooga, was named 'General-in-Chief of the Armies of the United States' and charged with the overall direction of Northern strategy. He attached his headquarters to the Army of the Potomac to supervise Lee's destruction. General Pleasonton, who had earned Meade's enmity for criticizing his feeble pursuit of the Rebels after Gettysburg, was exiled to the Department of Missouri. His place was taken by one of Grant's friends, Major General Philip Henry Sheridan, a short, bandy-legged, quick-tempered, foul-mouthed Irish bantam, with a massive torso, dangling arms and an infinite capacity for making men want to fight. 'Little Phil', as his troopers fondly called him, was resolved to make the Cavalry Corps an equal and independent arm of the Army of the Potomac, and he knew how to get what he wanted. He also had the means to attain all his desires. When he took the reins of the Cavalry

A sergeant of the 5th or 6th Michigan Cavalry holding a Spencer repeating rifle, circa 1863. These two regiments in George A. Custer's Michigan Cavalry Brigade made good use of this splendid firearm. As a Reb captured by the 5th at Gettysburg exclaimed, 'You'ns load in the morning and fire all day.' In 1864 Custer's 'Wolverines' exchanged their Spencer rifles for the shorter carbine version.

Corps, it was 20,000 men strong — 12,000 of them mounted.

After guiding Grant's doughboys into the Wilderness, Sheridan extricated his 10,000 troopers from the fighting, slipped around the left of Lee's army and made a lunge at Richmond. This was no ordinary cavalry raid. Little Phil was deliberately trying to draw Jeb Stuart out into the open, far enough away from the Army of Northern Virginia to have a man-to-man showdown without any outside interference. The proud Stuart could not overlook so blatant a challenge, and he tried to block Sheridan's road to Richmond on 11 May 1864, with 4500 horsemen at Yellow Tavern, six miles north of the Confederate capital. As Sheridan was arraying his divisions, the ebullient Custer spotted a vulnerable spot in the enemy line and received permission to take his Michigan Brigade, borrow another and punch through it. Jeb Stuart was mortally wounded in the resulting mêlée by one of Custer's Wolverines, and his disheartened followers were driven from the field.

The Confederate cavalry was badly beaten at Yellow Tavern, but it was by no means finished. Rallying behind Major General Wade Hampton, the survivors furnished Sheridan with staunch opposition every time he ventured within reach. Five thousand to 6000 Yankee cavalrymen were killed, wounded or captured in Northern Virginia from 5 May to 1 August 1864. But the Johnny Rebs lost many men and horses too, and they could no longer make good such casualties. Like Grant, Sheridan had sucked his opponents into a war of attrition, and that was the one type of war the South could not win.

By the beginning of August, Grant had placed the Army of Northern Virginia under siege at Petersburg, and he sent Sheridan to chase the last enemy soldiers out of the Shenandoah Valley, the granary of the Confederacy and a frequent invasion corridor into the North. Little Phil took along the First and Third Cavalry Divisions to serve with his new Army of the Shenandoah. His two boy brigadiers, Merritt and Custer, so distinguished themselves that fall that they were both promoted to major general and put in command of the two respective divisions. Cleaning out the Shenandoah Valley just as winter descended, Sheridan disbanded his army, and on 27 February 1865, he started his 10,000 veteran troopers on a circuitous march across Virginia back to Grant.

Aided by the V Corps of the Army of the Potomac,

Private George D. Clark, Company G, 6th Michigan Cavalry, a nineteen-year-old in Custer's Michigan Cavalry Brigade who was killed on 9 July 1863, while pursuing Lee's defeated army after Gettysburg. The shell jacket issued to Michigan cavalrymen was an exact copy of those worn by the regulars and had two strips of yellow lace and a pair of buttons on each side of the collar.

Sheridan's command, now expanded to four horse divisions, smashed the extreme right wing of Lee's army at Five Forks on 1 April 1865, inflicting 6000 casualties. With the last two railroad lines leading into Petersburg cut by Little Phil's demons, Marse Robert abandoned his earthworks there and at Richmond, trying to avoid starvation and Grant's massive legions by heading west. Yankee pony soldiers lashed at him every step of the way, paring away chunks of the

Army of Northern Virginia until it was a skeleton of its former self. And on 8 April 1865, it was Custer's Third Cavalry Division that got in front of Lee's exhausted and harassed soldiers at Appomattox Station. Custer overran twenty-four Rebel cannon. Then with the support of Thomas Devin's First Cavalry Division, he held Lee in place until the next day, when Federal infantrymen could hurry up to seal the trap. A few hours later, the Army of Northern Virginia was surrendered to General Grant at Appomattox Court House.

Appomattox would always have a special savor for the men of the Yankee Cavalry Corps. From the laughing-stocks of the Army of the Potomac, they had become the driving force in its ultimate victory. It was with perfect sincerity that Custer could proclaim his 'profound gratitude toward the God of battles, by whose blessings our enemies have been humbled and our arms rendered triumphant.'

Cavalry figured conspicuously in the fighting in the Western Theater, and both the North and South found their fair share of champions.

When the Civil War broke out, Nathan Bedford Forrest was a forty-year-old horse, cattle and slave trader living in Memphis, Tennessee. He had less than six months of formal education, but he had made a lot of money, and over the next four years he was to become what Ulysses S. Grant called 'about the ablest cavalry general in the South,' and possibly the greatest cavalryman in American history.

During Grant's Vicksburg Campaign of 1862–3 and Sherman's operations against Atlanta in 1864, Forrest played hell with Yankee supply lines. William Tecumseh Sherman was no man to hand out empty flattery, but he was so stung by those incessant raids he paid that imposing six-foot-two giant with the fierce face and piercing eyes the compliment of referring to him as 'that devil Forrest'. Forrest was not only a charismatic and daring leader, but an excellent organizer. He possessed a flair for whipping raw recruits into crack brigades and divisions. All too often he saw his commands snatched away and handed over to lesser men, but while he still held them in his power, they performed deeds of epic proportions.

In the early summer of 1864, Sherman sent an army of 7800 men and eighteen guns from Memphis to wipe out Forrest's troublesome cavalry. Forrest had only

PLATE 20: ROUGH DRESS AND HARD FIGHTING: CONFEDERATE CAVALRY, 1862–5

59. Private, 8th Texas Cavalry (Terry's Texas Rangers), 1862: *Uniform shortages forced Confederate cavalrymen to wear civilian items and clothing pilfered from Yankee stores. This fellow has an 1858 infantry-pattern 'Hardee' hat, a pull-over flannel shirt and a pair of unusual fur-covered gauntlets. The 8th Texas was armed with double-barrelled shotguns, which were employed with lethal effect at the Battle of Shiloh.*

60. Corporal, 12th Virginia Cavalry, 1864: *As stocks of grey cloth ran low, large numbers of Johnny Rebs appeared in 'butternut' (light brown) jackets and trousers. The 12th Virginia belonged to Thomas L. Rosser's 'Laurel Brigade,' known for the green sprigs they stuck in their hats. The checked pants are a gift from home. Accoutrements and arms were often taken from the Yankees, and this fellow's include a Model 1859 Wesson Cartridge carbine and 1860 light cavalry saber.*

61. Private, 43rd Battalion of Partisan Rangers (Mosby's Rangers), 1864–5: *Mosby's guerrillas were revolver mad, packing pistols in every conceivable place on their person and horses. This fellow has a Model 1861 Remington Army revolver in his holster, a Model 1860 Colt Navy revolver thrust through his belt and a Model 1860 Colt Army revolver lodged in his boot. Plain shell jackets were worn by both the Rebel cavalry and infantry.*

3500 horsemen, but he rolled into the Yanks on 11 June, at Brice's Cross Roads, Mississippi. Forrest struck with such ferocity and ingenuity that his foes were routed. The exulting Johnny Rebs killed 223, wounded 394 and took 1623 prisoners, sixteen cannon and 250 vehicles. In an effort to retard Sherman's movements in Georgia, Forrest and his tattered followers rode toward Johnsonville, Tennessee, in mid-October 1864, to shoot up Federal shipping on the Mississippi. In what must stand as one of the most unusual forays of the Civil War, Forrest's troopers and horse artillery destroyed four Union gunboats, fourteen steamships, seventeen barges, thirty-two pieces of artillery and 75,000 tons of supplies. Total damages were in the neighborhood of $6,700,000, and Forrest carried off 150 prisoners to boot.

By the end of the struggle, this indomitable warrior was a lieutenant general, and he was reputed to have slain or seriously injured more than thirty bluecoated adversaries with his own hands.

PLATE 20: 1862–5

59. Private, 8th Texas Cavalry (Terry's Texas Rangers), 1862

60. Corporal, 12th Virginia Cavalry, 1864

61. Private, 43rd Battalion of Partisan Rangers (Mosby's Rangers), 1864–5

*First Lieutenant William H. Beach of the 1st New York
(Lincoln) Cavalry, a regiment from Brevet Major General
George A. Custer's Third Cavalry Division, circa 1865. In
addition to his regulation frock coat and officer's sash, Beach
sports a scarlet cravat in emulation of his widely admired
divisional commander. This was the general practice in all of
Custer's Civil War commands, and the men of the Third
Division proudly called themselves the 'Red Tie Boys'.*

To Union men, John Hunt Morgan was nothing
more than a brigand and a horse thief, but to his own
people, he was the prince of Rebel raiders. A Lexington businessman who had served with Marshall's
Kentucky Cavalry in the Mexican War, Morgan
swept repeatedly through Kentucky and parts of
occupied Tennessee with such audacity and at such
trifling cost that it was almost as if he was skylarking
through Confederate territory. At the head of a brigade, and later a division, he would roam far behind

Yankee lines, seeking military stores, mounts and recruits. Morgan held the distinction of occasionally
bringing back more men from such expeditions than
he took in.

On 2 July 1863, Morgan took 2460 riders in two
brigades and mounted his most ambitious undertaking
of the war. Scudding across Kentucky, he crossed the
Ohio River into Indiana on 8 July, and then veered
east over southern Ohio. The entire North was thrown
into an uproar. Over 100,000 trained soldiers and
home guards were mobilized against Morgan. They
prevented him from recrossing the Ohio and getting
away to the South, but they could not catch him until
26 July, when he was only sixty miles from Lake Erie.
In the meantime, the Kentucky cavalier covered 700
miles, inflicted 600 casualties, captured and paroled
6000 Federal troops, destroyed $10,000,000 worth
of supplies, and tore up countless bridges and vast
stretches of telegraph lines and railroad tracks. At the
same time, however, Morgan had sacrificed his entire
division for little more than some passing glory. It was
a loss the Confederacy could ill afford.

The Yankees put Morgan in the Ohio State Peniten-
tiary, but they could not hold him. He escaped on
28 November 1863. Such was the magic of his name
that he was able to attract 2700 volunteers to his camp
at Columbia, Georgia, by the end of May 1864, but he
lost half of them in a reckless and ill-conceived raid on
Kentucky that following month. While awaiting a
court of inquiry, Morgan took his remaining 1600
troopers to investigate enemy movements in eastern
Tennessee. On the night of 4 September 1864, the
Yankees surrounded the house in Greenville where
Morgan was sleeping, far in advance of the rest of his
men. He was shot down as he tried to get away.

Despite his somewhat wild sobriquet of 'Fighting
Joe', diminutive General Joseph Wheeler, while every
bit as bold as Morgan, had enough hold on his ego to
subordinate the antics of his cavalry to the needs of the
Army of Tennessee. When Major General William S.
Rosecrans marched his Union Army of the Cumber-
land out of Nashville at the end of December 1862, to
fall on the Confederates at Murfreesboro, Braxton
Bragg sent Wheeler's 4237 cavalrymen to slow the
Yankees down. Fighting Joe so plagued and pestered
Rosecrans's 47,000 men that their progress slowed to a
crawl. Wheeler bought Bragg four days to prepare a
hot reception for his uninvited guests. In the ensuing
Battle of Stones River, which commenced on 31

Corporal Frederich Bush, Company D, 7th Michigan Cavalry, another one of Custer's Wolverines. His mount is outfitted with a variation on the McClellan horse equipment.

December, Wheeler's riders helped push the attack on the Northern right and rear, rounding up 2000 captives, 327 head of cattle, five guns and many wagons. Wheeler later rendered service at the Battle of Chickamauga in mid-September 1863, and while raiding a few days later, he intercepted a 500-wagon supply train meant for Rosecrans's beaten army hemmed in at Chattanooga.

Northerners had their own heroes on horseback in the fighting that raged beyond the Blue Ridge and Appalachian Mountains.

To mask Grant's envelopment of Vicksburg, Colonel Benjamin Henry Grierson left LaGrange, Tennessee, on 17 April 1863, to cause as much trouble as he could behind enemy lines. His brigade counted 1700 sabers from the 6th Illinois, 7th Illinois and 2nd Iowa Cavalry. A former music teacher who hated horses, Grierson presided over the most flawlessly conducted mounted raid of the Civil War. Every move he made kept the Confederates off balance and threw them off his trail. On 21 April, Grierson sent the 2nd Iowa to tear up a bit of the Mobile & Ohio Railroad and then head back north to LaGrange to divert the Rebs from the main body, which would continue on south. The ruse worked to perfection. On 2 May 1863, Grierson and his two remaining regiments linked up with Union forces at Baton Rouge. They had ridden

600 miles through the heart of the Confederacy in sixteen days, destroyed fifty to sixty miles of telegraph lines and railroad track, wrecked 3000 stands of arms and confiscated 1000 horses and mules. Grierson's troopers had killed or wounded 100 Confederates and paroled 500 prisoners – and all at the slight loss of twenty-six to themselves.

Born in 1837, young James Harrison Wilson revealed himself to be a talented administrator at the Cavalry Bureau, but he turned in a mediocre performance leading a mounted division under Phil Sheridan in Virginia. Nevertheless, he retained enough of Grant's confidence to receive the command of the four lackluster cavalry divisions Sherman had left behind from his 'March to the Sea' in October 1864. Wilson inherited 14,000 despondent troopers, 1500 of them without horses. But by careful training and inspired generalship, he turned them into an irresistible host.

When Major General George H. Thomas flattened the Army of Tennessee outside of Nashville on 15 and 16 December 1864, Wilson's troopers went charging in on foot on the right flank of the infantry, swinging around the Rebel left and rear. They took two redoubts, thirty-two guns, eleven caissons, twelve battleflags, one general and 3231 other prisoners, one pontoon bridge train and 125 wagons. Wilson's total casualties were 902. It was a grand achievement, but the commander of the Cavalry Corps of the Military Division of the Mississippi had even grander plans.

Wilson fervently believed that cavalry was primarily an offensive arm with the power to affect the course of the war by itself. He urged his superiors to hurl his corps 'into the bowels of the South in masses that the enemy cannot drive back.' What he had specifically in mind was a mounted invasion of Alabama, then under the tenuous protection of Lieutenant General Forrest. Building up three of his divisions to 12,500 sabers, Wilson launched his expedition on 22 March 1865, after he had received the proper authorization.

Brushing aside Forrest's thin brigades, Wilson doggedly declined to be swerved from his main goal, the city of Selma, one of the Confederacy's few untouched or uncaptured armories and manufacturing centers. On 2 April, Wilson stormed the works of Selma, which were stoutly held by 2500 of Forrest's cavalrymen, along with 2500 Reb militia. The citizen soldiers bolted, and Forrest's men were swamped in the blue tide. Ten days later, Montgomery, the first capital of the Confederate States, fell without a fight,

PLATE 21: YANKEE CAVALRY IN ON THE KILL, 1865

62. First Sergeant, 3rd New Jersey Cavalry, 1865: *They preferred to be known as the '1st U.S. Hussars', but the men of this outfit were called the 'New Jersey Butterflies' for their ornate, Austrian-style uniforms. The crown of the visorless forage cap tilted to the side – not the front as previously illustrated. NCOs of this regiment had orange cord borders on their trouser stripes. The 3rd New Jersey was issued the Remington Army revolver and Model 1860 saber in addition to the trusty Spencer carbine. The Third Cavalry Division adopted red neckties after Custer took command in October 1864.* **63. Major General (George A. Custer), Third Cavalry Division, Cavalry Corps, Army of the Potomac, Field Dress, 1865:** *When Custer was made brigadier in June 1863, he turned out in a personally-designed uniform of black velveteen piped with gold lace. Following his promotion to major general in the fall of 1864, he adopted a cut-down regulation frock coat and dark blue trousers with gold stripes. In either uniform he sported his personal trademarks – a broad-brimmed hat, a sailor shirt with white stars and trim on the collar, and a cravat of brilliant scarlet. Custer also designed his own guidon to mark his location on the battlefield. The flag he waves here was the fourth to serve him in the Civil War. It was made of silk by his wife, Elizabeth, and delivered the day before the Battle of Five Forks. Normally the guidon was carried by a sergeant, but Custer snatched it up on 1 April, after his color bearer was shot in the charge. (The bullet-ridden guidon is in the collection of noted Custer authority, Dr Lawrence A. Frost.)* **64. Private, 2nd Ohio Cavalry, 1865:** *The men of the 2nd Ohio commonly wore slouch hats and unusually long four-button fatigue blouses with civilianized collars and semi-lapels. The regiment was armed with the seven-shot Spencer carbine. The Blakeslee Quickloader cartridge box slung from the trooper's chest contained seven to thirteen tubular magazines for the repeater. The plate shows, George A. Custer leading his Third Cavalry Division in a successful charge on the Rebel earthworks at Five Forks, 1 April 1865.*

and on 20 April, Wilson's column clattered into Macon.

Although he wrestled with a nation that was even then on its deathbed, Wilson's record was not unimpressive. In less than a month, he captured five fortified

62. First Sergeant, 3rd New Jersey Cavalry, 1865

63. Major General, 3rd Cavalry Division, Cavalry Corps, Army of the Potomac, Field Dress, 1865

64. Private, 2nd Ohio Cavalry, 1865

cities, twenty-three enemy banners, 6820 soldiers and 288 fieldpieces. He had 725 killed, wounded and missing, but he dealt out 1200 casualties among those who opposed him. And then to top everything off, on 10 May 1865, some of Wilson's troopers captured President Jefferson Davis and snuffed out the last significant hopes of continuing Southern resistance.

There were other horsemen who made glowing names for themselves in every theater of the conflict – Elon J. Farnsworth, Ranald Mackenzie and George Crook for the North, and Fitzhugh Lee, Thomas L. Rosser, Lunsford Lomax, Thomas Munford and Matthew Calbraith Butler for the South. Among the Confederacy's most formidable mounted warriors

were such guerrillas as John Singleton Mosby, William C. Quantrill, M. Jeff Thompson, Harry Gilmor, 'Bloody Bill' Anderson, Frank and Jesse James, Champ Ferguson and Jesse McNeill. Most of them were sadistic

The dress coat of Brigadier General Thomas L. Rosser, the commander of a division of Confederate cavalry in the Shenandoah Valley. It was captured by Brigadier General George A. Custer when his Third Cavalry Division routed Rosser's troops at Tom's Brook on 9 October 1864. Custer used this coat to make good his escape when Rosser surprised Custer's headquarters at Lacey's Springs, Virginia, just before dawn on 21 December 1864.

A private of one of the six regiments of 'United States Colored Cavalry' that were raised by the North for the Civil War. Everything about this image bespeaks pride. Note the immaculate condition of his saber and his sky blue greatcoat.

murderers and robbers, but their very names brought terror to the hearts of their foes, and the Southerners tied up thousands of Union troops far from the front with their outrages and depredations.

The Civil War allowed the United States Cavalry, both regular and volunteer, to reach its summit, numerically speaking, to shake off outmoded European notions and adopt a more pragmatic and thoroughly American doctrine. Romantics like George A. Custer still practiced the saber charge with great effect, but even he accepted the new conception of mounted warfare. Cavalrymen were no longer mere pickets, scouts or shock troops, but highly mobile gunmen who could use their horses to deny strategic positions to the enemy and hold them with rapid-fire repeating carbines until infantry support arrived.

It was a hard earned lesson, and America would never fight another major war where it could be applied.

The designating guidon of the Reserve Cavalry Brigade, which contained almost all the regular mounted regiments with the Army of the Potomac. Nearly every brigade and division commander in the Union Cavalry Corps had his own personally designed guidon.

7 Policing the Plains
1865-90

With the surrender of the last Confederate armies in May 1865, the people of the United States welcomed peace with the same relish and fierce embrace as they took up war four years before. Within a year, nearly 1,000,000 Northern volunteers were mustered out of the service and their regiments disbanded. The regular army, which had been expanded and augmented during the Civil War, was now 30,000 strong, more than twice its antebellum size. However, the America of 1866 was an entirely different world and even the most anti-militaristic and miserly politician recognized the glaring need for more professional soldiers.

Congress regarded the Southern states as conquered provinces that would have to be 'reconstructed' before they were readmitted to the Union. As partisan politics shaped it, Reconstruction came to entail the acceptance of Republican state governments and the enfranchisement of the recently freed Negro. That was a bitter pill for ex-Rebels and ex-slave owners to swallow, and it took an army of occupation to force it down.

As white men in blue and grey exterminated each other on dozens of battlefields in the East, the plains and deserts of the West were ablaze with a series of Indian wars that made the clashes of the 1850s look like mere rehearsals. Although the Civil War drew most of the nation's regulars from the frontier, nearly 20,000 volunteers were recruited in California, Nevada, New Mexico, Minnesota, Kansas, Nebraska, Colorado and Dakota for home defense, or sent west from Ohio, Wisconsin and Missouri. These hard-headed and hard-hitting citizen soldiers subdued some tribes and checked a few more, but their operations stirred up many others. The regulars who relieved them in 1866 inherited a Great Plains and Southwest rife with hate and violence.

Even the most peaceful bands contributed warriors to the multitude of war parties that preyed on the stagecoach roads, wagon trails and homesteads for prisoners and plunder. Murder, robbery, torture and

PLATE 22: A HARSH INTRODUCTION TO INDIAN WARFARE, 1867-8
65. Private, 7th U.S. Cavalry, Undress, 1867: *Upon its organization in 1866, the 7th was issued .50-caliber and .52-caliber Spencer carbines, Remington Army revolvers and Model 1860 light cavalry sabers.*
66. Private, 7th U.S. Cavalry, Undress, 1867: *Out on the Plains, cavalrymen reinforced the seat and inseam of their trousers with white tent canvas.*
67. Captain (Albert Barnitz), 7th U.S. Cavalry, Campaign Dress, 1868: *Flannel 'firemen's shirts' were much favored by officers and men for field use due to their comfort and durability. Barnitz's shirt was sewn by his spouse, Jennie, from a pattern supplied by Elizabeth Bacon Custer, wife of the 7th's first lieutenant colonel. Note the partially hidden riding whip dangling from Barnitz's right hand. Uniforms of Civil-War vintage were worn by the Indian-Fighting Army up until 1872.*

gang rape became commonplace on the frontier, and each depredation was followed by a rising chorus for military retaliation. The West was developing more influence as a political lobby. The Civil War barely diverted the flow of emigrants spilling over the prairies and mountains, and the end of the War between the States unleashed an even greater deluge. Increasing population forced some action from Washington, and token gestures were made toward strengthening western security.

On 28 July 1866, President Andrew Johnson signed the momentous 'Act to increase and fix the Military Peace Establishment of the United States.' For the first time, the U.S. Army was radically expanded immediately *after* a war. The artillery remained constant at five regiments, but the infantry mushroomed from nineteen to forty-five regiments. The six regiments of U.S. Cavalry were joined by four more. Two of these new mounted regiments and four of those on foot

65. Private, 7th U.S. Cavalry, Undress,
1867

66. Private, 7th U.S. Cavalry, Undress,
1867

67. Captain, 7th U.S. Cavalry, Campaign
Dress, 1868

were to consist entirely of Negro enlisted men – although their officers were all white. The Army was permitted to raise a maximum of 1000 Indian scouts to be employed as cavalrymen on the frontier.

This legislation laid down a new organization for the cavalry, which was basically similar to the system employed during the Civil War. One colonel, one lieutenant colonel, three majors, one adjutant, one quartermaster, one regimental commissary, one veterinary surgeon, one sergeant major, one quartermaster sergeant, one commissary sergeant, one saddler sergeant, one chief trumpeter and one regimental hospital steward made up the regimental staff. There was also an additional veterinary surgeon, who functioned without a commission. The old twelve-troop table was retained. Company strength was set provisionally at one captain, one first lieutenant, one second lieutenant, one first sergeant, one quartermaster sergeant, five sergeants, eight corporals, two trumpeters, two farriers and blacksmiths, one saddler, one wagoner and seventy-eight privates. The law permitted the President to fix a company's size anywhere from fifty to a hundred privates, and at first the War Department recommended that the number should be sixty-four, giving the Army an authorized complement of 54,302 officers and men. In 1867, however, Johnson let all companies on the frontier have 100 privates, which brought the regular establishment up to an unprecedented peak of 56,815 by September.

These figures are misleading, for the Army did not enter into an era of bloated affluence. A third of the Bluecoats were stationed in the South. In 1868, twenty-eight of the 120 regular cavalry companies were on duty in the former Confederacy, upholding the rule of the detested 'Carpetbagger' and 'Scalawag' governments, chasing down the Ku Klux Klan and other terrorists and hoodlums, and making half-hearted efforts to preserve black rights.

That service brought the Army more than a little grief. As each Southern state was put in order and restored to full membership in the Union, the Federal troops were withdrawn. More and more economy-minded Republican congressmen started clamoring for Army reductions. They found allies among Northern Democrats and newly-elected Southerners, who viewed the large military establishment as the tool of their political opponents and oppressors. The knife was soon applied, and the Army skinned down to its usual skeletal shape.

The Army appropriation act of 3 March 1869, abolished twenty whole infantry regiments. Each cavalry regiment had a chief musician added to its staff, but the 120 companies were shrunk to sixty privates apiece. That left the Army with a total size of 37,313 officers and other ranks. A little more than a year later, Con-

A troop of the 9th U.S. Cavalry, one of the four mounted regiments created in 1866, on mounted parade at Fort Davis, Texas, in 1875. The two white officers and twenty-five black enlisted men are in the 1872-regulation dress uniform.

gress put a ceiling of 30,000 on the number of enlisted men. Further legislation struck the ranks of medical steward and commissary from the rolls of the cavalry regiments and removed four corporals from each company. Beginning in 1874, the annual Army appropriation acts forbade the recruitment of more than 25,000 common soldiers, which made for a sanctioned standing army of 27,000, counting the officers. The actual number of men on duty usually hovered down around 19,000, due to the ordinary causes of attrition.

Between 1874 and 1876, Congress deprived the cavalry regiments of their commissary sergeants and whittled each troop down to fifty-four privates. The near annihilation of the 7th Cavalry at the Battle of the Little Big Horn on 25 June 1876, shocked the frugal legislators into an abrupt about face and temporarily reversed the process of Army erosion — at least in favor of the cavalry. That same year Congress allowed the Army an extra 2500 men to raise each cavalry company to 100 troopers. When the emergency subsided, the 25,000-man ceiling was restored. The pony soldiers did not suffer from this new cut; infantry companies were simply limited to thirty-seven men. Naturally enough, this move roused a great deal of resentment in that branch, which was just as warmly engaged in fighting Indians and felt it was holding up much more

than its share of the burden. Colonel William B. Hazen of the 6th U.S. Infantry stormed:

> After the fourth day's march of a mixed command, the horse does not march faster than the foot soldier, and after the seventh day, the foot soldier begins to out-march the horse, and from that time on the foot soldier has to end his march earlier each day, to enable the cavalry to reach the camp the same day at all.

Hazen's derogatory remarks were certainly inspired as much by intra-service rivalry as by the facts, but the point cannot be made too strongly that the U.S. Cavalry's performance against the Indians of the Great Plains and the Southwest was nowhere near as brilliant or as successful as Hollywood has led millions to believe. It was not the Army that conquered the Indian, but the unstoppable sweeping advance of white civilization. The Bluecoats were just cogs in that machine; a dispersed and overworked police force rushing from trouble spot to trouble spot, with never enough numbers to do the job properly.

The root of most of the Army's problems grew from the financial and manpower limitations imposed by Congress. The cuts of 1869 left 430 companies of regulars to man about 200 posts. Even in the more bountiful days of 1868, ninety-two companies of cavalry were spread thin among fifty-nine forts in the West. It was hoped that a wide deployment would enable the pony soldiers to show the flag throughout the Indian country and awe potential hostiles. The men on the spot were supposed to prevent or snuff out any flare-ups, but the red men were not cowed by puny detachments, and whenever hostilities erupted local garrisons had to be heavily reinforced before they could send out strike forces of sufficient power to quell major disturbances. Before the railroads were completed, that was a complicated, costly and time-consuming operation.

The demands of geography and politics meant that once again the troop was the basic administrative and tactical unit. Some companies never saw each other for years. Many cavalry regiments were regiments in name only. A few able and ambitious leaders, like Ranald S. Mackenzie of the 4th, Wesley Merritt of the 5th, Eugene A. Carr of the 6th, and George A. Custer of the 7th, were able to keep enough of their companies together for sufficient periods of time to build real regimental esprit de corps and efficiency, but they were rare exceptions. Such circumstances made regi-

PLATE 23: THE 1872-REGULATION UNIFORM 68. Ordnance Sergeant, 2nd U.S. Cavalry, Dress Uniform, 1873: *Under the new dress regulations of 27 July 1872, enlisted cavalrymen received single-breasted coats faced with yellow. Two piped cloth straps were provided on the back of the coat to support the waistbelt. A brass regimental number was fixed on the four-inch yellow patch on either side of the collar. The dress cap was made of black felt, with a horsehair plume, and brass fittings and yellow worsted cords for enlisted men.* **69. Major, 10th U.S. Cavalry, Dress Uniform, 1873:** *Much to their delight, all regimental officers were given double-breasted coats by the 1872 regulations. Field officers wore nine buttons in each row; captains and lieutenants had seven. Braided non-regulation 'pillbox' caps were popular for wear on post. The officer's authorized dress cap was similar to the enlisted model except it had gold cords and fittings.* **70. Chief Trumpeter, 9th U.S. Cavalry, Dress Uniform, 1873:** *A musician's dress coat was ornamented by a streamlined arrangement of 'herring-bone' lace. The chevrons shown here were authorized on 25 June 1873.*

mental drill and training all but impossible, and even at the troop level such essential exercises were sadly neglected.

Enlistees in the cavalry received only the most rudimentary preparation at Jefferson Barracks, their recruit depot. Then they were shipped off to their unit. Most new arrivals were poor horsemen and poor shots, and they were not likely to polish up these skills in a hurry – even on the frontier. When they were not actually on campaign, commands were converted into construction crews, which sapped their energies and morale. As one new 7th Cavalryman complained from Fort Harker, Kansas, early in 1867:

> There has been no drills here the past winter, the soldiers being all occupied in building quarters. Isn't it a mistake on the part of the government to require enlisted men to work as common laborers with no opportunity to perfect themselves in drill? An officer cannot have proper discipline in his command under such circumstances. The men, too, labor somehow under silent protest; desertions are more than frequent.

Money was so short that the Army was forced to hoard ammunition, and small-arms target practice did

68. Ordnance Sergeant, 2nd U.S. Cavalry,
Dress Uniform, 1873

69. Major, 10th U.S. Cavalry, Dress
Uniform, 1873

70. Chief Trumpeter, 9th U.S. Cavalry,
Dress Uniform, 1873

Private John Comfort, Troop A, 4th U.S. Cavalry, as he appeared on campaign in 1877. He sports a privately purchased hat, cravat and a version of the blue 'fireman's shirt' that was so popular for field wear among pony soldiers of all ranks.

'Last Stop on Battle Ridge', a vivid and faithful recreation of the Battle of the Little Big Horn by Gary Zaboly. His remaining avenue of escape cut off by Crazy Horse and swarms of Oglala Sioux, Lieutenant Colonel George A. Custer rallies five companies of the 7th Cavalry for a final stand on a hogback ridge just east of the Little Big Horn River. The destruction of Custer's immediate command on 25 June 1876, is the most famous cavalry action and Indian battle in American history.

not receive official encouragement until 1872. Some imaginative and devious commanders were able to wrangle enough rounds to give their men enough experience with their carbines and pistols to render them combat ready. In the late fall of 1868, Lieutenant Colonel George A. Custer put his 7th Cavalry through an intensive program to hone up its marksmanship. Each man was sent to the firing range twice a day. Excellence was encouraged by incorporating the forty best shots into an elite company of sharpshooters, which would march independently of the regiment and would not be used for guard or picket duty. Colonel Ranald S. Mackenzie was just as dedicated to promoting straight shooting in his 4th Cavalry, although he was not as inventive in devising incentives as Custer.

Seven years after the Civil War, the Army finally began providing each trooper with ninety shells a year

Private F. W. Klopper, Troop H, 4th U.S. Cavalry, as he appeared on his arrival at Fort Stanton, New Mexico, fresh from the recruit depot at Jefferson Barracks, sometime in the 1880s. He wears the 1876 forage cap and the 1883 unpiped sack coat.

PLATE 24: THE FABULOUS 4TH CAVALRY, 1871–8

71. Corporal, 4th U.S. Cavalry, Texas Campaign Dress, 1871: *The Secretary of War authorized troops in the Department of Texas to wear white trousers and straw hats during the hot summer months – a privilege granted to all garrisons south of Washington, D.C., before the year was out. In 1871 ninety-four Remington half-cock and 150 Remington full-cock carbines were distributed to the cavalry for field tests. Some of the 4th also received Model 1869 Smith and Wesson revolvers.* **72. Captain, 4th U.S. Cavalry, Undress, 1875:** *Based on a contemporary engraving in* Frank Leslie's Illustrated Newspaper. *The 1872-pattern officer's undress coat was adorned with looped strands of black braid and five gilt buttons down the chest. On garrison duty the saber belt was worn under the coat, but such proprieties were flaunted on campaign. The sun helmet is a privately purchased sportsman's model.* **73. Private, 4th U.S. Cavalry, Campaign Dress, 1873:** *The 1872 plaited fatigue blouse was extremely unpopular and soon disappeared. This private also wears the 1872-pattern forage cap and handsome cavalry boots. From 1871 to 1873, the 4th was issued .50-caliber Spencer carbines.*

to fire on a rifle range and directed that the men take part in drills for estimating distances. Seven years later, in 1879, soldiers were ordered to fire twenty practice rounds a month. In 1878, post schools for the education of the enlisted men became mandatory. 'Companies of instruction' were instituted at the recruit depots in 1881 to furnish the new men with four months of basic training before they were shipped off to their respective regiments and troops. But units remained too dispersed, too overworked and too understrength to capitalize on this good foundation, and the cavalryman of the 1880s was hardly better prepared for duty than his predecessor of the two previous decades.

Such deprivations would have taken their toll on the best and the brightest, but the men who signed on with Uncle Sam between 1865 and 1890 were markedly inferior in quality to the idealistic volunteers who rallied to the colors of the North and South from 1861 to 1865. There was not much in the cavalryman's life of drudgery and danger to attract ambitious young Americans in an age that saw the rise of big business and the accumulation of vast fortunes. A trooper's monthly salary of $16.00, which was reduced to $13.00

PLATE 24: 1871–8

71. Corporal, 4th U.S. Cavalry, Texas
Campaign Dress, 1871

72. Captain, 4th U.S. Cavalry, Undress,
1875

73. Private, 4th U.S. Cavalry, Campaign
Dress, 1873

in 1872, attracted none but the most patriotic, the most foolish or the most desperate of the urban poor. As a Chicago newspaperman pontificated in 1874, 'The majority of the enlisted men in the army are simply human driftwood – men who have committed crime elsewhere, and are hiding in the service under assumed names; men who cannot brook the liberties and familiarities of society, and take refuge in military discipline; men who are disappointed, disheartened, and ambitionless, and find the lazy life of a soldier a relief.'

Half the men the Army recruited from 1865 to 1874 were foreign-born. Nearly 20 per cent of all the Bluecoats were Irish, and some 12 per cent were from Germany. These statistics fluctuated somewhat from regiment to regiment. When the 7th Cavalry rode into the valley of the Little Big Horn in June 1876, 42 per cent. of its troopers were foreign-born. Seventeen per cent. were Irish, 12 per cent. German, 4 per cent. English, 2 per cent. Canadian and a little more than 1 per cent. Scottish. As a general rule, many of these fellows were dirt poor and practically illiterate. Those who had to master English along with a soldier's routine posed a further handicap for their units. But once they learned the ropes, foreigners made reliable and devoted soldiers. If they found a home in a good regiment, the same could be said of many native Americans in uniform. As Lieutenant James Calhoun of the 7th Cavalry, an open-hearted and optimistic officer who had worked his way up from the ranks, observed in his diary on 20 June 1874:

> I have seen large bodies of troops in foreign countries on the march and in garrison, but I must candidly and honestly assert that for energy, bravery, and general appearance, American troops are far superior – in fact they take the premium. I am told, and believe that two-thirds of the American army is composed of foreigners. Foreigners as a general rule become initiated into the habits and customs of Americans pretty quick. The best remark that can be offered regarding our army is that the major portion are young men capable of sustaining any amount of hardship and fatigue imposed upon them.

Officers of the 5th U.S. Cavalry near their bivouac on French Creek in the Black Hills of Dakota at the end of the Sioux Campaign, October 1876. Most of them wear privately purchased hats and firemen's shirts, and a couple carry extra pistols stuffed through their belts.

The average run of rankers did not share Calhoun's jolly views. Discipline was petty and harsh – it was often the only way to get the men to perform well. There were few tangible rewards for exemplary conduct. The food was bad, quarters were cramped, isolated and wretched, and the pitiful pittance the troops were paid often arrived late. There was little to hold a man in the Army, except a strong sense of duty or a strong sense of fear. Of the 255,712 men who enlisted between 1867 and 1891, 88,475 – practically a third – deserted. Even the best organizations were not immune to the debilitating disease. The 7th Cavalry suffered 512 desertions between 1 October 1866, and 1 October 1867, and they nearly ruined the regiment during its first Indian campaign. On the night on 6 July 1867, thirty-five men deserted in a body, and at the

Lieutenant Colonel George Armstrong Custer, 7th U.S. Cavalry, in the 1872-regulation dress uniform.

PLATE 25: CUSTER'S 7TH CAVALRY AT THE LITTLE BIG HORN, 25 JUNE 1876

74. Private, 7th U.S. Cavalry, Campaign Dress, 1876: *The 1874 grey flannel shirt was often worn without a coat during a summer campaign. The 1872 campaign hat could be worn brim-up with the help of two pairs of hooks and eyes – or down for extra sun protection. This private is loading his 1873 Colt Army revolver, the famous .45-caliber 'Peacemaker' (or 'Thumb-buster' as the soldiers called it).* **75. First Lieutenant (William W. Cooke), 7th U.S. Cavalry, Campaign Dress, 1876:** *Custer and many of his officers campaigned in hardy buckskin coats. Some favored the issue sky blue trousers, while others preferred buckskin legwear. Cooke, the 7th's adjutant, holds the .45-caliber U.S. Carbine Model 1873, better known as the Springfield carbine. A 'fireman's shirt' is visible beneath his coat.* **76. Sergeant (Robert H. Hughes), 7th U.S. Cavalry, Campaign Dress, 1876:** *In 1874 enlisted men received a new sack coat piped with yellow cord to replace the plaited fatigue blouse introduced in 1872. Hughes carried Custer's personal guidon, which was lost at the Last Stand. Figures 74–79 are based on the uniform regulations of the day, contemporary photographs, the testimony of white survivors of the battle, and on recovered artifacts on display at the Smithsonian Institution, West Point Museum, Custer Battlefield National Monument, Monroe County Historical Museum and in private collections.*

noon halt the next day, thirteen troopers bolted from the column. This mutinous and disloyal behavior did not stop until Custer threatened to shoot deserters and sent his officers to carry out his pledge. The young cavalier was later court martialed for cruelty, but he had only done what was necessary to save his regiment.

Despite such strictness, hundreds of troopers could not resist the temptation to take 'French leave' or the 'grand bounce', as going A.W.O.L. was then so colorfully called. In 1877, the 3rd Cavalry had 170 desertions, the 4th 184, the 5th 224, the 7th 172 and the 8th 174. When desertion was joined with what the Army lost due to death and discharge, that produced an annual turnover rate of 25 per cent. to 40 per cent. Only about 1000 Bluecoats re-enlisted each year, but a seasoned cadre of 6000 to 7000 veterans with more than five years service was maintained. The average trooper who died with Custer had nearly four years of experience in the 7th Cavalry.

PLATE 25: 25 June 1876

74. Private, 7th U.S. Cavalry, Campaign Dress, 1876

75. First Lieutenant, 7th U.S. Cavalry, Campaign Dress, 1876

76. Sergeant, 7th U.S. Cavalry, Campaign Dress, 1876

Cavalry officers varied in quality. At first, they were nearly all veterans of the Civil War – many of them possessing enviable records. As the years went on, vacancies were customarily filled with West Point graduates, although by 1874, 13 per cent. of the officer corps had been promoted from the ranks. Whatever their backgrounds, even the most ardent and promising were liable to be spoiled in an Army of shrinking size and prospects. With the demobilization of the Union volunteers in 1865, career officers who had been breveted generals and colonels found themselves dropping several grades to their permanent ranks in the regular army. Men who had led corps, divisions and brigades now found themselves put in charge of a single regiment, battalion, squadron or troop. As Congress legislated further cutbacks in the Army's size, these men were often stripped of their commissions, and a stranglehold was clamped on further promotions.

The thought of growing old as a captain or major on some rude, lonely and God-forsaken frontier outpost was not very cheering to the fiery young gallants who had attained the heights of glory during the great War of the Rebellion. Some sought solace in the bottle, others through the corrupt sale of government property at the stations under their control, and others hatched jealous plots against their superiors, hoping to unseat them and clamber a bit higher up the totem pole. The extent of bickering in the postwar Army was phenomenal. There was, of course, a goodly proportion of officers who stood aloof from such reprehensible and childish goings-on and simply did their duty as best they could, but that made life no more pleasant for them or their families.

The officers of the Indian-Fighting Army had a right to be unhappy. Their responsibilities were heavier than they should have been, because commands were chronically under-officered. Seasoned hands were constantly being called back to departmental, divisional or national headquarters to assist with recruiting, staff work, administrative or logistical duties. George Armstrong Custer rode to his last battle with fifteen of his regiment's forty-six officers absent on detached service.

The prime source of frustration for all ranks was the nature of Indian warfare. The hardest thing about fighting the red man was not the actual fighting itself – but finding him. Americans fought to annihilate their foes; Indians fought for honors and loot. While white

A troop of the 6th Cavalry waiting for the word to hit the trail in Arizona, 1881.

troops were willing to take substantial casualties to come to grips with their opponents, the native warriors shunned such situations. They only gave battle on their own terms – or when their women, children, horses and other property were in danger. Even if they had an edge in numbers, Indians carefully avoided sizable concentrations of troops – who could do heavy damage even if they were overwhelmed – preferring instead to fall on single companies, small patrols, stagecoaches and isolated settlers.

The Indian was admirably suited for hit-and-run guerrilla warfare. He travelled and fought half-naked, carrying only his weapons, ammunition and a few other bare necessities. His small, swift pony could outdistance anything on the Plains, and as he normally owned at least two or three – he always had a fresh mount to put plenty of miles between himself and his pursuers. Both man and animal could live on whatever nature had to offer, which greatly increased an Indian's mobility.

The average cavalry trooper weighed 140 to 150 pounds, and even when he was stripped down for action, he burdened his horse with 100 pounds of indispensable clothing, equipment, rations and forage. The American soldier could not live solely off the

country, and had to pack enough rations to last as long as he planned to be out on campaign. His large, heavier horse was unable to survive on prairie grasses and required a diet supplemented by oats and other grains. The Indian-Fighting Army was a conventional army, and it needed a wide logistical base. The men had to have access to a wide range of extra items – from bullets to horse shoes – to keep them on the trail of the wily 'Redskins'.

These unalterable facts tied the Bluecoats to long, lumbering supply trains, which restricted their movements and added to their worries. Not only did the supply wagons slow them down, they had to be protected.

When they were in Indian country, cavalrymen were forced to move in large numbers – for their own protection. But the big columns were always easy for the Indians to spot and avoid. If they were pressed too hard, the bands would simply split up into smaller, family-sized groups – leaving the puzzled and exhausted troopers a myriad of small trails, none of which was worth following. Since the Indians knew the country so well, the members of the band could rendezvous at some predesignated safe spot, and then continue on their way. To confuse the Indian and so wear him down until he could do no more than stand and fight, the Army would flood hostile territory with converging columns – sometimes as many as three, four or five. This strategy sometimes worked,

but a number of officers always swore that the savages were virtually impossible to catch in the summer. Only hard-driving and relentless leaders like Custer, Mackenzie and that remarkable, fleet-footed infantryman, Nelson A. Miles, seemed to possess the energy and the will essential to overtake and surprise their foes.

George Crook, a bewhiskered outdoorsman and an avid student of Indian thinking and customs, introduced some startling innovations for combating Indians that brought about his rapid rise from lieutenant colonel of the 23rd Infantry in 1866 to brigadier general by October 1873. As the commander of combined expeditions of cavalry and infantry, Crook was indomitable in chasing down his adversaries – and just as cunning. He cut his troops free of the supply train by elevating the use of the pack mule to a high science. Other Army officers employed Indian scouts, but Crook was wise enough to pit Indians against Indians. This ingenious tactic solved both the problems of mobility and logistics. When he took the field against the Chiricahua and Warm Springs Apaches in the fall of 1882, Crook recruited 250 Apache scouts and organized them into five equal companies. Working in tandem with troops of the 4th and 6th Cavalry, they were more than a match for such chiefs as Chato and Geronimo.

After a backbreaking decade, the Army's unceasing war of attrition began to tell on the Plains Indians.

PLATE 26: CUSTER'S 7TH CAVALRY AT THE LITTLE BIG HORN, 25 JUNE 1876

77. Lieutenant Colonel (George A. Custer), 7th U.S. Cavalry, Campaign Dress, 1876: *25 June 1876 was a warm day, and the last 7th Cavalryman to see Custer alive recalled that he had removed his buckskin blouse. He is depicted here in his 'fireman's shirt' and a white sombrero as described by eyewitnesses. Officers of the 7th Cavalry wore crossed-sabers with the regimental number embroidered in yellow or white silk on the corners of the shirt collar. As for Custer's armament, Edward S. Godfrey, then a lieutenant in command of Company K, declared: 'General Custer carried a Remington Sporting rifle, octagonal barrel; two Bulldog, self-cocking, English, white-handled pistols, with a ring in the butt for a lanyard; a hunting knife, in a beaded fringed scabbard; and a canvas cartridge belt.' Custer borrowed a pair of strong field glasses from another subordinate who survived him, First Lieutenant Charles DeRudio.* **78. Captain (Thomas W. Custer), 7th U.S. Cavalry, Campaign Dress, 1876:** *Tom Custer faced death dressed much like his famous brother. However, he is shown in a double-breasted, military-style buckskin jacket for sake of illustration. He is armed with the Model 1875 U.S. Army officer's Springfield rifle, a deluxe half-stock version of the enlisted man's carbine.* **79. Corporal, 7th U.S. Cavalry, Campaign Dress, 1876:** *Corporal Daniel Ryan was photographed in this handsome 'fireman's shirt' before he rode off to die with Tom Custer's C Company. The 1872 campaign hat lost its shape and fell apart in the field – especially after a good drenching. Several 7th Cavalrymen purchased straw hats from a sutler aboard the steamer* Far West *on 21 June. Officers and men sewed canvas or leather loops to their belts to make the metallic cartridges more accessible.*

An officer of the 4th or 6th Cavalry at Fort Wingate, New Mexico, circa 1886. He has on a shortened version of the 1876 undress sack coat and Apache style leggings. His armament consists of a Springfield carbine and large hunting knife, and his ammunition is carried on a looped cartridge belt.

77. Lieutenant Colonel, 7th U.S. Cavalry, Campaign Dress, 1876

78. Captain, 7th U.S. Cavalry, Campaign Dress, 1876

79. Corporal, 7th U.S. Cavalry, Campaign Dress, 1876

Enlisted men from Troop C, 5th U.S. Cavalry, with squatters they arrested in the Indian Territory prior to the opening of Oklahoma. The uniforms and equipment of the troopers place this in the early 1880s. On the left are two Indian scouts.

They grew weary of always having to fight and flee, and there were fewer and fewer places for them to hide. In desperation, some bands laid down their arms and came in to settle on their reservations, but others chose to stand and fight to the death. Those who did frequently gave the Army a rude shock. Man-for-man, the Indian brave was far superior to the average soldier as a warrior. The Bluecoats' advantages lay in discipline and firepower, but when pushed too hard by their cornered prey, the effects of their superficial training speedily evaporated.

At the Battle of the Rosebud on 17 June 1876, Crazy Horse and 750 to 1000 Sioux and Cheyennes easily checked General Crook and a massive force of 1300 cavalry, infantry and Indian scouts. In the last half of 1877, 300 Nez Perce warriors, hampered by 500 women and children, made their valorous way over 1700 miles in three months in a futile effort to escape to Canada. At virtually every turn of the trip, they were hounded by soldiers from two different departments, but they successfully out-thought, outfought and out-maneuvered every detachment the Army could throw at them. Among the outfits they humiliated were the 1st and 7th Cavalry, and it was only the sheer press of white numbers and the exertion of Nelson Miles that brought them to their knees.

In the twenty-five years following Appomattox, the Army was locked in a continuous struggle for mastery of the American Indian. There were almost 400 separate actions recorded between parties of troops and the various bands and tribes – many of them small affairs with few if any casualties. It would take volumes to do justice to these affrays – major and minor – but a brief summary of the careers of four famous cavalry regiments might provide an adequate sampling of the triumphs and trials of the Indian-Fighting Army.

The most renowned regiment on the Great Plains was the 7th U.S. Cavalry, one of the four new mounted regiments created by Congress on 28 July 1866. By the end of September, the 7th's 882 fresh recruits had been assembled and organized into twelve companies at Fort Riley, Kansas, and on 3 November 1866, Lieutenant Colonel George Armstrong Custer arrived to take over the reins and snap the whip. Because the two

Surgeon Leonard Wood distinguished himself in the 4th Cavalry's pursuit of Geronimo in 1886, the year this picture was taken. Later obtaining a regular commission, this athletic Yale man made the Army his career, rising to become colonel of the Rough Riders, military governor of Cuba and one of the first chiefs of staff.

men who were appointed as the 7th's colonels were permanently detached for staff work during Custer's lifetime, the blond-haired cavalier was actually the regiment's commander. He was resolved to make his troopers the pride of the Army, and he did surprisingly well considering the materials he had to work with.

In April 1867, Major General Winfield Scott Hancock gathered eleven companies of Custer's 7th Cavalry, seven companies of the 37th Infantry and a battery of the 4th Artillery to form an awesome army of 1400 officers and men. Hancock's intention was to intimidate the Southern Cheyennes and their Sioux allies into pursuing the ways of peace, but the approach of this terrifying host scared them onto the warpath instead. From May until the middle of July, Custer led the 7th zigzagging and backtracking for over 1000 miles across the flat, boring prairies of Kansas and Nebraska, vainly tracking the rampaging hostiles. But both the young colonel and his green troopers were too inexperienced and naïve to get the better of the elusive braves. Hancock, who deserved severe censure for stirring up a needless war in the first place, shifted all blame from his own shoulders by making a scapegoat out of Custer and having him court-martialed for several trivial offenses and trumped-up charges.

Custer was convicted and sentenced to suspension

from pay and duty for one year, but he only served ten months of his punishment. He rejoined the 7th Cavalry on 6 October 1868, at the express request of Major General Philip H. Sheridan, who had taken over the pompous Hancock's western command. After another fruitless summer of attempting to snare marauding Indians, Sheridan had concluded that the best time to strike the savages was in the winter, when they were most vulnerable. With heavy snows covering the grass and incommoding travel, their ponies would be weak and the tribesmen themselves would be less vigilant.

To deliver this first decisive postwar blow against

the Plains Indians, Sheridan wanted Custer, who was his trustworthy lieutenant from the Civil War and one of the few officers whose enthusiasm for soldiering had not succumbed to the disappointments and doldrums of peacetime. Custer took charge of the 800 demoralized officers and men from eleven companies of his regiment and proceeded to breathe new life into them. He redistributed the horses to each troop by color, and he organized an elite corps of forty sharpshooters. By the time the 7th trudged out of Camp Supply on 23 November 1868, it was ready for business.

The snow was falling so thickly that the Osage scouts lost their bearings, but Custer guided the regiment back on the right track with his compass. At daybreak on 26 November, the soldiers discovered the trail of a war party leading into the valley of the Washita River, and under the veil of darkness, Custer carefully moved the 7th Cavalry to within a mile of an unsuspecting Cheyenne village of fifty-one lodges. As they waited for the sun to rise, Custer stealthily divided his command into four battalions – to swamp the village from all sides.

At dawn on 27 November 1868, the 7th Cavalry band belted out the first few strains of 'Garry Owen', the regiment's rollicking march, until the cold morning air froze the saliva in the instruments. As the last brassy note died away, the 7th Cavalry came crunching down the frigid wastes, the victory-starved troopers shaking the sides of the valley with their thunderous cheers and blasting volleys from their revolvers and Spencer carbines. Custer's surprise was devastatingly complete. One hundred and three Cheyenne men and boys were slain, and fifty-seven women and children were captured. Only one officer and three men were killed, and three officers and eleven troopers were wounded in overrunning the camp. One major and sixteen other ranks perished when they chased a group of fugitives downstream and ran into an overwhelming number of Cheyenne, Arapaho, Kiowa and Comanche warriors, whose winter camps stretched for ten miles further down the valley.

These enraged Indians pushed on to confront Custer. Though possibly outnumbered, he adroitly feinted toward the other villages, which sent the braves scrambling back to protect their families. To prevent their recapture, Custer ordered the destruction of the 875 Cheyenne ponies he had taken, and then he withdrew his regiment with no further losses.

The Battle of the Washita shattered the confidence

PLATE 27: FASHIONS ON THE PLAINS, 1879–90

80. First Lieutenant, 5th U.S. Cavalry, Dress Uniform, 1881: *The 1879 dress coat came without gold lace on the cuffs for officers below the rank of brigadier general. The 1881 cavalry dress helmet had a shorter back brim than the 1872 model and a buffalo-hair plume for officers. Note the U.S. Model 1872 cavalry officer's saber.*
81. Sergeant, 6th U.S. Cavalry, Campaign Dress, 1885–6: *This sturdy non-com is ready for a go with the Apaches with his drab 1885 campaign hat, unpiped 1883 sack coat and U.S. Model 1884 Springfield carbine, complete with Buffington rear sight. The red-and-white guidon pattern was restored in 1885, and the U.S. Cavalry carried it up into World War 2.* **82. Corporal, 7th U.S. Cavalry, Winter Campaign Dress, 1890:** *The 1880 enlisted man's overcoat had yellow lining in the cape for cavalry. General Order No. 38 of 6 June 1883, specified that chevrons be worn on the lower sleeves. Note the muskrat cap, first adopted in 1879, and the calfskin gauntlets.*

of the southern Plains tribes, and Sheridan was swift to capitalize on Custer's breakthrough. To alleviate his deficiency in mounted strength, Sheridan called on state authorities to muster about 1000 men in the 19th Kansas Volunteer Cavalry. Together with these citizen soldiers and the 7th Cavalry, he and Custer set out to pacify the Plains on 7 December. Eleven days later, the 1500 horsemen surprised a village of Kiowas and Comanches under Santanta and Lone Wolf. Instead of attacking, Little Phil had Custer arrest the two chiefs and hold them hostage until their people came in to the reservation.

Taking a mere fifty-seven 7th Cavalrymen and risking what seemed certain death, Custer searched out Little Raven and his Arapahoes and convinced them to come to terms with the whites. While Sheridan was in Washington receiving his promotion to lieutenant general, Custer sought his most stubborn adversaries, the Cheyennes, at the head of his 7th and the 19th Kansas. After the Washita, those people were particularly leery of white soldiers. Custer kept after them, however, and he had only 800 men still on horseback when he came upon the large village of Medicine Arrow and Little Robe on 15 March 1869. There were two white women held captive in the camp, so Custer did not jeopardize their lives by starting a battle.

80. First Lieutenant, 5th U.S. Cavalry, Dress Uniform, 1881

81. Sergeant, 6th U.S. Cavalry, Campaign Dress, 1885-6

82. Corporal, 7th U.S. Cavalry, Winter Campaign Dress, 1890

Instead, he courageously rode into the midst of the hostiles, accompanied by only his adjutant and orderly, to try to negotiate their release. When his words proved unavailing, he seized three chiefs as hostages and threatened to string them up. Bullying worked. The Cheyennes released their prisoners and promised to go to their reservation.

Following this run of good fortune, the 7th Cavalry was split up for Reconstruction duty in Kentucky, Tennessee and South Carolina. Sioux harassment of survey parties employed by the Northern Pacific Railroad to map the Dakota Territory brought the regiment a change of station after several years. By 10 June 1873, ten companies had been reunited at Fort Rice. Ten days later, Colonel David Stanley's Yellowstone Expedition headed west to shield the railroadmen. Besides the 7th Cavalry, there were twenty companies of infantry, two Rodman guns, ten white scouts and seventy-five Arikaras in the 1500-man column.

On 4 August 1873, while scouting out ahead with a squadron of eighty 7th Cavalrymen, Custer spotted six Sioux bucks who tried to lure him into an ambush. When he declined to follow the decoys, 300 braves burst from hiding and hurled themselves at his party. Custer calmly dismounted his two companies and held them off for three hours. Then with ammunition running low, he ordered the troopers to vault back into their saddles and scattered his assailants with a mounted charge, killing two warriors and wounding a few more.

Four days later, the site of a recently vacated Sioux village was discovered, and Stanley directed Custer to follow the trail with 450 of his men. At dawn on 11 August, 800 braves on the opposite bank of the Yellowstone began shooting over the river into the soldiers' camp. Custer shook his Bluecoats out into open order to return the fire. After more than two hours of scrimmaging, a lookout informed Custer that 300 warriors had crossed the Yellowstone below the camp and were endeavoring to get into the bluffs behind the 7th. Welcoming this challenge, the colonel mounted his command and chased the Sioux for eight miles, claiming a bag of forty warriors killed and wounded.

Indignant about the mounting Sioux militancy, the Army decided to send a strong expedition to survey their sacred Black Hills and possibly rough up a few war parties. One thousand men were deemed sufficient

for the task, and Lieutenant Colonel Custer was put in charge. In addition to ten troops from his regiment, he was furnished with two infantry companies, three Gatling guns, one Rodman fieldpiece, sixty Indian scouts and a train of 100 supply wagons. The Sioux wisely steered clear of 'Long Hair' and his bronzed veterans. The column was out from 2 July until 30 August 1874, and it charted 1205 miles without incident. The most sensational result of this foray arose from the reports some of its members carried of finding traces of gold in the Black Hills.

This news fell on the ears of a nation in the throes of a serious economic depression, and it sparked a wild gold rush into lands reserved for the Sioux. The government could not keep these trespassers out, so it cowardly tried to purchase the Black Hills. When the Sioux understandably refused to sell, Washington de-

Troops B, E, F, A and I, the regimental band and the staff of the 2nd Cavalry turned out in full dress uniform on the parade ground at Fort Walla Walla, Washington, in 1887. From left, the officers in the foreground are the regiment's colonel, major, surgeon, adjutant, quartermaster and assistant surgeon.

cided to provoke a war. In December 1875, the Sioux were informed that if they did not take up residence on their reservations and abandon the desired territory by 31 January 1876, they would be left to the tender mercies of the U.S. Army. This ultimatum set the stage for the Battle of the Little Big Horn.

For the first time since 1866, all twelve companies of the 7th Cavalry were concentrated at Fort Abraham Lincoln by 1 May 1876, for the imminent campaign against the Sioux and Northern Cheyennes. Custer's thirty-two officers and 718 enlisted men provided the real bite for the 925-man Dakota Column presided over by Brigadier General Alfred H. Terry, Long Hair's mild-mannered and bumbling departmental commander. Terry's force was one of three converging columns that were to comb the Sioux country from the east, west and south that spring.

By 22 June 1876, Terry had linked up with Colonel John Gibbon's Montana Column on the Yellowstone, and a recent scout by half the 7th Cavalry indicated that 800 hostile warriors and their families were encamped in the valley of the Little Big Horn. Custer was instructed to take his twelve troops, follow their trail and pitch into the enemy whenever and wherever he found them. Terry himself accompanied Gibbon's smaller and slower column of 450 men, four companies of the 2nd Cavalry, six of the 7th Infantry and a

Lieutenant Colonel George A. Custer in the buckskin coat and trousers, buffalo robe and fur cap he wore during his successful operations against the Southern Cheyennes, Arapahoes and Kiowas in the winter of 1868–9.

battery of Gatlings, to take up a blocking position at the northern end of the Little Big Horn.

There was no fear that Custer might find the hostiles too soon, or that the 7th Cavalry might not be able to handle whatever it ran into. Army estimates put the number of Indian males of fighting age off their reservations at 800 to slightly more than 1000 – and that amount had never been able to stand up to a full regiment of regular cavalry before. Terry was so confident of success he detached two officers and 152 men from the 7th to guard his supply depot. That left the regiment with a much-reduced complement of thirty-one officers and 566 troopers. Even with the addition of thirty-five Arikara, Sioux and Crow scouts, seven white guides and interpreters, six mule packers and a newspaper reporter, Custer had a mere 647 men. But he was not concerned. He even turned down offers to take along the Gatling guns or Gibbon's battalion of the 2nd Cavalry. What really worried Long Hair and every other officer in the field was that the Indians would scatter and run before their soldiers could get so much as a peep at them.

With his customary dispatch, Custer sniffed down the trail, brought his command to the edge of the valley of the Little Big Horn by dawn on Sunday, 25 June 1876, and had his Indian scouts point out the general location of the village, which was still hidden from sight by intervening lines of bluffs and ridges. Custer planned to move his regiment into the valley, hide it the rest of the day, have his scouts pinpoint the hostile camp and then strike at sunrise on the twenty-sixth. Before he could set his plan in motion, he learned that the column had been spotted by a number of Sioux out hunting in the morning. Convinced that if they warned their people the hostiles would scatter to the four winds, Custer had no other choice than to attack immediately.

At 12.07 p.m., the 7th U.S. Cavalry entered the valley of the Little Big Horn. Anxious lest his quarry slip away and escape to the south, Custer sent Captain Frederick Benteen and Troops D, H and K on a brief reconnaissance to the left. Then as the rest of the regiment neared the Little Big Horn, he ordered Major Marcus A. Reno to take Troops A, G and M, ford the river and charge the village head-on. Shortly after Reno moved out, Custer's scouts informed him that the encampment extended far to the north. Deciding to support Reno with a disconcerting flank attack, Custer swung to the right with Troops C, E, F, I and L.

It was not until George Armstrong Custer ascended the bluffs blocking his view of the valley that he finally realized what he had gotten the 7th Cavalry into. There was an enormous village stretching for miles below him – at least 1000 lodges housing anywhere from 2000 to 4000 warriors. The Army had never run into such a concentration before, and these Indians were not running away! With Reno's battalion already committed and the regiment widely divided, withdrawing would just invite disaster. The best Custer could do was brazen it out – keep moving, strive to knock the braves off balance and consolidate the 7th Cavalry as he went along. Dispatching couriers to recall Benteen and the troop (B) guarding the pack train, he continued north, looking for a break in the bluffs and a ford so he could get into the village.

In the meantime, Major Reno prudently stopped his attack short, rather than let his 141 soldiers and thirty-five scouts be swallowed alive by that monstrous camp. Unfortunately, Reno lost his nerve and led his three companies in a panicky flight back across the Little Big Horn, which saw half his troopers killed or cut off by the inflamed Sioux and Cheyennes. Just as Reno's men broke clear, they were spotted by Benteen, who was lethargically answering Custer's urgent plea for help. Ascertaining the crippled state of Reno's command, Benteen very naturally went no further. But with seven-twelfths of the 7th Cavalry out of the engagement, the hostiles were free to turn all their attention on Custer.

It is not clear whether Custer attempted to charge the village or not, but mounting numbers pressed his five companies back from the river up a broken hog-back ridge, where they were whittled down to nothing. It took between forty-five minutes and an hour and a half, and then Custer and every one of the thirteen officers, 193 soldiers and four civilians under his immediate command were dead. Once this threat was eliminated, the hostiles returned to deal with Reno and Benteen, who had entrenched their 339 survivors atop a hill. These frightened men had to endure a perilous siege the rest of that evening and all the next day. They were relieved by a tardy Terry and Gibbon on 27 June.

Counting the troopers who fell on that quarter of the battlefield, the 7th Cavalry lost 263 killed and fifty-nine wounded at the Little Big Horn. It was the Indians' greatest victory over the Army, but it only postponed the inevitable.

In the spring of 1870, Colonel Ranald S. Mackenzie became the colonel of the 4th Cavalry. This twenty-nine-year-old West Point graduate with a surfeit of valor had suffered six wounds during the Civil War,

but he had earned the rank of brevet major general in the process and the undying admiration of Ulysses S. Grant. Mackenzie was an irritable, fuming fussbudget, a tireless worker who gave no thought to his own comfort, and, like Custer, a merciless disciplinarian. Under his iron grip, the 4th shortly became what Robert M. Utley, the leading historian of the Indian-Fighting Army, has dubbed 'the best cavalry regiment in the army.'

The most logical posting for so fine a unit and so forceful a leader was Texas, still the favorite stomping ground for red raiders from New Mexico, the Indian Territory, Kansas and south of the border. Colonel Mackenzie served notice of his arrival by invading the Staked Plains in 1871 and 1872, and uncovering the pattern of the infamous *Comanchero* trade. On 29 September 1872, the 4th Cavalry surprised a Comanche camp at McClellan's Creek on the North Fork of the Red River. The troopers whizzed through the 262 teepees with lightning speed, gunning down twenty males and capturing 124 women and children. Unlike Custer at the Washita, Mackenzie did not take the precaution of slaughtering the pony herd, and it was recovered by the surviving braves.

While Mackenzie was cleaning out the north of Texas, depredations against her southern and western settlements committed by Kickapoos, Lipans and Mescalero Apaches living in Mexico increased in frequency and intensity. At the direct order of President Grant, the 4th Cavalry was shifted down to Fort Clark in March 1873. On 11 April, Mackenzie received secret instructions from General Sheridan and Secretary of War William W. Belknap, who had made the tiresome journey to that bleak outpost with the express purpose of delivering them in person. In effect, Mackenzie was directed to ignore the international boundary, cross over into Mexico and smash up the vulture bands that had been preying on Texas. When the unsmiling young colonel asked for written authority to sanction his violation of Mexican sovereignty, Sheridan pounded on a table and bellowed:

'Damn the orders! Damn the authority! You are to go ahead on your own plan of action, and your authority and backing shall be General Grant and myself. With us behind you in whatever you do to clean up this situation, you can rest assured of the fullest support. You must assume the risk. We will assume the final responsibility should any result.'

While he put the 4th Cavalry through its paces to raise the general level of fitness and marksmanship, Mackenzie slipped some spies into Mexico to locate his quarry. By the night of 16 May, they were back, reporting that there were three villages of fifty to sixty lodges pitched by the San Rodrigo River near Remolino. One camp belonged to the Kickapoos, another to the Mescaleros and the third to the Lipans. At sunset on 17 May 1873, Mackenzie led six troops of the 4th Cavalry over the Rio Grande. In addition to his 400 Bluecoats, he brought along Lieutenant John L. Bullis and twenty-five Seminole-Negro scouts, plus a fast-moving mule train. The 4th came upon the Kickapoo camp in full daylight the next day, but Mackenzie attacked so quickly the Indians had no chance to get away. Nineteen were killed and forty captured. Mackenzie then passed on to the other villages, which he found abandoned, and burned them to the ground. The 4th Cavalry recrossed the Rio Grande on 19 May, after riding 160 miles in thirty-two hours and spending nearly sixty without sleep. Mackenzie's only cost was one dead and two wounded, and he frightened 432 Kickapoos into returning to the United States to avoid further retribution.

A troop of the 9th U.S. Cavalry on dismounted parade at Fort Davis, circa 1875. Due to the prejudices of the day, black soldiers were assigned to the bleakest, rudest posts on the frontier.

The outbreak of the Red River War that following spring found Mackenzie operating in the Staked Plains again. On 20 September 1874, he led twenty-one officers and 450 men comprising eight troops from his regiment and five companies of infantry from Fort Concho. Eight days later, he fell upon several hundred Cheyenne, Comanche and Kiowa lodges grouped together in the upper reaches of Palo Duro Canyon. The hostiles scattered before the 4th Cavalry could descend to the canyon floor, but Mackenzie was swift enough to slay three warriors, raze the camp and seize the entire pony herd of 1424 head. Picking out the best horses for his soldiers, he had the remainder, more than 1000 animals, destroyed. This was a terrible blow to the warring tribes, and it helped immeasurably to persuade them to capitulate.

After the Custer Massacre, Mackenzie was rushed north with six companies of the 4th to chastise the Sioux and Cheyennes. At dawn on 25 November 1876, Mackenzie stole up on the icebound Cheyenne village of Dull Knife and Little Wolf with ten troops representing the 2nd, 3rd, 4th and 5th Cavalry. There were only 400 warriors in the camp, but they stood up well to the 1100 soldiers and 400 Indian scouts. Mackenzie was not able to take all 183 lodges until mid-afternoon, and he lost six killed and twenty-six wounded. But he had killed forty braves and impoverished the rest. They too would soon surrender.

For these and other victories, Mackenzie was handsomely rewarded. In October 1882, he was promoted to brigadier general, and in thirteen months he became commander of the Department of Texas. Mackenzie had always pushed himself too hard, and his mind, tortured by his poorly healed wounds, his erratic eating and sleeping habits, and the stress of an irascible temper, finally snapped under his added responsibilities. He went insane in December 1883, and died three years later.

Nowhere were the qualities of instant courage, good humor under adversity, devotion to duty and lasting loyalty displayed to better advantage in the Indian-Fighting Army than among the two black mounted regiments, the 9th and 10th Cavalry. On account of the prevailing white prejudices of the day, their exploits were ignored or belittled, and they were subjected to indignities that made the lowly lot of their pale-faced colleagues look luxurious. Harried by Army and civilian authorities, they were given old and damaged equipment, broken-down nags that had been lamed by other outfits or purchased during the Civil War, the most miserable quarters and the dirtiest jobs on the frontier. Derided by their white comrades as 'Moacs', 'Brunettes' and 'Niggers', they were called 'Buffalo Soldiers' by the Indians for their tight, curly hair and fierce fighting spirit.

After their establishment in July 1866, the 9th Cavalry set up shop in New Orleans, and the 10th at Fort Leavenworth. Recruiting was conducted throughout Louisiana, Kentucky, the Upper South, Philadelphia, Boston, New York and Pittsburgh – and there was no shortage of enthusiastic volunteers. By the middle of March 1867, the 9th had 885 enlisted men.

The real trouble came in the procurement of officers. Congress set very high standards for the first set of commissions it handed out in these two regiments. All candidates had to have served at least two years with the Union cavalry during the Civil War, and one third of all the field officers and troop commanders were to come from the regular service. Every applicant had also to pass an examination as to his fitness before a board of officers convened by the Secretary of War. These conditions must have scared away many, and there were those who looked upon service with Afro-Americans as demeaning and a sure road to social ostracism. Others, such as George A. Custer and

Eugene A. Carr, did not believe that Negroes would make steady soldiers.

To tell the truth, those early recruits had more than their share of rough edges. The harsh and submissive life of slavery or of the most-menial labor in the 'free' North had robbed many of them of pride and self-confidence. Illiteracy was almost universal in the ranks. Whereas in the rest of the Army, chaplains were normally assigned to posts, the 9th and 10th Cavalry each carried one on their rolls. Besides attending to religious matters, these reverend gentlemen were to engage 'in the instruction of the enlisted men in the Common English branches.' Until that was accomplished, however, the officers had to fill out the reports and paperwork that were supposed to be handled by their non-coms, and teach their troopers all their duties from scratch. As bothersome as all this overtime must have been, the additional contact it engendered had one unforeseen and beneficial effect. It bound the officers and men of the 9th and 10th Cavalry close together, far closer than any other units in the West.

For a white, enlisting was a step down on the social scale, an admission of defeat in trying to get by in the civilian world. During the era of black codes and Jim Crow, the Army offered a young and active Negro a relatively secure home and an honorable career. There he could prove his manhood, and if he applied himself, he might attain the status of corporal or sergeant. These conditions set the 9th and 10th Cavalry apart from the rest of the Indian-Fighting Army in a special way.

The Buffalo Soldiers took well to discipline, and no fighting men in the world could excel them for initiative and bravery in the face of the most daunting odds. After a punishing hard campaign against the Mescaleros, Major Albert P. Morrow of the 9th Cavalry reported on 1 June 1870:

> I cannot speak too highly of the conduct of the officers and men under my command, always cheerful and ready, braving the severest hardships with short rations and no water without a murmur. The negro troops are peculiarly adapted to hunting Indians knowing no fear and capable of great endurance.

Three years before, Major Eugene A. Carr of the 5th Cavalry had looked on in amazement as Companies H and I of the 10th Cavalry beat off 400 to 500 Cheyenne warriors with a sustained fire from their Spencer carbines. As the smoke lifted and the hostiles withdrew across the Kanasas prairies, he turned to the men he had so badly underestimated and whooped, 'I have never seen such superior marksmanship among soldiers, in all my military experience!'

The Buffalo Soldiers were very lucky in the choice of their first two colonels. General Grant possibly thought more of Colonel Benjamin H. Grierson of the 10th than any other cavalry commander who had served under him during the Civil War. Edward Hatch had commanded a regiment on Grierson's famous raid back in 1863, and he coincidentally received command of the 9th. Both men were more than competent, extraordinarily tolerant and ever ready to defend their men against slanders and discrimination. In June 1867, Grierson forbade his subordinates to use the word 'colored' in their official papers. 'The regiment is simply the Tenth Regiment of Cavalry, United States Army,' he decreed. Under such enlightened administration, desertion all but disappeared among the Buffalo

Soldiers. In 1877, only ten of Grierson's troopers took the grand bounce, and the 9th suffered only six cases of French leave. Three years later, the 10th Cavalry lost a mere five deserters, an all-time Army record. Furthermore, the black regiments boasted a high re-enlistment rate and a larger contingent of veterans than the rest of the U.S. Cavalry.

In the spring of 1867, Colonel Hatch was ordered to march the halftrained and under-officered 9th Cavalry into Texas. There it spent the next eight years sweltering in the stifling heat along the Rio Grande and in some of the rottenest forts ever to fly the Stars and Stripes. In September 1875, the 9th was transferred to the District of New Mexico, but that was not much of an improvement, and the Apaches gave the regiment no rest. The 10th Cavalry first saw action in Kansas and the Indian Territory, and then in March 1875, it was assigned to West Texas.

One of the severest tests the Buffalo Soldiers faced was the Victorio War, which blew up in September 1879. The 9th Cavalry practically dismounted itself in its valiant efforts to apprehend the elusive Victorio and his Warm Springs Apaches, but it did succeed in making things too hot for the Apaches in New Mexico and hounded them down south of the border. Guessing correctly that Victorio would next try to enter West

Sergeant John Bouck and Corporal Sampson of Troop K, 1st U.S. Cavalry, on duty at Crow Agency, Montana Territory, in the fall of 1887. Sampson was killed by Crow renegades shortly afterward, on 5 November.

Texas, Colonel Grierson astutely stationed his companies at the major border waterholes and let the hostiles come to him. A short but brilliant campaign drove Victorio back into Mexico by 11 August 1880, where he was killed by local soldiers two months later.

As the 1880s drew to a close, the last of the tribes were defeated and confined to reservations. Their power and freedom gone, everything else they held dear was threatened by the imposition of white culture on their children and the prostrating effects of alcohol. Some bewildered Indians tried to escape this horrible new world by losing themselves in mysticism, especially the new Ghost Dance that was being preached by a gentle Paiute shaman named Wovoka. The Sioux, however, put a militant twist on Wovoka's words, predicting the Ghost Dance would hasten an Indian armageddon in which whites would be exterminated.

By November 1890, the Ghost Dance hysteria had brought the Pine Ridge and Rosebud Agencies to the verge of anarchy. Major General Nelson A. Miles deployed half the Army in the vicinity to quiet things down, including the 1st, 2nd, 5th, 6th, 7th, 8th and 9th Cavalry. On 28 December 1890, the 7th Cavalry intercepted 320 Miniconjous and thirty-eight Hunkpapas who had jumped the reservation and escorted them into the valley of Wounded Knee Creek. The next morning the 500 troopers moved into the camp to disarm the 120 warriors of their Winchester repeaters. Instead of handing over their weapons, the agitated Sioux started shooting into the soldiers at pointblank range. The soldiers returned the fire with their Springfield carbines and, as they backed away, Light Battery E, 1st U.S. Artillery, brought four Hotchkiss guns into play. When the firing finally stopped, more than 150 Indian men, women and children lay dead and another fifty were wounded. But Wounded Knee was no massacre, it was a short vicious battle. Twenty-five Bluecoats had been killed and fifty hurt by bullets and arrows.

On 30 December, some vengeful Sioux braves trapped eight troops of the 7th Cavalry in a narrow valley at Drexel Mission, four miles north of Pine Ridge, and nearly cut them to pieces. Major Guy Henry and Companies I, K, D and F of the 9th Cavalry arrived in the nick of time, however, and extricated the grateful white troopers.

Intent on avoiding further bloodshed, General Miles skilfully alternated threats of force with deft diplo-

A lieutenant and a patrol of the 1st Cavalry surprise a pair of poachers in Yellowstone National Park in 1886. From that year until 1918, detachments of pony soldiers guarded the wonders and wildlife of one of America's great natural preserves.

macy, and he prevailed upon the remaining Sioux hostiles to surrender by 15 January 1891.

The Indian Wars were now over. By and large, the U.S. Cavalry had behaved creditably in their prosecution, but the conquest of the Great Plains had eliminated their primary reason for being. Yet it would take the nation and the conservative Army over fifty years to realize that the services of the pony soldiers were no longer required.

8 Fighting for Empire
1890-1918

As the curtain closed on the last of the Indian Wars, Congress came swooping in from the wings to slash Army manpower down to the barest minimum possible. In 1890, well before the guns fell silent at Wounded Knee, the U.S. Cavalry was virtually halved in size. The last two troops in each regiment, L and M, were disbanded. The ten remaining troops were kept to a fixed quota of forty-four privates apiece.

Curiously enough, the pacification of the Indian brought about a temporary resurgence in the Army's strength. There was no doubt that the tribes had been utterly vanquished, but government authorities harbored a very real fear that the young warriors might get into trouble if they were given nothing more exciting to do than farm. Some humanitarians proposed military service as an ideal channel for the Indians' lingering belligerent tendencies, and the discipline, routine and pageantry of Army life would help to assimilate the Indian into American culture.

Two 100-man companies of Indian scouts were raised on an experimental basis in the spring of 1890, one on the northern Plains and one to the south. Eight hundred more scouts were called out during the Wounded Knee Campaign in December. The success of these units encouraged the War Department to undertake an even grander venture. On 9 March 1891, the Adjutant General's Office issued General Order 28. This directive authorized the formation of eight troops of Indian cavalry and nineteen companies of Indian infantry – one for each regiment stationed west of the Mississippi, except the Negro outfits.

To encourage recruiting, the Indians were enlisted from the areas in which their regiments were serving, and they were promised that they would not be transferred away from home unless it was absolutely necessary. By the end of June 1892, 837 braves had submitted to the shears of post barbers and put on soldier blue. Some of the new pony soldiers were former allies, like the Crows of the 1st Cavalry's Troop L, but even more

were former foes. Troop L, 3rd U.S. Cavalry, consisted of Miniconjou Sioux; the eleventh troop of the 6th Cavalry was raised among the Brule Sioux on the Rosebud Agency; and the 7th Cavalry had a contingent of Arapahoes.

At first the Native Americans seemed to thrive in their new environment. Red soldiers were reputedly the best marksmen in the 2nd and 7th Cavalry. The Sioux troopers of the 3rd and 6th Cavalry were chosen as honor guards for the 1893 Chicago World's Fair, where they made a favorable impression on throngs of tourists. Within a short passage of time, however, there surfaced a number of problems that quickly doomed this noble experiment. The language barrier made it difficult for the Indians to master much more than rote drill movements. As the novelty of Army life was translated into monotony and hard work, enlistments dropped off and the braves already in uniform began to agitate for an early release. The recruitment of Indians was suspended, and attrition killed off each unit one by one. By mid-1894, only 547 Indians remained in six cavalry troops and four infantry companies. The last of them, Troop L of the 7th Cavalry, was finally discharged in 1897.

The conquest of the frontier did not quench the American thirst for expansion. Having blazed a wide swath across the North American continent, the citizens of the great Yankee republic cast their eyes across the seas and let their imagination roam. Imperialism had sunk its ugly roots into the hearts of the major Western powers, and Americans longed to see their own nation take its place in the scramble for colonies, empire, foreign markets and international prestige.

Cuba became the first object of these awakening ambitions. In 1895, the inhabitants of that island took up arms against Spanish misrule, and as the rebellion spread their overlords reacted with repression and cruelty. Americans took an uncommon interest in this bloody and seemingly endless affray. Cuba was

An unidentified cavalry sergeant leads his squad through the Southwest, circa 1893–4. He wears the 1885 drab campaign hat, the 1883 sack coat and the Model 1885 woven carbine cartridge belt.

situated just ninety miles from the southern tip of Florida in the Caribbean, which the United States regarded as her own backyard. Harkening back to the days of their revolution, ordinary Americans looked with sympathy on the Cuban struggle for liberty, and they were outraged by tales of indiscriminate Spanish atrocities against rebels and noncombatants alike. Businessmen were concerned because the continuing

The band of the 3rd U.S. Cavalry at Jefferson Barracks, Missouri, circa 1894–8. The musicians' tunics are of a purely regimental style, and service stripes are in evidence on the lower sleeves of the older men. The bass drummer in the center of the front row displays chevrons authorized for a saddler sergeant on 7 March 1892.

violence down there disrupted profitable commerce, threatened $50,000,000 in American property and investments on the island and posed a growing danger to the military and political stability of the entire region.

Spurred on by the hysterical warmongering of the lurid 'Yellow Press', more and more Americans began

to urge the administration of President William McKinley to kick the Spanish out of Cuba. On 25 January 1898, the battleship U.S.S. *Maine* steamed into Havana Harbor, a thinly veiled warning to Madrid that something had to be done at once to bring peace to Cuba. When the *Maine* blew up mysteriously twenty-one days later, most Americans concluded the disaster was the work of the Spaniards, and the nation succumbed to an irrational martial frenzy that had lain dormant since 1865.

On 9 March, Congress appropriated $50,000,000 to beef up the Army and the Navy, and on 19 April, it granted President McKinley's request to recognize Cuban independence and to approve American military intervention there to guarantee it. Within a week's time, the United States was officially at war with Spain.

As soon as hostilities appeared probable, the War and Navy Departments swung into action. There was not a moment to lose. The whole U.S. Army numbered a bare 2143 officers and 26,040 enlisted men, 6000 of the latter in the cavalry, at the start of April 1898, while the Spanish had 150,000 regulars and 80,000 native volunteers in Cuba alone! On 22 April, Congress empowered the President to raise a practically limitless amount of temporary volunteers, who would serve for two years or to the end of the war – whichever came sooner. McKinley was allowed to set each state's quota, and it was hoped that militia organizations would enter Federal service as units. Because the state forces could muster no more than 4800 cavalrymen, the Secretary of War was authorized to raise 3000 'United States Volunteers' from the nation at large and form them into three mounted regiments 'to be composed exclusively of frontiersmen possessing special qualifications as horsemen and marksmen.'

On 26 April, the day after it declared war on Spain, Congress enlarged the regular army to 64,719 officers and men. Troops L and M were reactivated in the ten cavalry regiments, and all 120 troops received an extra lieutenant, a sergeant, four corporals and thirty-four privates, producing a total of 104 officers and men apiece. Each cavalry regiment now had a recommended strength of 1262. In the same way, infantry outfits got back the two companies that had been mothballed in 1890 and received two more for good measure.

Anticipating this expansion for its professional soldiers, the War Department advised McKinley that it

PLATE 28: A PLACID PERIOD, 1890–8
83. Private, 3rd U.S. Cavalry, Summer Undress, 1892: *At this time the entire enlisted complement of the 3rd Cavalry's Troop L consisted of Sioux Indians. This Americanized warrior sports the 1889-pattern summer helmet, 1888 summer sack coat and trousers, and U.S. Model 1890 Springfield carbine.* **84. Major, 1st U.S. Cavalry, White Undress Uniform, 1895:** *The new white forage cap and undress coat were trimmed with flat white braid, but they bore no rank devices or any other ornaments until 1901.* **85. Second Lieutenant, 2nd U.S. Cavalry, Undress, 1895:** *The 1895 regulations prescribed shoulder straps and gilt collar devices for the blue undress coat. The braid was black mohair. The officer's forage cap had an embroidered eagle device on the front. The enlisted man's bore a pair of brass crossed-sabers, with the regimental number in the upper angle and the company letter in the lower.*

would need only 60,000 volunteers to humble the Spanish. The President, however, had a mind of his own, and he called out 125,000 on 22 April. A month later he appealed to the states for 75,000 more. The response was overwhelming. By the end of May, the U.S. Army listed 8400 officers and 160,000 men in its regular and volunteer regiments, and within two more months the sum had swollen to 271,000.

This flowering host was shipped off to camps all over the nation and quickly formed into eight separate corps, but only two of them were to see any real fighting.

The first large body of American troops to get into action was Major General William R. Shafter's V Corps, which assembled in the blistering summer heat at Tampa, Florida. Shafter's command included the greatest concentration of the Army's regular artillery, infantry and cavalry, plus nine of the best-trained and equipped volunteer regiments. There were 25,000 eager warriors in all, and they were divided between two divisions of infantry and one of cavalry.

Shafter's Cavalry Division was put in the very capable hands of Major General Joseph Wheeler, the same 'Fighting Joe' who had served the Confederacy so well during the Civil War. Like Fitzhugh Lee and other Southern officers, he had offered his services to battle the Spanish, and the McKinley Administration, glad to unite the entire nation behind the war effort, gra-

PLATE 28: 1890–8

83. Private, 3rd U.S. Cavalry, Summer Undress, 1892

84. Major, 1st U.S. Cavalry, White Undress Uniform, 1895

85. Second Lieutenant, 2nd U.S. Cavalry, Undress, 1895

ciously accepted. Wheeler's 4000 troopers were drawn from some of the most celebrated regiments of the Indian-Fighting Army, the 1st, 3rd, 6th, 9th and 10th Cavalry, but in the coming conflict they were all to be overshadowed by the much publicized exploits of the Johnny-come-lately 1st United States Volunteer Cavalry.

Created along with its two sister regiments on 22 April, the 1st U.S. Volunteer Cavalry was swiftly organized at San Antonio, Texas, with a full complement of forty-seven federally appointed officers and 994 other ranks, and it set something of a record by getting them all prepared for combat in less than a month. The man most responsible for this awesome feat was Colonel Leonard Wood, a Yale graduate and former Army contract surgeon who had made a name for himself in the 4th Cavalry's arduous pursuit of Geronimo. Originally, the Secretary of War had offered Wood's job to a rising young Republican politician and the current Assistant Secretary of the Navy, Theodore Roosevelt of New York. Roosevelt declined the honor, stating with uncharacteristic modesty that it would require at least a month for him to learn how to handle a cavalry regiment. Instead he nominated his friend Wood for the senior post and settled for the rank of lieutenant colonel.

Thanks to his career as a moderate political reformer, his many books about history and outdoor life, and a short but colorful stint as a Dakota rancher, Lieutenant Colonel Roosevelt was already a national celebrity, and the regiment was soon dubbed 'Roosevelt's Rough Riders'. Wood envied none of his chief subordinate's notoriety. He shrewdly capitalized on the lieutenant colonel's popularity, press coverage and political pull to attract the best sort of recruits and to provide them with modern Krag-Jorgensen carbines and other equipment of high quality. The U.S. Volunteers were supposed to be raised in the West, and many of the Rough Riders were genuine cowboys – not a few of them former outlaws. Nevertheless, they were all a select breed; only one applicant in twenty was accepted into the ranks. Ever a law unto himself, Roosevelt also signed up fifty 'gentlemen rankers' from the best colleges and clubs in the East to set the tone for his 'jim-dandy' regiment. The manners of these dudes must have excited a great deal of mirth among their less-advantaged comrades, but they were all superb athletes – football, track and crew stars from the Ivy League, tennis and polo champions, accomplished

huntsmen – and they made a unique and valuable addition to the outfit.

As the month of May drew to a close, the Rough Riders were itching for a fight, and on the twenty-ninth they began to load their 1200 horses and mules onto the seven trains that would take them to join Shafter's V Corps. On 2 June, they detrained on the pine flats six miles north of Tampa and shortly fell in with the rest of the Cavalry Division for brigade maneuvers and other mounted exercises.

There was not much time for further training. The day before the Rough Riders set out for Tampa, the U.S. Navy blockaded the main Spanish fleet in the port of Santiago de Cuba, a city on the island's southern coast and the capital of its easternmost province. If an amphibious American expedition could capture

Troopers of the 9th or 10th Cavalry at Montauk Point, Long Island, immediately after their return from Cuba. One of Roosevelt's Rough Riders who fought alongside these troops at San Juan Hill testified, 'I must say that I never saw braver men anywhere.'

the town and put those ships out of commission, the United States and her coastal cities would be free from any threat of Spanish attack and Cuba would be completely cut off from further enemy reinforcements. There were 12,000 Spanish soldiers at Santiago and 24,000 others scattered in eastern Cuba, but native guerrillas, impassable roads and mountainous jungle terrain kept them from co-operating with each other or receiving help from their fellows elsewhere on the island. Furthermore, nearly a third of the Spanish Army was sick with yellow fever. McKinley decided to strike before most of his volunteers could be organized and trained, and on 31 May, he ordered V Corps to sail for Santiago.

Shafter was not able to get V Corps embarked until 8 June, and even then there was only room for 16,286 of his 25,000 Bluecoats aboard the thirty-one cramped transports at his disposal. As a result, each cavalry regiment had to leave behind four full troops, its sabers and all but the senior officers' horses. After sweltering for six days in Tampa Bay, the men of V Crops finally began their voyage toward battle.

On 22 June 1898, 6000 American soldiers landed unopposed at Daiquirí, a small seacoast town seventeen miles east of Santiago. The next day they occupied Siboney, a port eight miles closer to their final goal. Up to this time, the advance had been led by Brigadier General Henry W. Lawton's Second Infantry Division, with the cavalry following in support. But Fighting Joe Wheeler was not the kind of man to choke on anybody's dust, especially not a Northern doughboy's. On the evening of 23 June, he directed Brigadier General S. B. M. Young to march past Lawton's men toward the enemy's lines at Las Guasimas, a mountain pass four miles away, and 'hit the Spaniards . . . as soon after daybreak as possible.'

Well before the sun rose the next morning, Young's 470 regulars from the 1st and 10th Cavalry and his 500 Rough Riders were on the move. Shortly after 7.00 a.m., they neared the Spanish detachment blocking the way to Santiago. Suddenly the jungle came alive with the eerie crack of Mauser rifles and a chilling ripping sound as Spanish bullets tore through the broad leaves and dug into human flesh and bone. The Americans formed skirmish lines and fanned out, groping their way toward concealed marksmen who were firing with smokeless powder, Roosevelt's volunteers fighting as bravely as the rest. Eventually the 900 troopers, aided by the fire of four Hotchkiss guns, flushed their 1500 Spanish adversaries out into the open and sent them packing for Santiago. Caught up in the exhilaration of the moment, Fighting Joe forgot which war he was in and screeched, 'We've got the damned Yankees on the run!'

The Battle of Las Guasimas was an auspicious debut for the Cavalry Division. Sixteen Americans had been killed and fifty-two wounded during the two hours it lasted, but their opponents had sustained 250 casualties.

Shafter let his men dawdle for a week before moving forward to invest Santiago. The Second Infantry Division was ordered to take the fortified village of El Caney and cut the city's supply route from the north. Then the Cavalry and First Infantry Divisions would storm San Juan Hill. Once that had fallen, the whole of V Corps would attack the San Juan Heights and peel away Santiago's outer defenses.

The grand assault was launched early on the morning of 1 July 1898, and it promptly bogged down. At El Caney, 500 Spanish troops held off a third of Shafter's army for nine hours. Meanwhile, the Cavalry Division marched through a heavy fire and 100 degree heat toward the base of Kettle Hill, an elevation to the right of its main objective. None of the cavalry

Tenth Cavalrymen at Tampa, Florida, march toward their transport, bound for Cuba on 8 June 1898. Except for their short Krag-Jorgensen carbines, there is little to distinguish them from American infantry.

officers had been briefed on the plan of attack for San Juan Hill – or even the part they were to play in it. For an hour and a half the dismounted troopers were kept in an exposed field of waist-high grass as shrapnel and bullets killed and maimed dozens. Sometime after noon, Lieutenant Colonel Roosevelt spied the First Infantry Division climbing the slopes of San Juan Hill, and he sent an urgent note to his brigade commander begging permission to take Kettle Hill.

When an affirmative reply finally came, Roosevelt leaped on his horse, rallied his rowdy Rough Riders, and led them through a startled line of the 10th Cavalry. The volunteers bounded forward, cheering and shooting, Roosevelt leading the way and their regular comrades joining in the spontaneous assault. A barbed wire fence forty yards from the crest stopped Roosevelt's mare, but he clambered off and kept going on foot. When he was ten yards from an enemy trench, up popped a Spaniard, but Roosevelt shot him first with a revolver salvaged from the sunken *Maine*. His faithful orderly killed two more. Within a few minutes, Kettle Hill was in American hands.

Roosevelt had his men use their Krags to support the infantry's faltering effort to overrun San Juan Hill. Then with the 1st and 10th Cavalry, the Rough Riders

Captain Letcher P. Hardeman of the 10th Cavalry was the first commander of the regional remount depot established by the Army in 1908 at Fort Reno, Oklahoma. He is shown here in this H. Charles McBarron, Jr, painting putting one of his horses through its paces for a group of cavalrymen in the 1907-regulation olive-drab service uniform and new russet-strap leather leggings.

PLATE 29: TAKING UP 'THE WHITE MAN'S BURDEN', 1898–1901

86. Private, 1st U.S. Volunteer Cavalry (The Rough Riders), Campaign Dress, 1898: *This regiment's makeshift uniform consisted of the 1884 enlisted man's brown canvas fatigue coat and trousers, the 1883 blue overshirt, a pair of canvas leggings laced down the sides or front, and the 1885 campaign hat. Once in Cuba, the Rough Riders fought in their shirtsleeves. They were issued the Model 1896 .30-caliber Krag carbine and Model 1884 Colt revolver. Ammunition was carried in a double-row cartridge belt of blue webbing.* **87. Lieutenant Colonel (Theodore Roosevelt), 1st U.S. Volunteer Cavalry (The Rough Riders), Field Dress, 1898:** *Roosevelt's tailor made him a uniform of khaki cotton. The blouse had a yellow collar with gilt regimental devices, and yellow shoulder tabs crisscrossed by shoulder strap rank insignia. Roosevelt also used a collar badge to pin up the left brim of his hat. His polka-dot bandana became the unit's trademark. So many other American officers wore khaki uniforms in Cuba they were adopted by the regulations of 1899.* **88. Cook, 1st U.S. Cavalry, Field Dress, 1901:** *The overshirt became the regulation drill and campaign uniform for 'extremely warm weather' in 1901. The cook's chevrons were authorized in 1899. Note the 1899-pattern khaki field trousers and Krag carbine.*

pitched into the fray and the Stars and Stripes were soon seen waving over the San Juan blockhouse. The Americans thought they had won a great victory, but in reality, little more than 2000 Spanish soldiers had fought off Shafter's entire command for most of the day. A third to a half of those brave defenders were struck down, and American losses were close to 1000. The Cavalry Division had suffered heavily. The 10th Cavalry had 20 per cent casualties, and half its officers were killed or wounded. The Rough Riders lost eighty-nine men, more than any other cavalry regiment engaged.

Fearing the consequences of another such bloodbath, Shafter had V Corps dig in on the heights overlooking Santiago and settle in for a siege. On 3 July, the outclassed Spanish fleet tried to make a desperate break from the city's harbor and was promptly shot to scrap metal and toothpicks by the waiting U.S. Navy. Two weeks later, Santiago surrendered to V Corps, just five

PLATE 29: 1898–1901

86. Private, 1st U.S. Volunteer Cavalry
(The Rough Riders), Campaign Dress,
1898

87. Lieutenant Colonel, 1st U.S.
Volunteer Cavalry (The Rough Riders),
Field Dress, 1898

88. Cook, 1st U.S. Cavalry, Field Dress,
1901

A sergeant and three privates of the 13th U.S. Cavalry pose on horseback behind the body of a Villista they helped slay during Pancho Villa's raid on Columbus, New Mexico, 9 March 1916. The men are wearing 1912 olive-drab flannel shirts, and their mounts have Model 1912 combination halter-bridles and service saddles.

days after malaria and other tropical diseases began to sweep through its ranks. To save the soldiers from a slow and lingering death, they were shipped to a quarantine camp at Montauk Point on healthy Long Island. There on 13 September, the Rough Riders were mustered out after 133 days of service. Shafter officially disbanded V Corps on 3 October.

At the outbreak of hostilities, Americans had declared that they had no territorial ambitions in Cuba. They kept that pledge, but they felt they deserved some tangible rewards for their noble little Caribbean crusade. So they used the war as an opportunity to strip Spain of some of her possessions, like Guam and Puerto Rico. The richest prize, the 7000 islands of the Philippine Archipelago, fell into their hands almost by accident. At 4.00 a.m. on 1 May 1898, Commodore

George Dewey's small Asiatic Squadron darted into Manila Bay, and by noon destroyed the Spanish Pacific fleet at a cost of one American dead. Never a man to pass up a bargain, President McKinley organized an army of occupation and eventually decided to annex the Philippines.

From 13 May until the end of June, the 20,000 troops of Major General Wesley Merritt's VIII Corps flocked to San Francisco. Most of them were volunteers from the western states, but Merritt had a nucleus of regulars consisting of three infantry regiments, an artillery battalion and six troops of the 4th Cavalry. Between 25 May and 29 June, enough ships were found to embark 10,600 of the men in three contingents for the Philippines. They found an unpleasant surprise awaiting them. Following the example of the Cubans, the Filipinos had revolted against the Spanish in August 1896. After Dewey's triumph, their president and generalissimo, Don Emilio Aguinaldo, surrounded Manila with an army of 30,000 insurgents and bottled up the 13,000-man Spanish garrison that was based there.

Without disclosing their true intentions, Dewey and Merritt used Aguinaldo as long as they needed him. After arranging a sham battle with the Spanish commander, American troops seized the Philippine capital without warning to their native allies on 13 August, and then refused the rebels admission to their own city! While the Filipinos were willing to accept the Americans as liberators, they were not prepared to exchange one set of masters for another. Keeping his followers in their siege lines, Aguinaldo made hasty preparations for a new revolt. By the end of January 1899, there were 21,000 American soldiers jammed into Manila and its immediate environs, 14,000 of them combat troops. Aguinaldo's host was approaching 80,000, but only half those men had rifles.

Gunfire unexpectedly erupted between American and Filipino outposts along Manila's northern quarter on the evening of 4 February 1899. The Filipino Insurrection was on. Though clearly outnumbered, the Yanks possessed superior discipline and firepower, and they brushed the rebels away from Manila and chased them out of large areas of Luzon without much trouble. The U.S. Army lost 281 officers and 1577 enlisted men in battle during the 'splendid little war' against Spain. Between 4 February and 10 June 1899, 2000 American soldiers were killed in action by the Filipino insurgents, and the end was nowhere in sight.

By the middle of May, Major General Elwell S. Otis, Merritt's successor as commander of VIII Corps, suspended offensive operations on Luzon. The rainy season had started, and campaigning would be impractical until the fall. It was also necessary for him to completely overhaul his forces. With the ratification of the Treaty of Paris on 6 February, and the official end of the war with Spain, the American volunteers in the Philippines were eligible for discharge. Otis took advantage of the monsoon lull to ship them home. Recognizing America's new commitments abroad, Congress granted the Army an ample supply of manpower to tackle its enlarged duties, in a measure passed on 2 March. The regular establishment was continued at 65,000 for the next two years, and 35,000 more volunteers were raised. To replace those that had been dissolved, three additional regiments of United States Volunteer Cavalry were authorized. Each troop was supposed to boast 100 enlisted men, every one a crack shot and skilled rider, who could serve as easily on foot as on horseback. Because of such high standards, only two such outfits were organized. The first of these, the 11th U.S. Volunteer Cavalry, was recruited mainly from discharged volunteers whose units were leaving the Philippines.

By 3 October 1899, the rains were letting up and

Brigadier General John J. Pershing and his staff splash across the Santa Maria River during one of his frequent inspection tours with the Punitive Expedition.

The 11th Cavalry hot on Pancho Villa's trail, spring 1916. Pershing kept his troopers in the saddle almost constantly in his determination to wear Villa down. As one officer complained in a letter home: 'Old Indian campaigners say that they have never seen men or horses [treated] as Pershing is treating them.'

General Otis had 47,465 regulars and volunteers poised at Manila for his dry season offensive. Some 16,018 more were en route from the United States, but Otis would not wait for them. He sent three massive columns racing through the central Luzon plain to smash Aguinaldo's army. American commanders made an imaginative use of their cavalry and their mounted Filipino scouts to scatter any significant concentrations of *insurrectos* and capture their supply depots and headquarters. Leading two squadrons of the 3rd Cavalry, some artillery and a battalion of the 22nd Infantry, Brigadier General S. M. B. Young effectively spearheaded the march of Major General Henry Lawton's First Division. Catching a scent of Aguinaldo's trail, Young reduced his column to one troop of the 3rd Cavalry and a battalion of 300 Maccabebe scouts. He hounded Aguinaldo just as mercilessly as he drove his own command, which is demonstrated in this dispatch he sent to Otis toward the latter part of November:

> Aguinaldo is now a fugitive and an outlaw, seeking security in escape to the mountains or by sea. My cavalry has ridden down his forces wherever found, utterly routing them in every instance, capturing and liberating many prisoners ... My men have had no supplies from the government for the past five days ...

Despite such strenuous efforts, Aguinaldo refused to surrender his people's independence. When things got too hot for him in central Luzon, he disappeared into the rough country to the north and inaugurated guerrilla warfare. As the contest entered this frustrating stage, the Americans' real ordeal commenced. Over 2000 of them were shot, speared or boloed as they tried to pacify the archipelago over the next two years. These deaths were not unavenged. By 4 June 1900, the War Department claimed the deaths of 14,643 insurgents and the wounding of 3297 more, but still the fighting and the killing went on.

Between 1899 and 1901, nine regular regiments of the U.S. Cavalry did duty in the Philippines. As the 11th Volunteer Cavalry and the other volunteer units raised in 1899 were due to be disbanded in July 1901, Congress took steps in February of that year to fill the void with regulars. A comprehensive act reorganized the artillery and increased the size of the other two combat arms. Five new cavalry regiments, the 11th, 12th, 13th, 14th and 15th, were created. The table of organization for all fifteen was altered with the addition of a chaplain, a captain, three second lieutenants, a commissary sergeant and two color sergeants. The President was further empowered to raise each troop from 100 to 164 enlisted men at his discretion. Usually the units that benefitted from this elastic clause were those stationed in the nation's new island possessions.

PLATE 30: ON VILLA'S TRAIL, 1916-7

89. Captain, 11th U.S. Cavalry, Field Dress, 1916: *The overshirt and breeches were worn without the service coat for summer campaigning. The Model 1911 service hat was issued to both officers and men, although goggles were privately acquired. The captain's Model 1912 officer's belt and accoutrements are held in place by the Model 1908 shoulder belt. High russet leather boots complete his outfit. He is armed with the Model 1911 Colt automatic pistol.* **90. Color Sergeant, 10th U.S. Cavalry, Service Uniform, 1916:** *The olive-drab 1912-pattern service uniform was made of wool for winter wear and cotton for summer. The 1912-pattern cavalry equipments included a cartridge belt and bandoleer. Mounted men were issued russet leather strap leggings in 1907. A trooper carried the .30-caliber U.S. Model 1903 Springfield rifle and .45-caliber Model 1911 Colt automatic pistol. Cavalry regiments received yellow silk standards in 1887, and the pattern was slightly modified in 1890. The Model 1912 experimental horse equipments are illustrated here.* **91. Colonel (H. J. Slocum), 13th U.S. Cavalry, Field Dress, 1917:** *Many of Pershing's officers provided themselves with short fur-lined overcoats to guard against the cold nights in the Chihuahua foothills. On 30 December 1916, the Army adopted an overcoat for cavalry officers similar to the one pictured here (except it had a rounded collar and flaps over both pockets). The objects displayed on the ammunition box in the foreground are, from left to right, a feedbag, a rasp, a nail puller, a field anvil, a picket pin and a hammer. The blue bottle contains Kreso disinfectant.*

Just as the five newborn cavalry regiments started recruiting, the Philippine Insurrection started to wind down. Frustrated by a cunning and elusive enemy some American soldiers grew as cruel as their Spanish predecessors. They murdered their prisoners and tortured suspected rebels. Others, however, treated the Filipinos honorably, winning them over with administrative, educational, economic and sanitary reforms. On 23 February 1901, Aguinaldo was captured in a clever ruse, and by 19 April, he had been persuaded to tell his followers to lay down their arms. Sporadic violence was to continue for quite some time, but by 4 July 1902, things had quieted down enough for President Theodore Roosevelt to declare an end to the uprising.

89. Captain, 11th U.S. Cavalry, Field
Dress, 1916

90. Color Sergeant, 10th U.S. Cavalry,
Service Uniform, 1916

91. Colonel, 13th U.S. Cavalry, Field
Dress, 1917

Flowering first among some progressive officers in the late 1880s, a new spirit of professionalism took hold in the U.S. Army as it settled into its Imperial mission and the twentieth century. In the never-ending quest for increased efficiency, the cavalry became the object of considerable experimentation. Influenced by European heavy cavalry, some officers convinced their superiors to implement a tighter six-troop organization and a two-rank tactical formation to facilitate massed charges with the saber. These innovations did not set well with most of the pony soldiers. They preferred to fight mounted in open order with the pistol, and the corps quickly reverted to those traditional American practices.

One lasting change came in 1906, when each cavalry regiment received a machine-gun platoon. Six years later a separate headquarters and supply detachment were grafted onto the regimental organization, and in 1915 these three adjuncts became experimental troops in their own right. By 1916, the U.S. Cavalry was 15,424 men strong. Each regiment consisted of a headquarters troop, a supply troop, a machine-gun troop and twelve rifle troops. Modernization had come without the sacrifice of national characteristics. Just how well this job had been done was soon to be seen.

With the ousting of the tyrant Porfirio Diaz in 1911, Mexico was plunged into a convulsive revolution as the believers in a genuinely representative government battled supporters of the old form of military dictatorship. By 19 October 1915, the Liberals under Venustiano Carranza were plainly in the ascendancy, and Secretary of State Robert Lansing announced de facto American recognition of Carranza's government. This gesture incurred the enmity of Pancho Villa, a former Liberal general and bandit chieftain who hoped to control Mexico himself. Villa had been defeated several times by Carranzista forces, but he believed he could recoup his losses by attacking United States soil. Such an act would inevitably provoke retaliation. Carranza was too weak to prevent any American violation of Mexican sovereignty, and if that happened his government could be discredited among the populace.

At 3.30 a.m. on 9 March 1916, 485 Villistas thundered through the border town of Columbus, New Mexico, shouting '*Viva Villa! Viva Villa! Muerte a los gringos!*' Eighteen Americans were murdered and eight wounded in the streets. Four rifle troops, the machine-gun troop and the headquarters of the 13th Cavalry were lodged in Columbus, and though surprised, the pony soldiers recovered quickly. After a sharp exchange, they cleared the Villistas out of Columbus and chased them back into Mexico, slaying 100 to 200.

President Woodrow Wilson reacted to Villa's Columbus Raid the next day by instructing the Army to send an armed force 'into Mexico with the sole object of capturing Villa and preventing further raids by his band.' Brigadier General John J. Pershing, a brilliant officer who had served with the 10th Cavalry in Cuba and the 15th Cavalry in the Philippines, took charge of this 'Punitive Expedition' at Columbus on 14 March. There were 192 officers and 4800 men under his command, and because of the nature of the task ahead, most of them were cavalry.

The Punitive Expedition was divided into three brigades. The 1st Provisional Cavalry Brigade consisted of the 11th and 13th Cavalry and a battery of the 6th Field Artillery. The 7th and 10th Cavalry and another battery from the 6th Field Artillery composed the 2nd Provisional Cavalry Brigade. The 1st Provisional Infantry Brigade contained the 6th and 16th Infantry and all of Pershing's support troops.

Some tired cavalrymen with the Punitive Expedition water their horses in a shady spot. Note the goggles on the campaign hat of the trooper adjusting his mount's bridle at left.

Never a man to waste a second, Pershing crossed over into Mexico on 15 March 1916, and pushed ahead with the 2nd Provisional Cavalry Brigade. Establishing his headquarters at Colonia Dublán two days later, he learned that Villa was lurking fifty to sixty miles to the south. Pershing boldly decided to split the brigade up into three parallel columns that would get behind Villa and cut off his escape to the south, east or west.

At 3.00 a.m. on 18 March, 675 weary 7th Cavalrymen clattered out of Colonia Dublán. The other two columns were drawn from the 10th Cavalry. One consisted of the 2nd Squadron and the machine-gun troop (275 officers and men), and the other consisted of the 1st Squadron (210 of all ranks). They departed by train the next day and separated further down the line.

When the rest of the Punitive Expedition reached Colonia Dublán on 20 March, the energetic Pershing broke his remaining cavalry up into flying columns and sent them out on 20, 21, 24 and 30 March, respectively. Their job was to traverse the areas intersected by the three parallel columns and wear Villa down. The first flying column was manned by five troops of the 13th Cavalry. The second was composed of the 3rd Squadron of the 10th Cavalry and the machine-gun troop and a squadron from the 13th. The third and fourth were two 'provisional squadrons' from the 11th Cavalry. A provisional squadron consisted of 265 to 300 of the very best men chosen from all the 11th's twelve rifle troops.

By flooding the deserts and foothills of Chihuahua with American cavalry, Pershing hoped to dig Villa out of his many hideouts and force him into the open. It was a sound plan, but it entailed a lot of tough work and hardship. Even Pershing, who was to be denounced as a slave driver by some of his subordinates, later admitted, 'I do not believe that the cavalry in all its experience has done as hard work as the cavalry with this expedition.'

Within a very brief period, Pershing's strategy was paying dividends. Although the Americans never captured Villa, they made life extremely unpleasant for him and dramatically diminished the size of his band. Following a strong lead, Colonel George H. Dodd, the commander of the 2nd Cavalry Brigade and the 7th Cavalry, force-marched his regiment for seventeen hours toward the village of Guerrero. At dawn on 29 March 1916, Dodd and the 370 troopers who were able to keep up with him surprised 500 to 600 Villistas at Guerrero. The Mexicans chose to flee, but the 7th

Private Keen, Troop B, 5th U.S. Cavalry, in camp at El Valle, Mexico, 27 July 1916. This candid close-up affords a good view of the trooper's 1916 olive-drab shirt (which had pocket flaps, unlike the 1912 pattern), goggles, Model 1903 Springfield rifle, and 1910 pattern russet leather strap leggings.

blocked some of their escape routes and cut down many of the fugitives. At least thirty-five of the bandits were slain, and a number of bodies lay unseen in the undergrowth and broken terrain. The Americans also captured two machine-guns, forty-four rifles, thirteen horses and twenty-three mules, and all for the price of just five slightly injured. Around the same time, the reunited 1st and 2nd Squadrons of the 10th Cavalry ran into 150 Villistas at Aguas Calientes. The Mexicans got away before the 10th could come to grips with them, but the skirmish was notable as the first in-

A group of 11th Cavalrymen at Troop C's open air barber shop at Colonia Dublán, the Mexican base of the Punitive Expedition. Two troopers have cut the sleeves off their under-shirts. Five of the others have on their 1916 olive-drab shirts, worn without coats in the summer.

stance in which American soldiers employed overhead machine-gun fire against a real enemy.

Had this kind of thing been allowed to continue, Villa and his marauders might well have been exterminated, but fate intervened. Instead of welcoming American aid against a common foe, the Carranzistas resented the fact that there was a foreign army killing Mexicans on Mexican soil. From the very outset, First Chief Carranza indignantly demanded the unconditional withdrawal of the Punitive Expedition, and relations with the United States strained to the breaking point. On 12 April 1916, a mob of Carranzista soldiers and civilians fell on a squadron of the 13th Cavalry as it cantered through the town of Parral. Less than 100 strong, the Americans bravely held their assailants at bay, killing more than forty, fought their way out into open country and then holed up at a ranch called Santa Cruz de Villegas. They held out there until nightfall, when they were relieved by the 10th Cavalry and a provisional squadron of the 11th.

Fearing that an all-out war with Mexico was in the offing, Pershing wisely called in his parallel and flying columns and confined his cavalry's searches to five constricted military districts. Luck was still with the Yankees. On 22 April, the 7th Cavalry cornered forty Villistas at Tomochic and scored thirty-one confirmed kills. Major Robert Howze, the machine-gun troop

and six rifle troops of the 11th Cavalry, and a detachment of Apache scouts fell in with 200 bandits at the ranch of Ojos Azules early on 5 May. More than sixty Mexicans were killed, and not an American was scratched.

All the while, Carranza was intensifying his complaints about the activities of the Punitive Expedition and mobilizing his forces to crush it if it did not get out of Mexico. To support Pershing, President Wilson ordered the 5000 National Guardsmen of Texas, New Mexico and Arizona into Federal service. As the crisis deepened, Congress passed the National Defense Act on 3 June 1916. This timely legislation aimed at expanding the regular army to 220,000 officers and men over the next five years. This increase envisioned the creation of ten new cavalry regiments and the formation of two full mounted divisions, with nine regiments apiece. The law also proposed a five-year increase of the National Guard to 450,000, and it provided that the state forces would come under complete Federal control in time of war or during what the President deemed was a grave public emergency.

On 16 June 1916, the Carranzista commander at Chihuahua City warned Pershing not to let his soldiers march south, east or west any more. He was not joking. There were now 22,000 Mexican government troops, eighty cannon and 100 machine-guns concentrated at Chihuahua City. Rather than curtail his operations entirely, Pershing resolved to test this new threat to the limit. Over the next two days, he dispatched Troops C and K of the 10th Cavalry to the east to reconnoiter Carranzista dispositions around Ahumada.

At the town of Carrizal on 21 June, 300 Carranzista soldiers placed themselves astride the Americans' line of march and warned them to go no further. There were only three officers and eighty ebony troopers in those two troops, but they were not about to let any number of Mexicans stop them from doing their duty without a fight. In the bloody confrontation that followed, two officers and ten black enlisted men were killed, ten were wounded and the rest were forced into a precipitate retreat. However, the Mexicans knew they had been facing the vaunted Buffalo Soldiers: even though they had the help of a machine-gun, seventy-four Carranzistas perished under American rifle fire, including their commanding general.

By now, war seemed unavoidable. President Wilson ordered out the remainder of the National Guard on

18 June, and by the end of July there were 112,000 citizen soldiers massed along the border. That same month the 16th and 17th Cavalry were organized at Forts Sam Houston and Bliss in Texas. Fortunately, there were no more major clashes and tempers cooled. As the year passed away, American diplomatic relations with Germany drastically worsened, and it became imperative to end what had become a fruitless minor adventure. Between 28 January and 5 February 1917, the Punitive Expedition evacuated Colonia Dublán and returned to the United States.

The Punitive Expedition was the U.S. Army's last major use of cavalry. Pershing's troopers never hung Pancho Villa up by his heels, but they accomplished their main objective by preventing additional Villista raids on American territory, and they made sure that many of the raiders never raided again. By 30 June 1916, 273 of Villa's band had been killed, 108 wounded, nineteen captured and sixty had given themselves up to the Carranzistas. Of even more importance was the fact that the Punitive Expedition went a long way toward preparing the Army and the nation for their entry into World War I on the side of the Allies.

The withdrawal of the Punitive Expedition. Troop E, 7th U.S. Cavalry, enters Camp Ojo Federico, Mexico, on its dusty march back to the United States, 31 January 1917. Note the troop's red and white guidon and the widespread use of goggles.

Ignoring the repeated protests of President Wilson, Imperial Germany announced the resumption of unrestricted submarine warfare in January 1917. Unwilling to endure the interruption of her trans-Atlantic trade and propelled by a deep-rooted sympathy for Great Britain and France, the United States declared war on 6 April 1917.

The nation was hardly prepared for what was in store, but thanks to the Punitive Expedition it had the perfect man to command the American Expeditionary Force, namely John J. Pershing. The regular army and National Guard had a rudimentary plan for expansion and there was a combat-seasoned cadre of professional officers and non-coms to train and lead a citizens' army; and the National Guard had received a practice run in mobilization. Because of all this, the 'Doughboys' would be in France in time to help administer the *coup de grâce* to the German military machine.

A month after hostilities commenced, Congress authorized the immediate implementation of the National Defense Act, which entailed the organization of the 18th through the 25th U.S. Cavalry Regiments, along with other regular units. On 18 May, the national legislature created twenty more cavalry regiments for the massive National Army that was being raised to fight Germany. Both of these measures were unrealistic. The fighting on the Western Front was being done from trenches, with bolt-action rifles,

machine-guns and artillery. It was no place for cavalry. A man on a horse made too good a target, and under the conditions then existing, his mobility could not compensate for his excessive vulnerability. Fortunately for all concerned, enough influential people recognized the mistake. On 1 October, Congress ordered the eight new regular cavalry regiments converted into field artillery. In August of 1918, the twenty National Army horse units were reorganized into thirty-nine artillery and trench mortar batteries.

The only pony soldiers to accompany the American Expeditionary Force belonged to the 2nd, 3rd, 6th and 15th Cavalry, but they were employed behind the lines as farriers and grooms to process remounts for the transport services, medical corps and artillery. Ever true to his old branch, General Pershing was importuning Congress as late as the summer of 1918 for eight full cavalry regiments to exploit any breakthroughs in German lines achieved by his Doughboys.

Finally toward the end of August, some American horsemen got their chance to taste modern combat. On the eve of the St Mihiel Offensive, Troops B, D, F and H of the 2nd Cavalry were formed into a provisional squadron of fourteen officers and 404 men mounted on convalescent horses from the veterinary hospital. Their commander was Lieutenant Colonel Oliver P. M. Hazzard, and their job was to serve as couriers and scouts. On the night of 11 September 1918, Hazzard led three of his troops into 'No Man's Land' in front of the trenches of the First American Division. Somehow they managed to slip by enemy patrols and penetrate to Nonsard, a spot five miles behind the original German line, by noon the next day. Once there, all hell broke loose, and the Yank cavalry was routed. Hazzard's squadron continued to serve through the Meuse-Argonne Offensive, but by mid-October, it was down to 150 mounted effectives and was withdrawn from the front.

Mexican-American relations took a long time to heal after the Punitive Expedition, and continuing strife in that unstable country kept most of the U.S. Cavalry along the border during and after World War I. On 9 January 1918, Troop E of the 10th Cavalry fought the Army's last Indian battle when it captured ten Yaqui renegades who had fled from Mexico to Arizona. Late on the afternoon of 27 August, a customs house dispute blossomed into a full-fledged shooting match at Nogales, Texas, when Mexican soldiers started firing across the international boundary.

An American cavalry sergeant photographed in 1918. His saber and horse equipment are circa 1906, which may mean that he belonged to a National Guard unit.

Troops A and C of the 10th Cavalry came to the town's defense, killing 129 Mexicans and forcing the rest to raise a white flag. Three American soldiers and two civilians also died in the senseless violence.

In the summer of 1919, Pancho Villa was strong enough to make another bid for power, and on the night of 14 June, he attacked the Carranzistas at Juarez, a town just across the border from El Paso, Texas. The fighting raged two full days, and as the final hours of the sixteenth ticked away, it became clear to Brigadier General James B. Erwin, the American commander at El Paso, that the Villistas were deliberately firing into his town. He decided to drive them from the border.

Throwing the 24th Infantry directly into Juarez, he had the 7th Cavalry and two squadrons of the 5th cross the Rio Grande a few miles downstream and try to head Villa off. The wily outlaw slipped out of the trap, but the American horsemen caught up with his band shortly after 9.00 a.m. on 17 June. In the skirmish that resulted, close to 200 Villistas were killed, and the gringos were out of Mexico by 5.00 p.m.

The Battle of Juarez ended Pancho Villa's days as a serious threat to the peace of both Mexico and the United States. His army was shattered by this total defeat and fell apart. In a very real sense, it was also the swan song of the U.S. Cavalry. With Villa and his ilk neutralized, the cavalry had outlived its usefulness.

9 Requiem for the Horse Cavalry
1918-44

With the end of World War I, the United States quickly demobilized the more than 3,000,000 citizen soldiers who had been called-up. By 1 January 1920, the U.S. Army held 130,000 men, most of them regulars. The General Staff hoped the nation would retain her position as a major world power and proposed a peacetime military establishment of 500,000 professional troops and a vast reserve created by universal military service. Congress was not ready for so bold a departure, however, and it devised a new National Defense Act, which became law on 4 June 1920.

The National Defense Act of 1920 set the size of the Army at 280,000, and it effected many organizational changes. It established an Army Air Service, Chemical Warfare Service and Finance Department. The four combat arms of infantry, field artillery, coast artillery and cavalry received their own administrative headquarters in the War Department. The first occupant of the new office of Chief of Cavalry was Major General Willard A. Holbrook, and he and his successors were the General Staff's main advisors on cavalry matters. Under the National Defense Act, Holbrook was responsible for 950 officers and 20,000 men, but as of 30 June 1920, the mounted arm numbered 965 officers and 15,812 troopers.

Curiously enough, Congress never provided enough money to support the National Defense Act. The watchword of government in the 1920s was economy, and amazing as it might seem, in those fabled days Federal budget cuts were made at the expense of the armed forces. This frugal impulse was encouraged by the widespread disillusionment fostered by World War I. Americans had entered the conflict to 'make the world safe for democracy', but they found their European cousins did not welcome Yankee solutions to their problems. This bruised naïveté and a general revulsion to the senseless slaughter that occurred on the Western Front brewed a strong mood of isolationism and anti-militarism, which pervaded the country for the next two decades.

Insufficient annual appropriations caused Army manpower to plummet from 150,000 in 1921 to 118,750 in 1927. Slashing cuts had to be made in every branch. The U.S. Cavalry was abruptly halved in 1922. The 15th, 16th and 17th Cavalry were deactivated. The remaining fourteen regiments were limited to a headquarters troop, a service troop and six lettered troops. That meant the mounted arm lost ninety-eight troops, in addition to three entire regiments. The only good news came from halfway across the globe, where the Philippine Scouts were permitted to organize a horse regiment. The Scouts were an integral part of the U.S. Army, with American officers and Filipino enlisted men. In the vain hope that its domain would someday reach the twenty-five regiments promised by the National Defense Act of 1916, the Office of the

General John J. Pershing and Colonel Harry N. Cootes inspect the machine-gun troop of the 10th Cavalry at Fort Myer, Virginia, in February 1932. Both Colonel Cootes and the buffalo soldiers are in the 1926 service uniform.

Chief of Cavalry named the new outfit the 26th Cavalry.

By mid-1923, the U.S. Cavalry had been pared down to 721 officers and 8887 men. There were supposed to be two mounted divisions, but only the First Cavalry Division was activated with the 5th, 7th, 8th and 12th Cavalry. The division was also assigned two machine-gun squadrons (one for each brigade), a battalion of horse artillery, a mounted engineer battalion, an ambulance company, and signal, ordnance and veterinary troops.

Until the end of the 1930s, the Army was little more than a struggling school for soldiers, with skeleton formations and antiquated arms. The pony soldiers had little more to do than train and look pretty for ceremonial functions. With no Indians to fight, their officers kept fit playing polo. The only action the cavalry saw during these years was against its own people. At the height of the Great Depression in the summer of 1932, more than 20,000 jobless veterans of the Great War descended on Washington, D.C., to demand the immediate payment of a bonus due to them in 1945. They erected shanty camps or occupied wrecked and abandoned buildings around the capital. Government leaders were convinced that the ranks of

Gas-masked 3rd Cavalrymen clatter down Pennsylvania Avenue on 28 July 1932, as they prepare to clear the Bonus Army out of Washington, D.C. They are in summer field dress, with the laced leather boots that were issued in 1931.

PLATE 31: OVER THERE AND BACK AGAIN, 1917–38

92. Private First Class, 2nd U.S. Cavalry, Field Dress, 1918: *American cavalrymen went to France in the woolen 1912 service uniform. Special combat gear included a steel trench helmet manufactured along British guidelines and a gas mask, which was housed in a pouch slung over the right shoulder. The 1917-pattern leggings were made of canvas and faced with russet leather.* **93. Captain, Machine-Gun Squadron, First Cavalry Division, Service Dress, 1924** *(at center): This officer's working attire consists of the 1921 service hat, the 1924-pattern service shirt and breeches, and pair of undress boots. Note the 1924-pattern squadron insignia on his collar (an MG separated by crossed-sabers). The 1921-pattern insignia had an MG surmounting crossed-sabers. The captain is tinkering with a jammed Model 1917 Browning .30-caliber heavy water-cooled machine-gun.* **94. Second Lieutenant, 2nd U.S. Cavalry, Service Dress, 1918** *(in background): Second lieutenants had plain shoulder loops on their service coats, but all other officers were issued metallic insignia to show their rank there. This subaltern's horse died in the Model 1917 officer's field saddle and Model 1912 combination halter-bridle.* **95. Major (George S. Patton), 3rd U.S. Cavalry, Full Dress Uniform, 1929** *(at right): This basic uniform was introduced in 1902, modified in 1907 and 1911, and finally replaced in 1938. The 1921-pattern officer's dress boots are worn with nickel-plated spurs and chains. Among Patton's medals are the Distinguished Service Cross and Distinguished Service Medal, which he won with the Tank Corps in World War 1.*

the 'Bonus Expeditionary Force' had been infiltrated by Reds intent on bringing a Bolshevik revolution to America. After the Bonus Marchers had a minor scuffle with local police on 28 July, the Army was summoned to clear them out. The 3rd Cavalry from Fort Myer, Virginia, was the first unit on the scene that very afternoon, fielding fourteen officers, 217 enlisted men and 213 horses. It was soon joined by a battalion of the 12th Infantry and a detachment of tanks. Together these units broke up large crowds of Bonus Marchers along Pennsylvania Avenue, using tear gas and drawn sabers to move them along, and by the next day they had levelled the veterans' camps. This highly publicized incident did not endear the pony soldiers to their fellow countrymen.

92. Private First Class, 2nd U.S. Cavalry, Field Dress, 1918

93. Captain, Machine-Gun Squadron, First Cavalry Division, Service Dress, 1924

94. Second Lieutenant, 2nd U.S. Cavalry, Service Dress, 1918

95. Major, 3rd U.S. Cavalry, Full Dress Uniform, 1929

The U.S. Cavalry faced a foe even more ominous in the interwar period, and that was mechanization. While mounted units had been practically banished from the Western Front early in the late war, the tank had emerged as the means to restore mobility to the battlefield. The American Army had raised a Tank Corps of 15,870 officers and men for this purpose, although less than half of them got to France before 11 November 1918. In 1920 the Tank Corps was abolished by the National Defense Act and its vehicles and personnel consigned to the infantry, but there were many people in the service and in the growing automobile industry who claimed that the machine should replace the horse.

Cavalry officers disagreed. They pointed out that America's next war would probably not be fought on the cleared, rolling fields of northern France, but on rougher terrain. The rickety motor vehicles of the day could be stopped by trees, underbrush or steep gradients, but horses could go anywhere. It was a strong argument, but the gentlemen in khaki riding breeches hedged their bet by greatly augmenting cavalry firepower.

In February 1928, the brigade machine-gun squadrons were disbanded and the machine-gun troop was reinstituted in each mounted regiment. It was equipped with eight .30-caliber Browning water-cooled machine-guns, three 37 mm guns to knock out enemy tanks and strongpoints, and three light cross-country cars mounting anti-aircraft machine-guns. One hundred and eight personnel were needed to man all these destructive new weapons, and their reassignment was made possible by reducing the number of lettered troops in each regiment from six to four. Counting 119 officers and men, a lettered troop was divided into three platoons of riflemen and one armed with .30-caliber Browning machine rifles. With the addition of a seventy-eight-man headquarters troop and a band of twenty-eight members, a cavalry regiment averaged 690 of all ranks. In October 1930, the machine rifle was replaced with the Browning air-cooled machine-gun. At war-strength a horse outfit could now bring sixteen water-cooled and forty-eight air-cooled machine-guns and 624 Springfield rifles to bear on an advancing adversary!

For all their love of animals, there were some cavalry officers who recognized that improved machines could join the horse in certain combat situations. In the January 1928 issue of *The Cavalry Journal*, Major

General Herbert B. Crosby, the current Chief of Cavalry, recommended that the First Cavalry Division receive an armored car squadron, a light tank company, an Air Corps observation squadron and more artillery. His proposals were soon implemented, but with a feebleness that characterized most Army reforms at the time. Authorized by the War Department on 15 February 1928, the armored car squadron was supposed to consist of a headquarters, three troops, thirty-six fighting cars, eighteen officers and 260 men. Only one troop with five officers, eighty-four troopers and twelve cars was activated during peacetime, but as late as July, only two dozen personnel had been assigned to the new unit. Nearly a year later, the 1st Armored Car Troop was making its patrols along the Mexican border in five small, open cars, five pick-up trucks and one large truck.

Cavalrymen figured prominently in the Army's two abortive experiments with a mechanized force in 1928 and 1930–31. On 17 November 1931, the War Department announced that the 1st Cavalry would be mechanized. Early in 1933, the regiment was shipped from Marfa, Texas, to Fort Knox, Kentucky, where it exchanged its horses for twelve armored cars and three dozen light tanks (then known as 'combat cars'). The 13th Cavalry was ordered to undergo the same process on 5 September 1936. Early in 1938, the 1st and 13th Cavalry (Mechanized) were joined by a battalion of field artillery and a quartermaster company and formed into the 7th Cavalry Brigade (Mechanized) under Brigadier General Daniel Van Voorhis. Van Voorhis was succeeded in September by Colonel Adna R. Chaffee, another far-sighted cavalryman who was destined to become the father of American armor.

Since 1927, the mounted arm had been carrying on experiments with 'portée cavalry' – using trucks and trailers to more-speedily transport horses and their riders to their zone of operations. Thirteen years later the 4th and 6th Cavalry became partially mechanized with the reception of new $2\frac{1}{2}$ ton 4×4 truck tractors and semi-trailers capable of carrying eight mounts and troopers.

With the outbreak of World War 2 in September 1939, the United States began taking cautious steps to prepare the armed forces for her possible entry into the struggle. By 1940, the U.S. Cavalry had 13,000 officers and men distributed in four mechanized or partially mechanized regiments, a regiment of Philippine Scouts and ten regular horse regiments. Within a year,

that number soared to 53,000, but the days of the pony soldier were numbered.

Military men around the world were astounded by the sweeping successes of the German *Panzer* divisions in the swift conquest of Poland, France and the Low Countries. For the Third Army Maneuvers held during the spring of 1940 in Georgia and Louisiana, Chaffee's 7th Mechanized Cavalry Brigade and some infantry tank battalions were organized into a provi-

The 3rd Cavalry marches along Pennsylvania Avenue toward the Capitol, shortly after its arrival from Fort Myer on 28 July 1932, to disperse the Bonus Marchers. Following unheralded in the pony soldiers' wake is an omen of their coming doom – the tank.

sional armored division. Chaffee's tanks and armored cars ran circles around the harried troopers of Major General Kenyon A. Joyce's First Cavalry Division, and they convinced the Army brass that the horse no longer had an important part to play in modern warfare.

After Pearl Harbor, the General Staff was saddled with the task of sending massive armies to fight in the Pacific, Asia, Africa and Europe, and it was decided to dismount the U.S. Cavalry. Horses would take up too much room on the transports. The First Cavalry Division compiled an admirable battle record as infantry in New Guinea and in the recapture of the Philippines. The Second Cavalry Division was partially deactivated in July 1942, when the 2nd, 3rd, 11th and 14th Cavalry were reorganized into 'armored regiments'. That left only the 9th and 10th Cavalry of the 4th Cavalry Brigade. In 1943 the division was revived when those four defunct regiments were recreated as mechanized cavalry, but it was dehorsed and deactivated once and for all by May 1944.

The only American outfit to fight on horseback during World War 2 was the 26th Cavalry, Philippine Scouts. As of 30 November 1941, this crack regiment numbered fifty-five officers and 787 enlisted men. When the Japanese landed on Lingayen Gulf in the north of Luzon on 22 December, the stoutest resistance to their inexorable drive inland came from the 26th. Although not equipped with anti-tank guns, the Scouts held off two enemy armored regiments and two infantry regiments at Damortis for six hours on the day of the invasion. On 24 December, the 26th Cavalry repulsed a tank assault on Binalonan, checked a drive by enemy infantry and then launched a blistering counterattack. The Japanese had to call in more tanks to stop the frenzied Scouts. Although reduced to 450 effectives, the cavalrymen kept Binalonan in their possession until dusk, when they neatly extricated themselves.

The 26th was shortly pulled off the line and built back up to 657 officers and men. During the first week of January 1942, it held open the gateway to Bataan as the half-trained native divisions and the dazed American battalions streamed onto the mountainous jungle peninsula for a final, desperate stand. Food was so short on Bataan that the 26th Cavalry had to turn its horses over to be butchered, and it was converted into a motorized rifle squadron and a mechanized squadron manning scout cars and Bren carriers. The Scouts

PLATE 32: OUT WITH A BANG: THE 26TH CAVALRY, PHILIPPINE SCOUTS, 1941–2

96. Sergeant Major, 26th U.S. Cavalry, Class-A Uniform, 1941: *For garrison duty at Fort Stotsenburg, the 1926-pattern service coat and breeches, 1912 garrison belt with holstered .45-caliber automatic, and 1931-pattern laced boots were worn. The Department of the Philippines shoulder patch was displayed on the coat. The sun helmet was donned at the discretion of the officer of the day.*

97. Private, 26th U.S. Cavalry, Summer Field Dress, 1942: *Suntan colored shirts and breeches served as the regiment's campaign uniform during the withdrawal to and siege of Bataan. World War 1-style tin helmets were given a coat of slick-finish green paint and then sprinkled with sand when the paint was still wet. The 26th was armed with the M1 .30-caliber rifle and .45-caliber automatic pistol. Mounts were decked out in the Model 1928 modified McClellan saddle and full packs.* **98. Captain (C. Cosby Kerney), 26th U.S. Cavalry, Summer Field Dress, 1942:** *The 26th's officers were still attired in the 1924-pattern service shirt and breeches. A compass case occupied a spot on the 1921 officer's field belt in front of the holster. Officers and men always secured their pistols to a lanyard draped around the neck. The gas mask case rested on the left hip from a strap slung over the opposite shoulder. Kerney was the only man in the 26th to use the old Model 1903 Springfield rifle in action against the Japanese. This plate based on information and artifacts furnished by Colonel C. Cosby Kerney, U.S. Army (Retired), who served as a captain with the 26th Cavalry in the Luzon and Bataan campaigns.*

fought on bravely to the bitter end. When Bataan was surrendered on 9 April 1942, the 26th was one of the few units that had not been broken and was still keeping the Japanese at bay. Its performance wrote a noble ending to the saga of the U.S. Cavalry.

The dash and spirit of the pony soldier lived on among the Army's Armored Force in the person of Lieutenant General George S. Patton, a former colonel of the 3rd and 5th Cavalry. He taught his tankers a pair of dicta, which he had coined during his days with the horse cavalry: 'Get around if you can't get through,' and 'The secret of success in mounted operations is to *grab the enemy by the nose and kick him in the pants.*' Whether they ride today in tanks or helicopters, that élan is still shared by the troopers of the U.S. Cavalry.

96. Sergeant Major, 26th U.S. Cavalry,
Class-A Uniform, 1941

97. Private, 26th U.S. Cavalry, Summer
Field Dress, 1942

98. Captain, 26th U.S. Cavalry, Summer
Field Dress, 1942

Select Bibliography

Bauer, K. Jack, *The Mexican War, 1846–1848*, Macmillan Publishing Co., Inc., New York, 1974.

Blumenson, Martin (ed), *The Patton Papers* (2 vols), Houghton Mifflin Company, Boston, 1972–74.

Carroll, John M. (ed), *The Black Military Experience in the American West*, Liveright, New York, 1971.

Clenenden, Clarence C., *Blood on the Border: The United States Army and the Mexican Irregulars*, The Macmillan Company, New York, 1969.

Cosmas, Graham A., *An Army for Empire: The United States Army in the Spanish-American War*, University of Missouri Press, Columbia, 1971.

Elting, John R. (ed), *Military Uniforms in America*, (2 vols) Presidio Press, San Rafael, California, 1974–77.

Gates, John Morgan, *Schoolbooks and Krags: The United States Army in the Philippines, 1898–1902*, Greenwood Press, Inc., Westport, Connecticut, 1973.

Gray, John S., *Centennial Campaign: The Sioux War of 1876*, The Old Army Press, Fort Collins, Colorado, 1976.

Guthman, William H., *March to Massacre: A History of the First Seven Years of the United States Army 1784–1791*, McGraw-Hill Book Company, New York, 1975.

Hayes, John T., *Connecticut's Revolutionary Cavalry: Sheldon's Horse*, Pequot Press, Chester, Connecticut, 1975.

Herr, John K., and Wallace, Edward S., *The Story of the U.S. Cavalry 1775–1942*, Little, Brown and Company, Boston, 1953.

Hutchins, James S., *Boots & Saddles at the Little Big Horn: Weapons, Dress, Equipment, Horses, and Flags of General Custer's Seventh U.S. Cavalry in 1876*. The Old Army Press, Fort Collins, Colorado, 1976.

Jacobs, James Ripley, *The Beginning of the U.S. Army 1783–1812*, Princeton University Press, Princeton, 1947.

Kohn, Richard H., *Eagle and Sword: The Federalists and the Creation of the Military Establishment in America, 1783–1802*, The Free Press, New York, 1975.

Leckie, William H., *The Buffalo Soldiers: A Narrative of the Negro Cavalry in the West*, University of Oklahoma Press, Norman, 1967.

Loescher, Burt Garfield, *Washington's Eyes: The Continental Light Dragoons*, The Old Army Press, Fort Collins, Colorado, 1977.

Mahon, John K., *History of the Second Seminole War 1835–1842*, University of Florida Press, Gainesville, 1967.

—— *The War of 1812*, University of Florida Press, Gainesville, 1972.

Merrill, James M., *Spurs to Glory: The Story of the United States Cavalry*, Rand McNally & Company, Chicago, 1966.

Morton, Louis, *The Fall of the Philippines*, Office of the Chief of Military History, Department of the Army, Washington, D.C., 1953.

Prucha, Francis Paul, *The Sword of the Republic: The United States Army on the Frontier, 1783–1846*, The Macmillan Company, New York, 1969.

Reedstrom, Ernest Lisle, *Bugles, Banners & War Bonnets: From Fort Riley to the Little Big Horn: A Study of Lt. Col. George A. Custer's 7th Cavalry, the Soldiers, their Weapons and Equipment*, The Caxton Printers, Ltd., Caldwell, Idaho, 1977.

Smythe, Donald, *Guerrilla Warrior: The Early Life of John J. Pershing*, Charles Scribner's Sons, New York, 1973.

Starr, Stephen Z., *The Union Cavalry in the Civil War* (Vol. 1); *From Fort Sumter to Gettysburg*, Louisiana State University Press, Baton Rouge, 1979.

Steffen, Randy, *The Horse Soldier 1776–1943: The United States Cavalryman: His Uniforms, Arms, Accoutrements, and Equipments* (4 vols), University of Oklahoma Press, Norman, 1977–79.

Stubbs, Mary Lee, and Connor, Stanley Russell, *Armor-Cavalry* (Part 1); *Regular Army and Army*

Picture Credits

Reserve, Office of the Chief of Military History, United States Army, Washington, D.C., 1969.

Todd, Frederick P., *American Military Equipage 1851–1872* (3 vols), The Company of Military Historians, Providence, Rhode Island, 1974–78.

Urwin, Gregory J. W., *Custer Victorious: The Civil War Battles of General George Armstrong Custer*, Fairleigh Dickinson University Press, Rutherford, Madison and Teaneck, New Jersey, 1983.

Utley, Robert M., *Frontiersmen in Blue: The United States Army and the Indian 1848–1865*, The Macmillan Company, New York, 1967.

—— *Frontier Regulars: The United States Army and the Indian 1866–1890*, Macmillan Publishing Co., Inc., New York, 1973.

Weigley, Russell F., *History of the United States Army*, The Macmillan Company, New York, 1967.

Index